SEVENTH EDITION

THE ACTOR AT WORK

Robert Benedetti
California Institute of the Arts

Allyn and Bacon
Boston • London • Toronto • Sydney • Tokyo • Singapore

Series Editor: Carla F. Daves
Vice President and Editor in Chief, Humanities: Joseph Opiela
Editorial Assistant: Andrea Geanacopoulos
Marketing Manager: Karon Bowers
Sr. Editorial Production Administrator: Susan McIntyre
Editorial Production Service: Ruttle, Shaw & Wetherill, Inc.
Composition Buyer: Linda Cox
Manufacturing Buyer: Megan Cochran
Cover Administrator: Suzanne Harbison

Library of Congress Cataloging-in-Publication Data

Benedetti, Robert L.
    The actor at work / Robert Benedetti,—7th ed.
      p. cm.
    Includes bibliographical references and index.
    ISBN 0-205-26139-6
    1. Acting. I. Title.
  PN2061.B39 1997
  792'.028—dc20   96-16034
                                      CIP

Printed in the United States of America

10 9 8 7 6 5 4 3 2 1   01 00 99 98 97 96

CONTENTS

LIST OF EXERCISES

FOREWORD

BY TED DANSON

I met Bob Benedetti twenty-seven years ago, when I was in his second-year acting class at Carnegie Tech. As long as I have known him, he has been exploring, discovering, and sharing what it means to act.

His classes filled me with the kind of excitement athletes must feel when they are in full stride. He taught me how to get acting out of my mind, out of theory, and into my body, into action; he gave me a point of concentration, so that my mind would not be censoring every impulse.

He was also fun to be around, and he planted in me the thought that acting, performing, could be joyous. I will cherish him always for that, because as far as I'm concerned acting, if it is nothing else, had best be joyous, both in the childlike spirit of play and as a profound celebration of life. For me, acting is a wonderful excuse to live life as fully as possible.

My mother had a prayer that has always stayed with me: "Dear Lord," she would say, "please help me to become fully human." The job of all of us in life is to experience the human condition and our own humanity fully; your job as an actor is to reflect what you have experienced in a way that clarifies and enhances people's lives.

As an actor, you are a pleader of causes. The characters you play have a cause, a purpose, and it is up to you to plead it with utmost integrity and commitment, as if a life depended on it—for in fact, it does.

To be able to do this, you must master the techniques of acting. You stretch your body, your voice, your thoughts and feelings so as to encompass as much of the human condition as possible; you must develop the capacity to reflect it all, not just that small portion with which you feel comfortable.

You must also live the same way: You must push past the comfortable, easy answers and explore the scary side of life and of yourself, for finally you have nothing to offer but yourself, your insights, your truth, your slice of the human condition. As you grow and expand, remember that at any moment in your personal journey as an actor, you have only yourself to offer: who you are at that moment is enough.

As you work to master technique, then, keep your attention focused outward. Don't worry about yourself, think about everybody else; don't worry about being interesting, just be interested in everybody else, in life itself. All the technique in the world will be meaningless unless you have something worth sharing through it; technique is the tool you will use to communicate whatever you have to say, through the characters you choose to play, about the human condition.

To me, acting has itself become a life process. Whatever is next in my development as a human being will happen either through my everyday life or through my acting; they are completely intertwined. This blending of acting and living is never more obvious to me than when I am working on a film (or a play or any other creative group effort); when everyone is aligned toward the common purpose, then there are no more "accidents"; everything that happens at home, on the way to work, in front of the camera, all contributes to your creative purpose. Only when you hold your acting separate from your life do they interfere with one another; when they are aligned, they feed each other. You can become a better actor by becoming a more complete human being, and you can become a more complete human being by becoming a better actor.

Back to technique!

PREFACE

It is hard for me to believe that *The Actor at Work* has been in print for twenty-six years, and that seven editions have gone by, each reflecting some substantive change in my understanding of the acting process.

This edition is more direct, simpler, and contains several new ideas which I think are helpful. It addresses the needs of the camera a bit more than previous editions, because it is obvious that a working actor must deal with the camera as well as the live stage if he or she is to make a living.

It is obvious that this edition, like the sixth, is much influenced by my present career as a producer–writer for film and television. Though I still teach part-time at the California Institute of the Arts, my relationship with actors has changed considerably. I understand better how hard a working actor must fight to maintain a career that has an artistic and ethical basis, and how hard it is to find pride and satisfaction in the kind of work that puts food on the table.

At the same time, I see that there is nothing stopping working actors from doing their best in every moment of every performance, from continuing to challenge themselves, and even from taking time off to do work that excites them.

I hope that the approach to acting embodied in this book will assist the beginning actor, and even established actors wishing to renew their skills, to develop the sense of purpose and self-esteem that will bring them both artistic satisfaction and career success.

HOW TO USE THIS BOOK

Buddhists describe the process of personal growth as the "threefold way." It begins with preparing the *ground,* in the way a gardener cultivates the soil to make it ready to accept the seed. Next a *path* is opened, as when the gardener plants the seed and waters the young plant. Finally, the *fruition* follows naturally, as when the gardener perfects the plant by pruning and tending, always with respect for its own nature.

We will use this idea of the threefold way of *ground, path,* and *fruition,* to organize our study of acting. The first part of this book will begin with *you,* your body, voice, thoughts and feelings. You are the "ground," the instrument, of your work as an actor.

The second part will open the "path," which is the concept of *action.* Here we will explore your ability to experience the needs and thoughts of the character within his or her circumstances, and to experience for yourself the things the character does to try to satisfy those needs.

The "fruition" of this process will make up the third part of the book, the *characterization.* Building on what you discovered in action, you develop an artistically heightened creation which serves the purposes intended by the author.

The Exercises and Readings.   There are exercises in each lesson in this book. They are a program of self-discovery and self-development and are arranged roughly according to a "natural" acquisition of skills and insights. The experiences provided by the exercises are essential to a true understanding (in the muscles as well as in the mind) of what this book is about. These exercises have no "right" outcome, so just follow the instructions and see what happens!

In addition to the exercises, later lessons will contain examples taken from five popular plays, and a sample scene from each is included in Appendix A at the back of this book. However, if you will take time to read the entire play from which these scenes come, you will benefit much more from the examples themselves. The plays are Miller's *Death of a Salesman,* Williams' *The Glass Menagerie* and *A Streetcar Named Desire,* Brecht's *Mother Courage,* and Albee's *The Zoo Story.*

ACKNOWLEDGMENTS

I'm grateful that I have had the chance to clarify my evolving understanding of the acting process by producing a new edition of this book every four years or so over the more than twenty years that it has been in print. In turn, I thank the editorial and production team at Allyn and Bacon for publishing this seventh edition. I thank all of the teachers and students who have given me their reactions to the book over the years, and I thank the reviewers of this edition, J. Laurence Lowenstein, *Brookdale Community College;* George W. Sorenson, *Texas Tech University;* and Dr. Bill Hutson, *Creighton University.*

My thanks also to my friend Ted Danson, who made my new career possible, and above all, to my parents Lola and Dino, for all they have given me in my life. I dedicate this book to them.

Lesson 1

THE ACTOR IN YOU

You are already an actor. You "play a role" every time you present yourself in a social situation. In various circumstances, in various relationships, you pursue your needs by behaving in certain ways, doing things to other people and reacting to the things they do to you. It is this interaction with your world, this give and take of acting and reacting, that shapes and expresses your personality, your *character*, in everyday life.

In a popular book of the fifties, *The Presentation of Self in Everyday Life*, social psychologist Erving Goffman analyzed social behavior as if it were a stage performance. He found that most of us have a highly developed capacity to play our social roles successfully:

> It does take deep skill, long training, and psychological capacity to become a good stage actor. But...almost anyone can quickly learn a script well enough to give a charitable audience some sense of realness. ...This is so because ordinary social intercourse is put together as a scene (in a play) is put together, by the exchange of dramatically inflated actions, counteractions, and terminating replies. Scripts even in the hands of unpracticed players can come to life because life itself is a dramatically enacted thing.... In short, we all act better than we know how.[1]

The fact that you are "acting" most of the time does not mean that you are insincere: behaving in ways that achieve your objectives in given circumstances is a natural and necessary way of coping with life. You adapt your social behavior to the demands of your situation automatically and unconsciously. In fact, you play several characters every day—student, son or daughter, friend, employee—each with its own appropriate behavior, speech, thought and feelings: your own little repertory company!

This fact was noticed many years ago by the psychologist William James, who said that our personalities are actually composites of many social roles; he called these roles our various "me's." Behind the "me's," of course, there is one consciousness, which he called our "I." But our "I" is not rigid and is expressed through all of our "me's," even though some of them may be quite different from one another.

We may even experience situations in which two or more of our "me's" come into conflict with one another. If you're busy being "buddy" with your friends, or "lover" with that special other, the arrival of parents or a boss may cause an uncomfortable conflict between your role as "buddy" or "lover" and your role as "child" or "employee."

As you become aware of this, you also notice that your sense of "I" tends to flow into whichever "me" you are being. As an actor, you still have your "I," but you learn to let it flow into new "me's," some of which may be very different from any of the roles you have already experienced. And of course, the qualities of these new "me's" are determined not by you but by your playwright, who also creates a new set of circumstances, a new world, in which this new "me" lives. *One of the actor's most important skills is to allow his or her "I" to flow fully and freely into this new "me" and its world, while still maintaining an awareness of the artistic purposes for which this new "me" was created.*

The art of acting, then, is based upon everyday life principles, so to that extent you already know how to act.

Exercise 1.1: The Actor in You

Life Study. For the next few days, observe your own behavior and that of those around you. Make note of the ways in which you present yourself differently in various circumstances.

1. Notice changes in your behavior.
2. Notice changes in your voice, manner of speaking, and choice of words.
3. Be aware of your choice of clothing and the "props" you use.
4. Most of all, note the changes in the way you think and feel.

Notice how you naturally tend to "become" each of the roles you are presenting.

An Acting Journal. Record these observations in a journal that you either carry with you, or complete at the end of each day. The actor is an explorer of emotional, physical, and psychological dimensions, and explorers have always found it valuable to record their journeys: begin now to keep a journal as you work. Record thoughts, observations, and experiences that relate to your development as an actor. Writing things down can help you to clarify and intensify your experiences. Make it a regular discipline.

THE SKILLS OF THE ACTOR

Although acting is based on everyday life skills, acting for the stage or camera demands that these everyday abilities be heightened, purified, and brought within the control of a purposeful discipline. As Brian Bates of the Royal Academy of Dramatic Art says in his book, *The Way of the Actor,*

> *Almost everything that actors do can be identified with things we do in less dramatic form, in everyday life. But in order to express the concentrated truths which are the life-stuff of drama, and to project convincing performances before large audiences, and the piercing eye of the film and television camera, the actor must develop depths of self-knowledge and powers of expression far beyond those with which most of us are familiar.[2]*

The development of your everyday acting skills into the greater power of artistic technique is the aim of this book. You will work on three kinds of skill as you develop your acting techniques: physical, intellectual, and spiritual. The physical skills develop your body and voice as expressive instruments. The intellectual skills enable you to analyze plays and scenes, and to recognize how the characters you perform function within their plays. The spiritual skills involve your ability to relax, to be centered, to observe and focus, to be aware on several levels at once, and—most important—to experience transformation, to "become" the character.

Each of these skills requires a different learning process. Physical skills are best developed through regular repetition over time, but intellectual skills require shorter and intensely focused periods of study. The spiritual skills are the most difficult to describe or teach; they can be developed through physical and intellectual disciplines, but they depend more on your own initiative and life experience.

Your task now is to recognize, focus, and strengthen the natural actor you already are. Only you can do this, but the ideas and exercises in this book can provide insights and experiences to help you fulfill your natural talents.

ACTING AND YOUR PERSONAL GROWTH

The development of what Bates calls the actor's "depths of self-knowledge and powers of expression" is an unending process of personal as well as artistic growth. It is exactly this opportunity for ongoing personal growth that attracts many people to the profession of acting. Even if you do not commit to the profession, your study of the acting process can enrich you in many ways. Bates, who is both an acting teacher and a psychologist, lists some of the ways in which the study of acting can contribute to personal growth:

> *Finding our inner identity. Changing ourselves. Realizing and integrating our life experience. Seeing life freshly and with insight into others. Becoming aware of the powers of our mind. Risking and commitment. Learning how to concentrate our lives into the present, and the secrets of presence and charisma. Extending our sense of who we are, and achieving liberation from restricted concepts of what a person is.*[3]

In all these ways, the study of acting, even if it does not lead to actual performance, is a meaningful journey of personal discovery and expansion.

WHY YOU ACT

There are nearly as many reasons to study acting as there are acting students. For some of you, it seems like an easy or enjoyable way to fulfill an academic credit (and it is!). Some of you think it might be a way to meet interesting women or men (and it is!). Some of you may have serious career intentions. Some of you may feel that acting might offer the possibility of satisfying some deep personal needs. And some very few of you may feel irresistibly compelled toward acting.

Many great actors have spoken of their inescapable need to act in spite of many misgivings about it. As Sir Laurence Olivier once told some reporters, "It does seem sometimes that acting is hardly the occupation for an adult... I can't stand it any more... But without it I would die, I suppose."[4]

For those who, like Olivier, have made acting not just a career but a way of life (and this includes all our greatest actors) it is clear that acting addresses needs far deeper than the desire for attention or material success. These actors often speak of the release that playing a role gives them from what Alec Guinness called "my dreary old life;" acting gives them permission to have experiences they would never dare have in real life. For others, the special position of the actor compensates for a sense of personal unworthiness. Whatever the needs may be, those with the deepest needs seem to have the best chance for a professional life, for acting is a dreadful way to earn a living and only very deep needs provide sufficient motivation to sustain a career.

Whatever your motives in studying acting may be, they are the source of your personal satisfaction as an actor, as well as a source of tremendous power on stage. Take a moment to consider your motives.

Exercise 1.2: Why You Act

Working with a partner, take turns repeating and completing each phrase spontaneously. Answer from your feelings; tell the truth.

1. The theatre experience I remember most vividly is...
2. Some of the actors I admire most are...
3. The thing I think I'd like most about being an actor is...
4. The thing I think I'd hate most about being an actor is...
5. The kind of acting I most want to do is...
6. The thing I want most out of acting is...
7. Some of the things I would rather do than act are...
8. What I would need for a career in the theatre would be...

After completing the phrases, relax and recall your earliest memory of theatre. Imagine yourself there again, and ask yourself these questions:

1. How did you come to be here?
2. What is it making you think about?
3. How is it making you feel?
4. Are you making any choices, conscious or unconscious, that have affected you since?
5. Is there anything about this that relates to studying acting later in life?

Review the results of these experiments. Do you see a pattern? Did you uncover anything that surprised you? What seemed the most true? Record your thoughts in your journal.

This exercise may have helped you recognize why you're interested in acting; the answers may even have surprised you. In any case, remember that one reason is no better, no more noble, no more effective than another. Your motives and needs change as you grow, and you may outgrow these early motives. As you work, you may discover new reasons for acting that are even stronger than the reasons with which you begin. What is important is that you have *your* reasons now, and they motivate you to take this journey of discovery. Let them.

DISCIPLINE

Before you begin your journey into acting in earnest, think about the one skill that will make all others possible: *discipline.*

Real discipline is not a matter of following someone else's rules: in the best sense it is *your acceptance of the responsibility for your own development through systematic effort.* You accept this responsibility not to please someone else, not to earn a grade, or a good review, or a job, but because you choose to become all that you can be.

Discipline is rooted in your respect for yourself, as well as your respect for your fellow workers, for your work, and for the world you serve through that work. Poor discipline is really a way of saying, "I'm not worth it" or "what I do doesn't matter." Discipline comes naturally if you acknowledge your own value, the importance and seriousness of your work, and the great need for your work in the world. The director Eugenio Barba put it this way in a letter to an undisciplined actor:

> *First of all, one gets the impression that your acts are not dictated by that interior conviction or undeniable need which would show itself in the execution of an exercise, or of an improvisation or a scene.... You have not proven to yourself the importance of what you want to share with the spectators. How, then, can you hope that the spectator will be captivated by your actions?...*
>
> *The second tendency which I see in you is the fear of considering the complete seriousness of our work: you find the need to laugh, to snigger, to pass humorous remarks upon whatever you and your classmates happen to be performing. It is as if you wanted to flee that responsibility which you sense is joined to our work and which consists of establishing a communication with other people and of facing up to the consequences you discover thereby....*
>
> *I believe you have never considered that all you are doing, delivering, shaping in your work belongs to the phenomena of life and that as such it deserves consideration and respect.*[5]

Discipline also involves regularity. Your work, especially on technical skills, must be a daily affair. Stanislavski, looking back late in his life, had this to say:

Let someone explain to me why the violinist who plays in an orchestra on the tenth violin must daily perform hour-long exercises or lose his power to play? Why does the dancer work daily over every muscle in his body? Why do the painter, the sculptor, the writer practice their art each day and count that day lost when they do not work? And why may the dramatic artist do nothing, spend his day in coffee houses and hope for the gift [of inspiration] in the evening? Enough. Is this an art when its priests speak like amateurs? There is no art that does not demand virtuosity.[6]

Patience and a sense of striving together—being able to accept the momentary failure for the sake of the long-range success—are the attitudes that you must nurture. The pressures of our educational system and of professional acting work against these attitudes, as does the normal desire of all of us to be "successful" right now. Resist your desire for immediate success and instead begin to enjoy the journey, the exploration itself.

And take the long view: enjoy your freedom as a student to explore a variety of approaches and experiences. Most of your explorations will lead up blind alleys, but it is better to suffer momentary failures now than to commit yourself to an approach or an attitude that may limit you later. Your discipline is dedicated to the whole of your career. As playwright David Mamet says:

Those of you who are called to strive to bring a new theatre, the theatre of your generation, to the stage, are set down for a very exciting life.

You will be pulling against an increasingly strong current, and as you do so, you will reap the great and priceless reward of knowing yourself a truly mature man or woman—if, in the midst of the panic which surrounds you, which calls itself common sense, or commercial viability, you are doing your job simply and well.

If you are going to work in the true theatre, that job is a great job in this time of final decay; that job is to bring to your fellows, through the medium of your understanding and skill, the possibility of communion with what is essential in us all: that we are born to die, that we strive and fail, that we live in ignorance of why we were placed here, and, that, in the midst of this we need to love and be loved, but we are afraid.[7]

SUMMARY

You are already an actor. You "play a role" every time you present yourself or adjust your behavior to achieve some desired goal. As an art, however, acting requires that these everyday abilities be heightened and purified.

The development of your everyday acting skills into the greater power of artistic technique is the aim of this book. Your task is to recognize, focus, and strengthen the natural actor you already are.

There are three types of skill involved in becoming an actor: the physical skills of voice and body, the intellectual skills of play and scene analysis, and the spiritual skill to experience transformation. The spiritual skill is the most difficult to describe and teach; it depends mostly on your own initiative and life experience.

Even if you do not commit to the profession, your study of the acting process can help you to grow in many ways. For many actors, acting addresses needs far deeper than the desire for attention or material success. Whatever your reasons, they motivate you to take this journey of personal discovery and expansion.

One skill makes all others possible: discipline. Real discipline is not a matter of following someone else's rules, it is *your acceptance of the responsibility for your own development through systematic effort*. Discipline comes naturally if you acknowledge your own value, and the importance of your work and the great need for it in the world.

Lesson 2

THE CREATIVE STATE

Many of us are distanced from our physical, intellectual, and emotional lives; we don't permit ourselves to use some aspects of our body and voice and some forms of expression, and we block out some feelings, thoughts, and experiences.

To be an actor, you can no more maintain this distance from yourself than a violinist could refuse contact with the violin. Your job requires that all aspects of your self—body, voice, thoughts, and feelings—be available, integrated, and controllable. They are the tools of your trade.

In Lessons 2 and 3, you explore your own body, voice, and mind. You may begin to rediscover the natural integration of mind and body that you enjoyed as a child, when "making believe" was a total and natural process. As we grow up, we begin to inhibit and censor this childlike ability to play; we can recapture it best when we are relaxed and unjudgmental—when our internal "parent" allows our "child" to come out and play. This is the condition that some psychologists have called "the creative state." For this reason, the first step in preparing yourself to act is *to relax.*

RELAXATION

When we speak of relaxation for the actor, we do not mean it in the ordinary sense of reduced energy or slackness; rather, we mean that all unnecessary tensions have been removed, the remaining energy has been purposefully focused, and awareness is acute.

The kind of relaxation you want is a state in which you are *most ready to react,* like a cat in front of a mousehole. Tensions that would inhibit movement are gone and you are in a state of balance, which leaves you free to react in any way required.

The best description of the relaxed actor's state is what meditators call "restful alertness." You are already capable of restful alertness; you don't need to do anything to achieve it, you only need to become still enough to experience it. You can do this right now, through a simple meditation.

Exercise 2.1: A Meditation

Sit comfortably in your chair, both feet flat on the floor, back and neck straight but not rigid, and hands resting on your thighs. Look at a spot on the floor eight feet in front of you. Focus your awareness on your breath flowing in and out of your nose. Allow any thoughts that come up to play across your consciousness, then simply return your awareness to your breath. Nothing is to be resisted. If you like, close your eyes. Sit for as long as you are comfortable. Whatever experience you have is correct.

Your meditation was focused on your breath for a very good reason: the breath is life. The word *psychology* means "study of the soul," and the word for soul, *psyche,* originally meant "vital breath." A common superstition is that the expiring breath of a dying person is the soul leaving the body.

Your breath constantly reflects your relationship to your world. It is through the breath that you literally bring the outside world into your body and then expel it again; the way you feel about your world is expressed in the way you breathe it in and breathe it out. This is why your natural voice, which is profoundly affected by your breath, is so expressive of your inner state. You can see sobbing, laughing, gasping, sighing, and all the other forms of breathing as the reflections of your relationship to your world. Unfortunately, television has turned many of us into "talking heads," breaking our natural connection between upper and lower body, causing us to lose touch with our natural breathing and therefore with our natural voice.

Now that you have begun to experience restful alertness, however, you can begin to rediscover the unity of your entire body and breath. As you do, you may become aware of bundles of chronic tension in your body, some of which may have become so familiar that you have lost consciousness of them. In the next two exercises you will take time to inspect the tensions within your body; invade your own privacy!

Exercise 2.2: Playing Cat

Lie on the floor comfortably in a surrounding that is not too distract-ing. Stretch yourself out face up, hands at your sides. Put yourself at rest by yawning and stretching.

> *To see yawning and stretching at their luxurious best, watch a cat just awakening from a siesta. It arches its back, extends to the utmost its legs, feet, and toes, drops its jaw, and all the while bal-loons itself up with air. Once it has swelled until it occupies its very maximum of space, it permits itself slowly to collapse—and then is ready for new business.[1]*

Act like a cat. Stretch, arch your back, extend all your limbs to their utmost, drop your jaw, wiggle your arms and hands, and breathe deeply (not once, but many times); each time taking in more and more air. When a real yawn comes, encourage it; let the full natural sound of the yawn pour out. Then settle back with your knees raised enough to make the small of your back touch the floor. Place your toes, heels, hip joints, and shoulders on two imaginary parallel lines. We call this our *floor alignment:* The head is level (a small pad should be placed under it); the waistline is also level. The knees are raised to avoid any strain on the lower back.

CHECKING FOR BLOCKS

Using stretching like a cat as a preparation, now take systematic inven-tory of your body, looking for any long-standing bundles of tension. These bundles of tension act as *blocks* to the flow of energy within your body, and may limit your ability to move freely, or to portray certain kinds of characters. They also have a psychological aspect, and may have been developed by blocked aspects of your past experience. If they remain, they may continue to limit your ability to experience and express certain thoughts, feelings, and traits.

Make an inventory of any potential physical blocks using the follow-ing exercise. It was developed by a pioneer in the field of relaxation, Dr. Edmund Jacobson. The exercise is more effective every time you repeat it, because your "relaxation response" develops with repetition just like any other skill. As you achieve greater and greater relaxation, bundles of chronic tension are dissolved by the natural wisdom of the body.

Remember that you are dealing with habits and structures that have formed over a lifetime; have the patience and discipline to adopt a long-term program of correction and maintenance. (Though this exercise can be quickly learned, a tape recording of these instructions with the necessary pauses would be useful at first.)

Exercise 2.3: Phasic Relaxation

Begin in floor alignment. Breath is again the focus of your awareness: Imagine that each inhalation is a warm, fresh, energy-filled fluid flowing into your body. Each exhalation carries away with it tension and inhibition, like a refreshing wave. Breathe deeply and easily in a slow, natural, regular rhythm; don't "act" your breathing or artificially exaggerate it.

Each successive breath is sent into a different part of the body, awakening that area. As the breath flows into a new area, let the muscles there contract as much as they can; then, as the breath flows out, the muscles release and the breath carries all the tension away with it, leaving the area refreshed and at ease. *Exhaling is letting go.*

The sequence of breaths moves from the top of the body downward, and the regular rhythm of your breathing should make the muscular contractions and relaxations flow smoothly down the body like a slow wave. Allow only one area at a time to be involved.

1. *The forehead and scalp,* furrowing the brow, then releasing it; the eyes are at rest, closed and turned slightly downward;
2. *The jaw,* clenching it, then letting it fall easily downward until the teeth are about one-half inch apart;
3. *The tongue,* extending it, then letting it lie easily in the mouth;
4. *The front of the neck,* extending the chin down to touch the chest, stretching the back of the neck—then rolling the head easily back down;
5. *The back of the neck,* rolling the top of the head under to touch the floor, stretching the front of the neck—then rolling the head slowly down and lengthening the neck;
6. *The upper chest,* swelling outward in all directions so that the shoulders are widened—then easily subsiding, feeling the shoulder blades spread and melt into the floor, wider than before;
7. *The arms and hands,* becoming stiff and straight like steel rods; the hands clenching into fists, then easily uncurling and melting into the floor, uncurling;
8. *The pit of the stomach,* clenching, becoming a small, hard ball—then, with a sigh, releasing;

9. *The buttocks,* clenching, then releasing and widening so that the hips are wider than before;

10. *The knees,* stiffening as the legs straighten, the feet being pushed downward by this action—then releasing the legs and feeling them melt into the floor;

11. *The toes,* reaching up to touch the eyes (but the heels remain on the floor)—then releasing and falling into a natural position;

12. *The heels and the shoulder blades,* simultaneously pushing downward into the floor so that the whole body lifts in a long arch—then, with a sigh, you slowly fall, the body lengthening as it relaxes, melting deep into the floor.

Now take ten deep, slow, regular breaths, and with each breath move more deeply into relaxation, remaining alert and refreshed. The flow of breath is a continuous cycle of energy that is stored comfortably in the body; with each breath this store of energy is increased. If a yawn comes to you, enjoy it fully; vocalize the exhalation, letting the sound of the yawn pour out.

As you repeat this exercise on successive days, you can begin to give yourself the instructions silently, reminding yourself of the specific activities in each phase. Keep a steady rhythm that follows the tempo of deep, relaxed breathing. Gradually the action of the exercise will become natural, and you will no longer need to think of the instructions. Your full awareness is given to the flow of contractions and relaxations that follow the breath as it travels down the body like a wave, awakening, refreshing, and relaxing it, making you ready for work.

You can use this exercise as an easy, quick preparation for all future work. Over time, it will help chronic bundles of tension within your body to break up and dissolve.

THE HERE AND NOW

Did you notice that relaxation allowed you to immerse yourself in the present instant, in the *here and now?* It is only now that you exist, and only now that you can act. In everyday life you rarely achieve complete contact with the present: you prefer to create a sense of comfortable continuity by blurring the lines that separate the present from the past and future. The past, in memory, and the future, in expectation, can be controlled by your consciousness; but the present can be met only on its own terms. Although you can never specifically isolate it, you can put yourself in touch with the unending flow of the present. As the psychologist Fritz Perls put it,

> *The wish to seize the present and pin it down—to mount it, as it were, like a butterfly in a case—is doomed to failure. Actuality forever changes. In healthy persons, the feeling of actuality is steady and continuous but, like the view from a train window, the scenery is always different.*[2]

When you act, you must work in the here and now. Even though your character may be lost in memory, consumed with desire for the future, or dreaming of being far away, you perform all this in the here and now.

MINIMIZING EFFORT

Acting, like all creative activity, arouses anxiety. This can be both pleasurable (in the quest for creative discovery) and unpleasurable (in the fear of failure and ridicule). In either case, this arousal tends to disrupt your breathing, and to raise the level of your bodily tension. In turn, this tension interferes with your readiness to react; it "freezes" you and reduces your creativity.

When you find yourself scared or "stuck" in this way, you may attempt to compensate by trying harder, putting more effort into the work and trying to muscle your way through your difficulty. Unfortunately, this is exactly the wrong thing to do. It only *increases* your tension and further reduces your freedom of creative response. It is common to see students in beginning acting classes make the mistake of trying harder, and the harder they try, the worse they get.

This excessive effort makes you self-aware, obscures your own experience of your work, and reduces your control. Movement therapist Moshe Feldenkrais uses the example of trying to open a sticking drawer: If you tug indiscriminately at it, chances are that it will let loose all at once and go flying out, spilling the contents. Because you were using excessive force, you failed to perceive the exact moment when the drawer loosened; you had ceased to experience the drawer and were experiencing *only your own effort.*

Unfortunately, many actors are driven to excessive effort; in their desire to deliver an acceptable performance, they do too much. Their assumption seems to be that they are unworthy of the audience's attention unless they *do* something extraordinary to earn it; the option of doing nothing, of simply allowing themselves to "be there," is terrifying.

They feel naked, exposed, and become desperate to do something—anything! As a result, they have difficulty experiencing what is really happening on stage and instead experience only *their own effort.*

Do you feel unworthy of our attention? Can you let your simple, unadorned presence be enough, or do you feel that you must do something extraordinary to earn our attention? See if you can let go of this need so that your stage choices are positive and not compensations for a sense of unworthiness.

Exercise 2.4: Being There

Take turns standing in front of the group. Place yourself in restful alertness and simply "be there." Let go of your need to do something until you are quite still.

Fully experience stillness both as actor and as audience; support one another with quiet attention. See how interesting the simple, unadorned presence of a human being can be!

SUMMARY

Acting requires that all aspects of your self—body, voice, thoughts, and feelings—be available, integrated, and controllable. They are the tools of your trade. Your work as an actor requires that you rediscover the natural integration of mind and body that you enjoyed as a child at play. It is this relaxed, unjudgmental condition that we call "the creative state." The first step in recapturing it is *to relax.*

The kind of relaxation best for the actor is a state in which you are most ready to react, the state meditators call "restful alertness." The breath is deeply involved with relaxation because it constantly reflects your relationship to your world. Unfortunately, our cultural disintegration has caused many of us to lose touch with our natural breathing.

Bundles of unconscious tensions within the body can be blocks to energy and experience. Achieving relaxation over a period of time helps break up and dissolve these blocks. Have the patience and discipline to adopt a long-term program of correction and maintenance.

Relaxation in the sense of simply "being there," ready to react, allows you to immerse yourself in the present instant, in the *here and now.*

Acting, like all creative activity, arouses anxiety, which disrupts your breathing and raises the level of your bodily tension. In turn, this tension "freezes" you and reduces your creativity. When you find yourself "stuck" in this way, you may attempt to compensate by trying harder.

Unfortunately, this only *increases* your tension and further reduces your freedom of creative response; excessive effort makes you self-aware.

Unfortunately, many actors are prone to excessive effort; they feel unworthy of the audience's attention unless they *do* something extraordinary to earn it. See if you can let go of this need and let yourself just "be there."

Lesson 3

CENTERING AND MOVING

Incarnation: bodying forth. Is this not our whole concern? The bodying forth of our sense of life?... We body forth our ideals in personal acts, either alone or with others in society. We body forth felt experience in a poem's image and sound. We body forth our inner residence in the architecture of our homes and common buildings. We body forth our struggles and our revelations in the space of theatre. That is what form is: the bodying forth....[1]

This thought is from a book called *Centering* by Mary Caroline Richards, a poet and potter. As a potter she knows how the centering of the clay upon the wheel is essential to creation of a pot, for only from perfectly centered clay can the motion of the wheel and the potter's hands bring the pot's shape freely and naturally toward its ultimate form. As a poet she also knows how the experiences of one's life must touch a personal center before they can, in turn, flow outward and be embodied in the form of a poem. As an actor you must also center yourself so that your energy, like the clay, flows outward into the new form of yourself demanded by your role.

The idea of a personal center is not just a metaphor; it has a tangible physical dimension. Finding and activating your bodily center is a necessary first step in laying a foundation for good stage movement and voice; the sense of center can integrate your responses and give you strength by involving your total organism in your actions.

Developing your physical center is also a way of developing a psychological and spiritual centeredness as well, because at this deep level your energy exists simultaneously in physical and psychological forms; movement, feeling, thought, and the beginnings of sound, all intermingle here. This deep *psychophysical* energy is the raw material of the acting process; like the potter's clay, you must gather it, make it responsive, and center it so that it can be shaped easily into new forms.

As you work on a role, this psychophysical energy flows outward into new forms of behavior demanded by your character's actions and the style of the play. As this happens, you begin to experience yourself anew. As you come to experience this new form of yourself more fully, you begin to enter into a new state of being, which in turn summons new energies from you; this is the creative cycle of the acting process.

This lesson explores the physical dimension of centering. Part III shows how its psychological dimension can be a primary tool of characterization. Here is an exercise to help you localize a specific sense of your physical center.

Exercise 3.1: Finding Center

Place yourself in standing alignment, clear your mind, and witness your body as it performs the following activities:

1. Move either foot out to the side about two feet; rock from foot to foot, feeling your center of gravity moving from side to side. Quickly make your rocking smaller and smaller, like a bowling pin that almost falls down; come to rest on center.

2. Move either foot forward about two feet; find your center with front-to-back motions as described above.

3. Move your center around rotationally, exploring the limits of various stances. Feel the weight of your body flowing into the ground and out of your center through the legs.

4. Point into your body at the spot that you feel is your center; don't be concerned about where it "ought" to be; sense where it really is.

5. Explore how your center is involved in moving and speaking.

As you become aware of your center over a period of days, you notice that it moves within the body as your mood changes; frequently, your center rises upward when you are in an excited or fearful state or downward in states of well-being or determination. You notice, too, that different people have different characteristic centers and that the locations of their centers are very appropriate to their personalities. Such diversity can be found in people who have a "lot of guts," who "follow their nose," "lead with their chins," are "all heart," "drag their feet," "have their heads in the clouds," and so on.

This sense of centeredness is, for the actor, rooted in a literal, specific recognition of a physical center from which all impulses to move or make sound flow outwardly and into the external world. That physical center is experienced in specific relationship to gravity.

YOUR RELATIONSHIP TO GRAVITY

As our species evolved, we gradually became more and more erect, standing within the field of gravity. (This adaptation is far from complete; our common lower back problems may be due partly to an incomplete adaptation to standing erect.) Your relationship to gravity is continuous; even when lying down, you are making constant adjustments within the field of gravity.

The way in which you experience gravity, like your breathing, is a fundamental expression of your relationship to your world. Some days, it seems that we wake up heavier, with "the weight of the world" on our shoulders. At such times, we speak of feeling "down," and at the saddest times we say we have a "heavy heart." On the other hand, sometimes we feel "light as a feather," "floating on cloud nine," and the most "light-hearted" moments are often expressed by a physical action that ignores gravity, skipping. Try to imagine being sad and skipping at the same time!

A person's attitude toward gravity can be seen in their posture. When Arthur Miller opens *Death of a Salesman* with Willy Loman crossing the stage, back bent under the weight of his sample case, his sense of defeat and his hopelessness are directly expressed in the way he is losing his fight with gravity.

We also seem to receive strength from gravity when we feel at one with it; at such times we speak of "knowing where we stand," or "holding our ground." One of the qualities of some classical heroes (like Oedipus or Electra, for example) is their oneness with the earth and the way the power of nature flows up through the earth and into them. Perhaps for this reason, I have noticed that it is impossible to play a strong character if the feet are kept too close together. Not only do strong characters need a wide, stable base, but they also need to be open to receive the flow of energy that is coming upward from the earth.

THE PURE CENTER AND THE VOICE

The martial arts teach a "pure" sense of center, which is the natural biomechanical center of an undistorted body. This "ideal" center is deep within the body, in an area roughly three finger-widths below your navel. It is here that the breath (and therefore the voice) originates, as well as

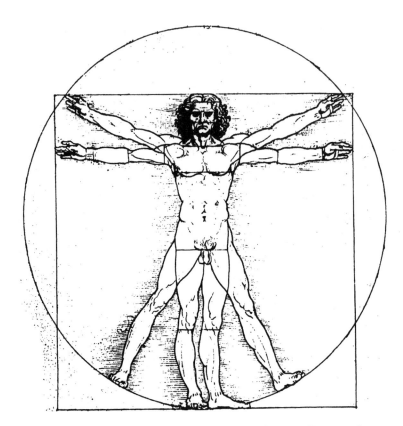

FIGURE 3.1   The Bodily Center According to Leonardo

all large motions of the body. This area is the literal center of gravity of your body, as shown by Leonardo Da Vinci's famous drawing (see Figure 3.1).

You must develop a sense of your pure center, for it is from this center that your deepest impulses spring. If you are operating instead from some higher center (such as the chest, or even the neck) you inevitably look and sound "stiff" and "superficial"; the movements and sounds you produce are not deeply motivated or complete because they do not originate from the true center of your being, and your voice in particular does not have the fullness and expressiveness required for good stage speech.

The committed worker is often the noisy one—humming, singing, laughing, or grunting; all action usually flows into the world through sound as well as motion. The student of karate learns this—the outward flow of energy from our deepest center naturally carries the breath, and hence the voice, with it. Unfortunately, we sometimes inhibit this natural flow of sound out of fear or because our upbringing has taught us to restrain our natural impulse to move, breathe, and sound. The following exercise gives you an experience of the breath flowing from your center, carrying sound and motion with it.

Exercise 3.2: Moving and Sounding from Center

Align and center yourself as in the previous exercises.

1. As you breathe easily and slowly, become aware of the breath rising and falling in the body from the center.

2. As the breath travels outward, make sound lightly; do not disturb the breath, just allow it to vibrate. This is your voice: your vibrating breath carrying energy from your center into the outside world.

3. Reach effortlessly with your vibrating breath into the world around you. Put yourself, at random, into new positions and experience the vibrating breath flowing through each. What changes are there in the voice?

4. As you continue to produce sound, feel the vibrations of that sound spreading into every part of your body: out of the neck into the head and chest, into the back, the stomach, the buttocks, into the arms and hands, into the legs and feet, and into the scalp. Feel the sound radiating from every part of your body! With a light fingertip touch, check every surface of your body. Are there "dead spots" that are not participating in the sound?

Examine your experience during sounding: Were there parts of your body that did not join in the vibration? Did you have a new sense of the capacity of your entire body to join in the act of sounding? Did you feel more in touch with yourself, and with the space around you, as if your sound were literally reaching outside yourself in a tangible way? Are you now more alert, refreshed, and relaxed?

Those areas of your body that are not available for sounding relate in some way to the distortions and chronic tensions that you identified during your phasic relaxation work; examine each and find the relationship. A disused abdomen causes a shallow, unsupported tone because the breath is not flowing freely from the center. A rigid or pinched chest and shoulders withhold the chest from sound, robbing the voice of the deep resonances that give it richness; a tense neck and jaw pinch the tone and force it into a narrow channel, causing a strident or sharp quality.

Whatever your findings, you see that vocal and physical qualities are integral with one another, because the breath, body, and voice are all integral with one another. As you begin to gain freedom and ease in one, you enhance the other; enhancing, too, a quality of mind important to your work, for your consciousness is itself a partner in this same wholeness.

THE ACTOR'S USE OF CENTER

Just as we experienced relaxation as a readiness to react, so our aim in aligning and centering the body is to put ourselves in the most responsive physiovocal condition. The "pure" center is an undistorted condition from which we begin our work so that we may develop in any direction required by the role without the impediment or bias of our personal distortions.

Although we *begin* from a pure center, however, we certainly do not *end* there. We are not interested in "correct" posture or voice for performance, for the actor has no "correct" voice or posture until they are determined by the demands of the role. Each character you play has his or her own center, which functions as the source of that character's breathing, motion, and sound.

In fact, any dramatic characterization is *a set of distortions* created to express the particular nature of that character. Whole and healthy people are rare in plays; dramatic characters are usually caught in difficult situations, driven by neurotic needs, or in other ways bent out of "normal" shape. A major aspect of your work consists of discovering the particular "abnormalities" that comprise the unique nature of each role you play.

To do this, you begin from as undistorted or "neutral" a base as you can, exploring and testing the particular qualities useful in creating the role. In truth, of course, you can never eradicate *all* your personal idiosyncrasies, nor should you; they give your work special and individual qualities that enable you, when at your best, to bring special insights and qualities to the roles you play. But those personal misalignments, inhibitions, and unconscious mannerisms—like regional dialects, unnatural postural or breathing habits, repetitive gestures—must be brought within the control of your conscious artistic discipline or they may forever limit the roles and qualities you can play.

And note that we wish not to *eliminate* these habits and qualities, but rather to bring them within our control. We actors shouldn't throw anything away; any quality, mannerism, way of speaking, or experience might be needed someday! But we must hold all these in such a way that *we are controlling them instead of them controlling us.* In these lessons we are working to achieve a neutral but energized condition where you are ready to move in any way necessary to fulfill your dramatic task.

THE CYCLE OF ENERGY

Next, we consider the *cycle* of energy that flows from our center outward toward the world *and back again.* Whenever we try to do something, to achieve some objective—in short, whenever we *act*—we send energy flowing out from our center into forms of sound, speech, or gesture in the outer world. We then receive a *reaction* to our action, and this energy flows into us and touches our center, in turn eliciting a further reaction from us, and so on. As this cycle flows out, then in, then out again, we see that there is no truly unilateral action; we do not *do* unless we have been *done to,* and vice versa. In the theatre, we like to say that *acting is reacting.*

This sense of a cycle of energy is central to the Oriental martial arts, such as T'ai Ch'i Ch'uan, and study in these arts can be of great benefit to the actor. Developing this sense of the cycle of energy can also help to open and free the passageway through which our voice naturally flows.

Exercise 3.3: The Cycle of Energy

Sit up, directly on the bony points you can feel just below the surface of each buttock; spread your legs as wide as is comfortable, with the knees slightly raised (see Figure 3.2 on page 24). Feel lifted from your center out of the top of your head so that your back and neck are long and wide. The head is level, eyes ahead, and the waist is level as well.

1. Breathing out, reach forward and down, keeping your back and neck long and shoulders wide. Imagine that you are bowing to someone sitting at the back of a theatre.

2. As you begin to breathe in, draw the breath into the lower part of your body by drawing the small of your back to the rear and scooping "energy" into the funnel formed by your legs with your hands.

3. As the breath begins to fill you, feel its warmth and power flowing up within you. Follow its upward movement with your hands.

4. As the breath rises in your body, it lifts you, straightening and lengthening the upper torso and neck, lifting the head, widening

FIGURE 3.2   Sitting in Balance

the shoulders and the throat as it flows upward like a wave moving you in a slow undulation. You unfurl like a fern opening.

5. The breath then flows into the outer world; give an "ah" sound to that imaginary person sitting at the back of the theatre, and accompany it with an unfolding gesture of the arms toward them.

6. As the power of the breath begins to diminish, close your mouth so that the "ah" sound becomes an "oh" and then an "m," and you experience a tingling sensation in your mouth and nose areas. The smooth flow of the sound produces a trisyllable word, "ah-oh-m" or *om.*

7. As the breath and sound die away, your body again bows forward and down, your back is still long and wide, and your arms are reaching forward to scoop in a new quantity of breath energy.

8. As the breath and sound are completely used up, your body has sunk low in its bow, and the cycle begins again. Feel the continuity of inward and outward breaths so that the entire exercise becomes one unbroken, flowing experience with no "sharp corners."

GROUNDING

As you begin to sense your physical center more acutely, also begin to feel the way your energy interacts with gravity. Your energy flows downward into the ground as well as upward, and there is also energy coming up into your center from the earth. We can speak, therefore, not only of being "centered," but also of being "grounded."

There is great power in being grounded, and several contemporary theatre makers have placed special emphasis on developing this quality, most notably the Japanese director Tadashi Suzuki, whose actor training system is based on a series of walks, many of which attack the earth as if to penetrate it. At the same time, some types of characters can be best expressed by a *lack* of grounding, by a floating or even flying quality. Here is an exercise to help you experience the various ways in which we can experience gravity.

Exercise 3.4: Roots

Imagine yourself standing on a mirror. Below you is your other self with its own center; imagine a bond between your center and that in your mirror image. This imaginary bond of energy is like a root, giving you stability, strength, and nourishment.

As your energy flows into your root, it also flows upward, so that your rootedness permits you to stand taller, to be stronger. As you move, your rootedness moves with you; you "detach" your rooted center, and at your destination you "plant" or ground yourself again.

1. Select a destination; lift your rooted center, move to the destination, and *plant* yourself there.

2. Now move to a destination without lifting the root; *plow* yourself there. Don't act this out; simply experience moving with this image and feel what it is like to *plow*. Extend this feeling so that you are pushing your way through the air itself, as if you are *molding* space as you move through it.

3. Now lift your root and leave it dangling all the time, whether moving or still: *float*. Again, give yourself time to experience *floating*.

4. Now imagine the root being drawn upward, still attached at your center, but now lifting your center upward and out of the top of your head. Move with the sense that you have to reach down to touch the floor: you are *flying*.

There is a distinct difference between the experiences of *molding, floating,* and *flying,* though each state offers numerous possibilities. Molding, for instance, can feel like dejection or defeat, but it might also feel like determination or commitment. Floating can feel like joy or enthusiasm, but it might also feel like confusion or vulnerability. The particular emotional quality of any one of these states can be determined only by *context,* and our bodily expression cannot be understood according to any sort of fixed vocabulary. (In the nineteenth century, however, there were attempts to construct such systems of acting, notably the Delsarte system, in which various body centers were related to emotions and qualities of thought.)

PHRASING MOVEMENT

In the last exercise you began to move through space by "lifting" your rooted center, moving, then "planting" your rooted center again at your destination. Review this experience; did it give you a heightened sense of clarity and purposefulness in your movements? The exercise made you more aware of the *shape* of your movements, the fact that each had a beginning, middle, and end. Just as our thoughts are shaped into words and sentences that are eventually reflected in the way we speak, so our movement on stage needs to be organized and shaped into clear phraseology.

Exercise 3.5: Phrasing Movement

As in Exercise 3.4, begin by "seeing" your own rooted center in relationship to your mirror image beneath the floor. Now make a movement by following each of these steps:

1. Select your destination: locate a specific spot with your eyes and let your face turn toward it so that your movement "follows your nose."
2. Begin to move by *lifting* the root; exaggerate this motion at first.
3. Carry your root to your destination and "land" there.
4. As you land, "spear" your root into the floor to complete your movement.
5. Repeat this action several times, paying special attention to the sense of beginning, middle, and end to each movement phrase.
6. Now begin to play with variations of this cycle, extending them beyond realistic movement. For instance, try lifting the root slowly and heavily, then drag it to the destination and *dump* it there so that it "plops" into the ground. Or make your lift light and high, moving *away* from your destination, then *throw* your root toward your destination and *fly* there, landing with a light jump. These are the kinds of "stylized" movement we associate with *commedia del l'arte.*

The states we have named "molding, floating, and flying" are different bodily *dynamics,* and are adapted from the analysis of "effort shape" made by Rudolf Laban (who also developed the system used for notating dance choreography). Besides the dynamic quality of physical energy, he spoke also of two other qualities: *flow,* which was either "direct" or "indirect," and *charge,* which was either "weak" or "strong." Let's extend this exercise to explore these other qualities of our "effort shape."

Exercise 3.6: Effort Shape

1. As you move, be aware of the quality of energy flowing from your center into that movement: is it *weak* or *strong?* Experiment with each.

2. As your energy leaves your body and enters the outside world, how does it contact others: is it *direct* or *indirect?* Experiment with each.

3. Now randomly select qualities from Table 3.1 and experience various effort shapes: for instance, try molding with a strong charge and a direct flow, and then try floating with a weak charge and an indirect flow, and so on.

Virtually any quality of movement can be created by using these variables. On stage, your performance is partly a dance, which, without appearing to be dancelike, is nevertheless composed, intensified, and purified through repeated testing and rehearsal (even if this process is rarely a conscious one). Your aim here is *not* to become self-consciously controlling of your movements, but rather to begin to experience the almost limitless range of movement qualities of which we are capable: this is one of the "palettes" from which you will "paint" as an actor, and you want to be sure that you have a wide choice of colors available to you.

TABLE 3.1   Effort Shape

Motion Quality	Effort Quality		Appearance
	Firm	Gentle	
Dynamic	Molding	Floating	Resistant or Effortless
Flow	Bound	Free	Stopping or Releasing
Charge	Strong	Weak	Fighting or Yielding
Speed	Sudden	Sustained	Quick or Slow

SUMMARY

A potter knows how the centering of the clay upon the wheel is essential to the creation of a pot; the actor must also be centered so that his or her energy, like the clay, flows outward into the new form of the role. This idea of a personal center is not just a metaphor; it has a tangible physical dimension. Finding and activating your bodily center is a necessary first step in laying a foundation for good stage movement and voice.

Developing your physical center is also a way of developing a psychological and spiritual centeredness, because at this deep level your energy exists simultaneously in physical and psychological forms. The center moves within the body as your mood changes; also, different people have different characteristic centers that are appropriate to their personalities.

The center functions in relationship to gravity, and the way in which you experience gravity, like your breathing, is a fundamental expression of your relationship to your world.

There is an "ideal" center deep within the body, roughly three finger-widths below your navel. The breath (and therefore the voice) originates here, as well as all large motions of the body and all your deepest impulses. The "pure" center is an undistorted condition from which we begin our work so that we may develop in any direction required by the role, but there is no "correct" voice or posture for the actor until they are determined by the demands of the role. Any dramatic characterization is *a set of distortions* created to express the particular nature of that character.

Our energy moves as a *cycle* that flows from our center outward toward the world *and back again.* It also flows downward into the ground, and energy also comes up into our center from the earth. We can speak, therefore, not only of being "centered," but also of being "grounded."

Various kinds of energy states produce different experiences. There is a distinct difference between *molding, floating,* and *flying,* between *strong* and *weak* energy, between *direct* and *indirect* energy flow. These different qualities of energy express different conditions, though the particular emotional quality of any one of these states can be determined only by *context.*

Lesson 4

BODY GESTURE

When you have an impulse, feeling, or idea it arouses an energy at your deep center that naturally flows outward, reaching the outer world in many forms: words, sounds, motions, or postures. Broadly speaking, any such external sign of a feeling or thought may be called a *gesture*.

In fact, the word *express* literally means "to move outward." When you have a feeling or idea, it is natural to externalize it, to "move it outward" through gesture and speech. Although this expressive behavior communicates your feelings and ideas to others, it is also an automatic part of your thought process and goes on even when you are alone. Watch people driving alone on the highway, for instance; you can see some amazingly animated conversations.

This lesson examines gestures of the body; Lesson 5 explores gestures of the voice, which are both verbal (the speaking of words) and nonverbal (the many sounds we make other than words).

COMMUNICATING THROUGH GESTURE

Our culture uses a large vocabulary of body gestures to augment and often to substitute for verbal communication. Although our verbal language communicates fairly precise meanings, our gestural language provides information about feelings and actions with greater expressiveness than words alone. Simply put, words can best say *what we mean* and gestures can best tell *how we feel* about what we mean.

Psychologists have for years been interested in body language, and this area of study has been given the name "Kinesics" by Professor Raymond Birdwhistle. Several of his basic premises are of interest to you as an actor: first, body gestures are socially learned; second, no gesture carries meaning by itself, so that all gestures must be interpreted in context; third, it is the physiological similarity of our bodies and the generally similar influences of our environment that cause some gestures to develop roughly standardized meanings within our culture.

Here is a brief example of nonverbal expression at work as observed by Professor Birdwhistle. He recorded this scene from real life and describes the nonverbal action just as a playwright would give "stage directions."

(The situation is that a guest of honor at a party arrives forty-five minutes late. Three couples besides the host and hostess had been waiting. The doorbell rings.)

Hostess: Oh! We were afraid you weren't coming; but good.

(As the hostess opened the door to admit her guest, she smiled a closed-toothed smile. As she began speaking she drew her hands, drawn into loose fists, up between her breasts. Opening her eyes very wide, she then closed them slowly and held them closed for several words. As she began to speak, she dropped her head to one side and then moved it toward the guest in a slow sweep. She then pursed her lips momentarily before continuing to speak, nodded, shut her eyes again, and spread her arms, indicating that he should enter.)

Guest: I'm very sorry; got held up you know, calls and all that.

(He looked at her fixedly; shook his head, and spread his arms with his hands held open. He then began to shuffle his feet and raise one hand, turning it slightly outward. He nodded, raised his other hand, and turned it palm-side up as he continued his vocalization. Then he dropped both hands and held them palms forward, to the side and away from his thighs. He continued his shuffling.)

Hostess: Put your wraps here. People are dying to meet you. I've told them all about you.

(She smiled at him, lips pulled back from clenched teeth, then, as she indicated where he should put his coat, she dropped her face momentarily into an expressionless pose. She smiled toothily again, clucked and slowly shut, opened, and shut her eyes again as she pointed to the guests with her lips. She then swept her head from one side to the other. As she said the word "all" she moved her head in a sweep up and down from one side to the other, shut her eyes slowly again, pursed her lips, and grasped the guest's lapel.)

Guest: You have! Well, I don't know.... Yes.... No.... I'd love to meet them.

(The guest hunched his shoulders, which pulled his lapel out of the hostess' grasp. He held his coat with both hands, frowned, and then blinked rapidly as he slipped the coat off. He continued to hold tightly to his coat.)[1]

As you reconstruct this scene in your mind's eye, it is obvious that the nonverbal behavior is very eloquent; you get a great deal of specific information from the gestures. The "logic of the body" has, within our culture, provided some gestures with conventionalized meanings: the clenching of the teeth beneath the smile, the making of fists, the shuffling of feet, all tend to have similar meanings when they appear in similar situations.

Moreover, many of the gestures tend to express feelings that run *counter* to the surface meaning of the words being spoken. This is an extremely important aspect of nonverbal expression: it often "counterpoints" or even contradicts our verbal expression and "safely" expresses feelings that would otherwise be impolite or embarrassing. For example, while the guest and the hostess are being very polite to one another, what is going on physically is that she is grabbing him and pulling him into the room against his will. To the very end, he continues to clutch his coat as a way of saying "I want to run away!" even while his words are saying "I'd love to meet them."

In acting terms, these nonverbal gestures are conveying a *subtext*, feelings running beneath the surface of the dialogue that are different from those being expressed on the surface of the scene. (Subtext is examined in greater detail in Part II.)

Though most of us read "body language" on an almost unconscious level all the time, the actor needs to heighten this skill through observation and analysis. You need to become an expert, like the famous fictional detective Sherlock Holmes:

> *He had risen from his chair and was standing between the parted blinds, gazing down into the dull neutral-tinted London street. . . . On the pavement opposite there stood a large woman with a heavy fur boa around her neck, and a large curling red feather in a broad-brimmed hat which was tilted in a coquettish Duchess of Devonshire fashion over her ear. From under this great panoply she peeped up in a nervous, hesitating fashion at our window, while her body oscillated backward and forward, and her fingers fidgeted with her glove buttons. Suddenly, with a plunge as of the swimmer who leaves the bank, she hurled across the road and we heard the sharp clang of the bell. "I have seen these symptoms before," said Holmes, throwing his cigarette into the fire. "Oscillation upon the pavement always means an affair de coeur. She would like advice, but is not sure that the matter is not too delicate*

for communication. And yet even here we may discriminate. When a woman has been seriously wronged by a man she no longer oscillates, and the usual symptom is a broken bell wire. Here we may take it that there is a love matter, but that the maiden is not so much angered as perplexed, or grieved. But here she comes in person to resolve our doubts."[2]

In his book *The Silent Language*, Edward Hall says that Sherlock Holmes "made explicit a highly complex process which many of us go through without knowing that we are involved. Those of us who keep our eyes open can read volumes into what we see going on around us."[3] The actor has special need to engage in this kind of acute observation. As Brian Bates reports in his book, *The Way of the Actor:*

Liv Ullmann regards observing other people as an essential path to "becoming other people" more fully and truthfully.... Actors have been observers for centuries, for without this keen attention to others, performances are limited to the prison of one's own personal life.[4]

To see how explicit a playwright can be about such details of non-verbal behavior, read the scene from *The Glass Menagerie* in the Appendix now, and pay special attention to Williams' stage directions.

Exercise 4.1: The Science of Deduction

Through observation over the next few days, find for yourself a brief real-life scene involving subtext, and record it in the same way as the hostess–guest scene recorded by Professor Birdwhistle.

Analyze it as if you were Sherlock Holmes. Recreate as completely as you can the reasons for the behavior of the characters, and create a personality profile for each.

With a partner, recreate the scene for the group. Let everyone develop their own ideas about the subtext, then compare your accounts to see what similar deductions you have made. What areas were the most commonly agreed upon, and what evidence was the most persuasive? Be specific: Why did you draw the conclusions you reached from each bit of evidence?

Although the scientific study of body language is fairly new, our interest in it is very old. One of the first studies of the "silent language" (which may have been influential on the style of acting of its time) was John Bulwer's *Chirologia and Chironomia*, written in 1644. The book calls itself a study of "the Speaking Motions, and Discoursing Gestures, the patheticalle motions of the minde." The book discussed and illustrated an enormous number of feelings as expressed by nonverbal gestures (see Figure 4.1 on page 34). Similar attempts to categorize physical gestures for the performer were made throughout the seventeenth, eighteenth, and nineteenth centuries. Even a few modern systems of acting use, in a very modified form, a formalized approach to the physical expression of emotion by locating "emotional centers" in the body, an idea borrowed from Oriental acting and medicine.

THE GENESIS OF GESTURE

As we have seen, some of our body gestures have developed a common meaning within similar situations, forming a gestural subvocabulary. This is because these gestures have a common origin.

Some of these gestures derive their meaning from the structure of the body itself. For example, a man hitching up his pants is usually asserting his masculinity, because this action refers attention to his genitals. Likewise, a woman covering her cheeks with her hands is probably expressing embarrassment, and her gesture is a *substitute blush* as the hands rise to the face in the same way that the blood would have risen to the cheeks in a real blush.

Other gestures derive their meaning by being leftovers of animal behavior that we would have used at an earlier, more primitive stage of our evolution as a species. These vestiges of animal behavior live on as symbolic activity long after the action has ceased to be practical. This idea was developed by Charles Darwin as part of his theory of evolution in *The Expression of Emotion in Man and Animal*. Darwin's ideas are expanded on here by my teacher, the late Robert S. Breen:

Consider the expressive value of behavior that was once in our human history adaptive, but is no longer so except in a vestigial sense—for example, the baring of teeth in the preparation for attack or defense. In primitive experience, the use of the teeth for tearing and rending an enemy was common enough, and a very effective means of adapting to an environmental necessity. Today, the use of teeth in this primitive fashion is rare, but the baring of the teeth is still very much with us. In an attitude of pugnacity, men will frequently clench their teeth and draw back their lips to expose their teeth. This action is a reinstatement of the primitive pattern of biting, though there is no real intention of using the teeth in such a fashion. The "tough guy" talks through his teeth because he is habituated to an attitude of aggressiveness. When

FIGURE 4.1   From *Chirologia and Chironomia,* 1644

he bares his teeth, it is a warning to all who see him that he is prepared to attack or to defend himself. His speech is characterized by a nasality because his oral cavity is closed, and his breath escapes primarily through his nose. Lip action in speech is curtailed because the jaw is held so close to the upper jaw that there is little room between the lips for even their normal activity. Restriction of the lip action results in the tough guy's talking out of the corner of his mouth.

When we see a person bare his clenched teeth, curl his lip, narrow his eyes, deepen his breathing, etc., we conclude that he is angry. These are the signs of attack in our ancestors which have become for us social symbols expressive of an emotional state *known as* anger.[5]

Exercise 4.2: Animal Gestures

Select a strongly physical action directed toward another, such as intimidation, seduction, rejection, or approval. Adopt the characteristics of an ape or prehistoric man performing the same function. When you have begun to experience the activity on a purely physical, "animalistic" level, begin gradually to "civilize" the behavior. If you begin by grabbing at your partner and pulling her toward you, let the grabbing turn into a beckoning finger, or a beckoning gesture of the head. Let the activity itself lead you as it gradually becomes less and less practical and more and more "symbolic."

Using the hostess–guest scene, or your own subtext scene, work with a partner to develop the scene as it might have happened between two animals.

You will probably notice that the "animalized" version of your scene brought the subtext to the surface, since the purposeful suppression of feelings is an exclusively human ability. You also noticed that the animal version involved a great deal more overt movement of the lower body than its civilized offspring. Consider, however, that all these same "animal" impulses are at work in you even when you are engaging in highly civilized behavior. They are felt as muscular arousal even though they may not result in observable movement, and they affect your voice and movement quality no matter how polite and symbolic you are being.

GESTURES IN THE TEXT

When performing scripted material, the playwright has provided the words. You must develop the many nonverbal aspects of your performance—the physical gestures, postures, vocal inflections, facial expressions, and so on. In doing this, you may find some guidance in the script, either in stage directions or by implications in the highly physical language that is the mark of a good playwright. As you gain experience, you begin to recognize and expand on these implications.

Exercise 4.3: Implied Gestures in the Text

With a partner, read some of the scene from *The Glass Menagerie* in the Appendix aloud, *including the stage directions that pertain to your character*. Act out the behavior Williams describes. Do you begin to feel the inner states that the behavior expresses?

The following speech from Shakespeare's *King Lear* suggests gestures of all four types; read it aloud and feel the strong, specific impulses to gesture it gives you.

> *When I do stare, see how the subject quakes. I pardon that man's life. What was thy cause? Adultery? Thou shalt not die. Die for adultery? The wren goes to't, and the small gilded fly does lecher in my sight. Let copulation thrive, for Gloucester's bastard son was kinder to his father than my daughter's got 'tween the lawful sheets. To't luxury, pell-mell! for I lack soldiers. Behold yond simpering dame, whose face between her forks presages snow, that minces virtue, and does shake the head to hear of pleasure's name: The fitchew nor the soiled horse goes to't with a more riotous appetite. Down from the waist they are centaurs, though women all above. But to the girdle do the gods inherit, beneath is all the fiend's. There's hell, there's darkness, there is the sulfurous pit: burning, scalding, stench, consumption. Fie, fie, fie! pah, pah! Give me an ounce of civet, good apothecary, to sweeten my imagination. There's money for thee.*

Now perform an "animalization" of the speech; see how far you can go, allowing the impulses for gesture to return to their deepest animal origins in biting, hitting, spitting, vomiting, embracing, and so on. Allow the words themselves to "regress" into the sounds of these activities.

SUMMARY

Any external sign of a feeling or thought may be called a gesture. When you have a feeling or idea, it is natural to express it, to "move it outward" through gesture and speech. This is an automatic part of your thought process and goes on even when you are alone.

Words can best say *what we mean* and gestures can best tell *how we feel* about what we mean. Body gestures are socially learned; no gesture carries meaning by itself, though the "logic of the body" has provided some gestures with conventionalized meanings in similar situations.

Body gestures sometimes express feelings that run *counter* to the surface meaning of the words being spoken. In acting terms, these nonverbal gestures are conveying a *subtext.* Though most of us read "body language" on an almost unconscious level all the time, the actor needs to heighten this skill through observation and analysis.

Some gestures derive their meaning from the structure of the body itself. Others are vestiges of animal behavior; when we see a person bare his clenched teeth, curl his lip, narrow his eyes, and deepen his breathing, we know that these were signs of attack in our ancestors, and have become for us *social symbols expressive of an emotional state* known as *anger.*

When you perform scripted material, the playwright may have provided gestures in the stage directions. Gestures are also implied in the highly physical language that is the mark of a good playwright.

Lesson 5

VOICE AND SPEECH

The emphasis our culture places on words as a way of communicating information sometimes makes us forget that the voice, apart from the speaking of words, also carries gesture. Articulated speech is a learned ability, but vocal gesture is instinctive. Perhaps for this reason, vocal sounds are universal in appeal. As Margaret Schlauch puts it in *The Gift of Language:*

> *A cry, a tonal inflection, a gesture, are means of communication far more universal than language as we understand it. They are, in fact, universal enough to be conveyed to animals as well as other human beings.*[1]

In this lesson, you begin exploring the wide range of vocal behavior that surrounds and supports the speaking of words. Some theorists believe that these nonverbal sounds are, in fact, the source from which our spoken language evolved. In any case, they are still used to express those deep feelings that often cannot be put into words.

THE VOICE AND EMOTION

Your voice is totally involved with your most basic bodily functions because it is produced by so many deep and important muscles and organs. As linguist Edward Sapir points out, "There are properly speaking no organs of speech. There are only organs that are incidentally useful in the production of speech sounds."[2] For this reason, your voice is called an "overlaid function," a sort of double duty performed by organs and muscles that evolved originally for other, more basic activities: the dia-phragm and lungs for breathing, the larynx for swallowing, the tongue, the teeth, and the lips for chewing, the palate and tongue for tasting. In fact, the network of muscles that produce the voice are so complex and far reaching that they ultimately involve the entire body.

We said in Lesson 4 that your natural impulse is to externalize your feelings and that these externalizations are part and parcel of your emo-tions. Because the voice is produced by the deep muscles that are the seat of emotion, your voice is completely integrated with your emotional life. As Sapir puts it:

> *The sound of pain or the sound of joy does not, as such, indicate the emotion, it does not stand aloof, as it were, and announce that such and such an emotion is being felt. What it does is to serve as a more or less automatic overflow of the emotional energy: in a sense, it is part and parcel of the emotion itself.*[3]

There are two important ideas here: first, that the vocal sounds can be an emotional "overflow," a sort of safety-valve action when our inner dynamic becomes so high that we can no longer "contain ourselves"; second, that such vocalizations of our inner feelings are an automatic and integral part of the feelings themselves because *the voice is produced by the same muscles and organs that are central to our emotional life.*

THE VOICE AND INNER DYNAMIC

There is an old story about a highly mannered, flamboyant actress who gestured so indiscriminately that her movements ceased to have any organic relationship to the scene she was performing. Her director tied her hands together with a string. "When your impulse to move is so strong that you must break the string," he said, "then you may move." The director was forcing her, through the string, to hold her responses in (to suppress them); a psychologist would say he was "raising her thresh-old of response" so that only the strongest (and therefore the most dra-matically important) responses would flow over her threshold; the less deeply felt impulses would be filtered out.

I once saw a short film showing the great cinema director, Jean Renoir, working with an actress in preparation for a highly emotional close-up. He sits her before the camera with the script and instructs her to read the words of her speech without emotion. She goes over the speech several times, and each time her natural response to the highly charged material starts to take over. At the slightest sign of emotion, however, Renoir sternly says, "No, no, just the words!" You can literally see the emotional pressure rising in her as the suppressed responses struggle harder and harder to break free. Finally, when she is about to explode, Renoir calls "action!" and the camera captures a splendid performance. Here is an exercise in which you can experience this for yourself.

Exercise 5.1: Overflow

This is an exercise in experiencing the "overflow" of vocal and physical gesture. Repeat Exercise 4.3: read the speech by King Lear aloud, but force yourself to remain perfectly expressionless and still, suppressing all impulses for vocal and physical gesture. Do this several times until you feel the demand for physical and vocal gesture growing so strong that you can no longer "contain yourself" and are finally forced to move.

As you may have felt in this exercise, the repeated suppression of the impulses tended not only to filter out the weaker, less deeply felt ones, but it also strengthened those that remained by building their "inner pressure," or *inner dynamic*. This is why we often say that "less is more," and why Stanislavski encouraged actors over the course of a rehearsal process to "cut eighty percent" of the activity they began with: with less external activity to release it, internal energy has a chance to build.

In fact, inner dynamic is essential to the sense of drama, because it arouses suspense. A person with a lot of energy "inside" but without much being released "outside" is dramatically interesting; they command our attention and make us wonder "What is he or she going to do?" This inner dynamic produces the quality of excitement or even danger we sense from actors like Robert DeNiro, James Woods, Gary Oldman, or Ed Harris. Here is an exercise that will enable you to experience this inner dynamic and to hear its profound effect on the voice.

Exercise 5.2: Running on the Inside

You are to stand and run in place, counting every other step aloud from one to fifty, but when you reach thirty, stop running "outside" but continue to run "inside;" hear the effect this has on your voice.

As you noticed here, the voice automatically carries much of your "hidden" energy out into the world, even when you are trying to suppress it! For instance, it is extremely moving to hear newscasters reporting a great tragedy, like the assassination of President John F. Kennedy, because they are trying to remain "objective," yet despite their disciplined efforts the emotion is forcing itself through.

This is why what you *don't* do on stage is often much more important than what you *do*. What you are holding *in* enriches your performance and makes it more dramatic. It also automatically enriches your voice.

THE VOICE AND ATTITUDE

As we said earlier, the words we speak carry the information we wish to impart, while our attitude about that information is usually carried by our tone of voice. If, for example, I feel strongly about what I am saying, I may increase the volume of my voice, elevate my pitch slightly, and enunciate sharply by hitting the hard consonants as a sort of vocal "pounding on the table."

We also pointed out that the voice may communicate attitudes contrary to the meaning of our words. You already recognize such "hidden" meanings as *subtext*. The most obvious example is sarcasm: If, during an argument, I say to you, "Well, you certainly are an expert on the subject," it is my tone of voice that lets you know that I really mean "You don't know what you're talking about!"

In such instances, it is the quality of my voice that communicates my true meaning. It is because these sounds have their source in the common construction of our bodies and in our evolutionary history that they are so powerfully communicative. Remember Charles Darwin's explanation of physical gesture as a vestige of animal behavior in Lesson 4; he also believed that many vocal gestures were symbolic of general bodily functions, as explained here by Robert Breen:

> *Darwin pointed to the primitive practice of children who expressed their dislike for someone or something by sticking out their tongues and making a sound something like a bleating sheep. Sticking out the tongue was for Darwin a primitive reflex of vomiting or rejecting something distasteful; so, too, was the sound, which got its peculiar vocal quality from the extremely open throat through which it came. The open throat was, of course, a feature of the regurgitation, or vomiting, reflex. It is interesting that the civilized adult will show his contempt or distaste in much the same fashion, though much repressed. We are all familiar with the tone of voice which we recognize as "superior" or "contemptuous" because it has that "open throat" quality.*[4]

Think back to the hostess–guest scene in Lesson 4; as the hostess greeted the overdue guest, she *"smiled a close-toothed smile."* The quality of voice that would go with this gesture has the sound of biting, and although she says "Oh, we were afraid you weren't coming. But good," her gesture and tone of voice express the subtext, "I'm so furious with you for being late I wish I could bite you!"

USING YOUR OWN VOICE

From all we have seen so far, we realize that the voice is a tremendously personal thing. In fact, the word *personality* comes from the root *per sona,* meaning "through sound." Your voice travels from your deepest center on its way toward the outer world and it carries with it the qualities of your "inner world." The act of speaking literally *turns you inside out.*

This is true when your voice is allowed to function in its normal, undistorted way. But sometimes actors choose to adopt an artificialized voice for the sake of "creating a character," or "playing age," or—especially with Shakespeare—"being poetic." If you do this, your voice is no longer authentically personal. Your aim is to let your "I" flow into the "me" of the character, and you make that journey first and most actively by *saying* what the character says. If you do not say it with your own voice—if *you are not there*—you are cut off from this primary point of entry into the experience of the character. Although it is true that your voice may undergo some degree of transformation in the course of working on a role, this transformation must be the result of other, deeper changes that cannot be replaced by vocal fakery.

Exercise 5.3: Using Your Own Voice

Select a speech from a play, preferably by a character who is quite "different" from you, or whose way of speaking is quite different from your own. Standing before the group, read this speech in your own voice; become aware of any urge to alter your voice in order to "perform" and simply release any such impulse. Don't try to do anything, simply *allow* yourself to speak the character's words in your own voice.

Of course, if you intend a professional acting career you must expand the range and responsiveness of your vocal instrument, but no matter how much you may work on your voice you must always do so with an aim to perfecting its own natural qualities. You can do this by becoming aware of good vocal technique and relearning any bad habits you have developed. It is a slow and gentle process, which must be pursued with the guidance of a qualified teacher.

SPEECH

Humankind was once described as "the animal who talks." Speech is an amazing capacity: it is based on the ability to *symbolize*. (Nowadays we are examining the possibility that animals such as whales, dolphins, and chimpanzees are also capable of using symbols.)

Philosopher Ernst Cassirer, when theorizing about how the capacity for speech develops in us, observed that at first the sounds we make are part of feelings like hunger, pain, or joy. In this infantile "sensuous" phase, we are not trying to express these feelings to others, but rather are making sounds as part of the feelings themselves:

> *When we seek to follow language back to its earliest beginnings, it seems to be not merely a representative sign for ideas, but also an emotional sign for sensuous drives and stimuli. The ancients knew this derivation of language from emotion from the pathos of sensation, pleasure, and pain...it is to this final source which is common to man and beast and hence truly "natural" that we must return, in order to understand the origin of language.[5]*

Speech, then, begins with our most fundamental experience of pleasure and pain, though at this stage it is only nonverbal sound, a kind of vocal gesture. In this earliest stage of development, the baby explores the world by grabbing it and literally "taking it in" to its mouth.

Later, the baby notices that making a certain sound makes Mommy appear, or causes food to be given. It is at this point that the baby notices that *the voice can reach farther than the hand;* it realizes that it can affect the world by producing certain sounds, and the capacity for symbolic speech is born.

Viewed in this way, speech is *a special kind of doing;* it is the most specific way in which we send our energies into the world in our effort to satisfy our needs.

This is a particularly useful view of speech for the actor. In creating a play, the writer has channeled a total human situation full of feelings and actions into the relatively few words of the dialogue. In a novel or short story, many more words are used to describe feelings, thoughts, and actions. In a play these words are eliminated in favor of the dialogue alone and all it can imply and suggest. Above all, the primary function of good dramatic language is *to transmit action.*

Remember: dramatic speech is *a form of doing.* When you deliver that speech on a stage or before a camera, your voice must also be *doing.* Your words should be hitting, or caressing, or grabbing, or whatever the action underlying the speech may be.

THE PROCESS OF SPEECH

In our technological world, speech has become primarily a means for the communication of information. But for the actor, speech must retain the feelingful and active qualities we have been describing. Think of speech as *a physical process whereby feelings, needs, and thoughts find their expression in muscular activity that produces articulated sound.* As such, speech is a special type of active gesture intended to produce a real effect on your world.

As you form your thoughts into the physical activity called speech, you make a great many choices that are expressive of your feelings, needs, values, background, and personality. In this way, your process of verbalization expresses the kind of person you are (character) and the way in which you try to cope with your world (action).

It is this living quality of speech *coming to be for the first time* that you must relive to enter fully into your character. If you deliver your lines merely as memorized words, you deprive yourself of the transformational power of participating actively in the character's thought processes that lie behind the words he or she speaks.

This does not require halting speech, long pauses, or the mumbling that too often are used as easy substitutes for an honest participation in the character's thought processes. You don't want to *show* us that you are thinking, you want to be *really thinking*. The words of the dialogue are both your starting point and your final judge: you "take them apart" in rehearsal to discover the thoughts and feelings that drive them; in performance you relive these thoughts and feelings and the words come out "under their own power."

Exercise 5.4: Bringing a Speech to Life

Choose a short speech (perhaps only a few lines) and, after memorizing it thoroughly, go through it so as to experience the thoughts and feelings that drive the words. Begin with movement and sound rooted in the needs and feelings that lie beneath the words, but without the words themselves. Then, allow the words of the speech to come gradually out of your movement, like a picture coming into focus. Do this with each phrase or sentence, letting the words come from the need to communicate the idea or feeling involved.

Does a sense of character begin to emerge as you experience the character's words coming to life? Think of it this way: playwrights, knowing that an actor will eventually speak their words, write not for the eye but for the human voice; the human voice is deeply involved in the body's muscles; the body's muscles are deeply involved in emotional life and thought. This is why the words your character speaks reflect both the psychology and physiology of that character and through this "psychophysical" process, the character's words can help provide a direct route to a living experience of that character. This is why some schools of acting encourage you to "just say the words," because "saying the words" in the most complete sense involves a total expression of the mind and body of the speaker!

SUMMARY

Vocal gesture is instinctive and universal in appeal and may be the source from which our spoken language evolved. Your voice is an "overlaid function," a sort of double duty performed by organs and muscles that evolved originally for other, more basic activities: the network of muscles that produce the voice begin deep within the body, and are central to our emotional life as well.

The arousal of these deep muscles in the act of sounding or speaking builds our *inner dynamic.* Inner dynamic is essential to the sense of drama, because it arouses suspense. A person with a lot of energy "inside" but without much being released "outside" is dramatically interesting. This is why what you *don't* do on stage is often much more important than what you *do.*

The word *personality* comes from the root *per sona,* meaning "through sound." The act of speaking literally *turns you inside out.*

You make the journey into the character's mind first and most actively by saying what the character says. If you do not say it with your own voice you are cut off from this fundamental point of entry into the character.

Speech begins when a baby notices that *the voice can reach farther than the hand.* Viewed in this way, speech is *a special kind of doing;* it is the most specific way in which we send our energies into the world in our effort to satisfy our needs. On stage, especially, speech is *a form of doing.*

Think of speech as *a physical process whereby feelings, needs, and thoughts find their expression in muscular activity that produces articulated sound.*

Playwrights write not for the eye but for the human voice; the human voice is deeply involved in the body's musculature; the body's musculature is deeply involved in emotional life and thought. This is why the words your character speaks reflect both the psychology and physiology of that character. Your ability to revitalize the process of word choice is crucial to your understanding and creation of the character.

Lesson 6

THE PERFORMANCE SPACE

So far you have been exploring your inner world. Now turn your attention outward, to the world outside your skin. Begin by exploring the space in which you work.

The famine in ancient Thebes; a child trying to leave home; mankind confronting nothingness: anything can happen on a stage. You can make a stage seem like any place and any time; but before it becomes the world of the character, it must first of all be your world as an actor. You work in the here and now; the stage is the "here." Being fully in touch with your space provides a point of contact that anchors your work. What you create is made more real by its derivation from your physical actuality on stage.

Unfortunately, most of us go through life largely unaware of the space we inhabit, and sometimes even feel isolated from it; this sense of physical isolation inside our "bags of skin" reflects a psychological and spiritual isolation from the world in which we live that is all too common in our culture. Philosopher Alan Watts expressed it this way:

We suffer from a hallucination, from a false and distorted sense of our own existence as living organisms. Most of us have the sensation that "I myself" is a separate center of feeling and action, living inside and bounded by the physical body—a center which "confronts" an "external" world of people and things, making contact through the senses with a universe both alien and strange. Everyday figures of speech reflect this illusion. "I came into this world," "You must face reality," "The conquest of nature." This feeling of being lonely and very temporary visitors in the universe is in flat contradiction to everything known about man (and all other living organisms) in the sciences. We do not "come into" this world; we come out of it, as leaves from a tree. As the ocean "waves," the universe "peoples." Every individual is an expression of the whole realm of nature, a unique action of the total universe.[1]

The following exercise helps you develop an open and responsive relationship to the physical space that you inhabit. You may discover that it also inhabits you.

Exercise 6.1: Swimming in Space

As a group, move freely through the space of the room. Be aware of the fluidity of your movement, of the eddies and currents in space that your are making as you move. Uncover as much of your skin as possible, and feel the resistance of the air as you move, swimming in the ocean of air.

Now become aware that every breath you take actually takes in space; you are not only swimming through space, but space is swimming through you; the space of the room is also in every joint and cavity of your body. Swim until you feel at one with your space, moving through it, it moving through you, and being carried along by it.

As you move, notice that you carry along a certain amount of space; awareness of this will help you to move smoothly, so as not to violate the momentum of your "envelope" of space.

Now become aware of the total space of the room and everything it contains; see how every movement of your own and every movement of every other person in the space influences the total space and everything in it.

THE STAGE

What exactly is a stage? It is *any* space in which actors create for their audience the patterned experience called drama, including the film or television "sound stage." Stages come in many sizes, shapes, and types: a circle scratched in the dirt, a rug spread in a marketplace, the back of a truck in a field, or an elaborate building filled with high-tech machinery. Never before has such a wide variety of stage types confronted the actor.

A stage is defined by its relationship to the audience, and there are four basic types of theatre configurations: *proscenium, thrust, arena,* and *environmental* (see Figure 6.1). Let's consider what each of the basic types means to the actor.

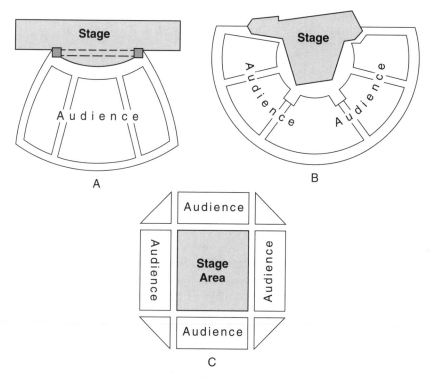

FIGURE 6.1   Types of Stages: (A) traditional proscenium; (B) modern thrust; (C) arena

Proscenium.   The traditional proscenium stage features an arch through which the audience sees the action. This "picture frame" evolved as a way of establishing a point of reference for settings painted in perspective (hence the word *pro-scenium* which means "in front of the scene"). To enhance the illusion of perspective, the stage floor was originally sloped upward away from the audience; thus moving away from the audience is called going "upstage," and staying there during a scene so that the other actors are forced to turn their backs on the audience to speak to you is called "upstaging."

The actor on the proscenium stage must, of course, realize that the audience is limited to one side of the playing area, but it is certainly not necessary to "cheat out" (to turn your body partly out toward the audience). Doing so makes your character appear to be more interested in speaking to the audience than to the other characters in the scene. And don't underestimate how much acting you can do with your back.

Although you may make some adjustments because of the audience's location, you must do so without destroying the internal logic of the character's environment.

Thrust.   In the 1950s the thrust stage (so called because it "thrusts" into the midst of the audience) became very popular. It features the same stage–audience relationship as the classical and Elizabethan theatres and places the actor into close proximity with the audience, but also limits the use of scenery. For this reason, it is very much an "actor's" theatre. There is some added responsibility to keep *open* to audience view, or at least to distribute your presence equally to all sections of the house, but the increased sense of audience contact inherent in the thrust stage makes such accommodation easy and natural.

Arena.   The arena and other types of full-round stages stand at the opposite extreme from proscenium stages. Here the audience completely surrounds the stage and the actor enters through the audience area, either down the aisles or from openings in the auditorium called "vomitoria." The actor's problem of keeping open to all sections of the audience is even more acute here than on a thrust stage. In both thrust and arena, it is important not to stand too close to one another because you will block each other from audience view.

The full-round offers a sense of intimacy unlike any other type of stage, and such theatres are usually quite small. For this reason, audiences tend to expect a more detailed and subtle performance, something closer to what is required for the camera.

Environmental.   Although most stages are of the three basic types described above, we sometimes create special environments for specific productions, some of which may abandon entirely the separation of stage and audience. Here, of course, the proximity of the audience demands total commitment and attention to detail, just as the camera does in film acting. For example, my production of Kafka's *The Trial,* at the California Institute of the Arts, was mounted as an enormous fun house; small audience groups moved from room to room, each accompanied by an actor performing the role of the hero, and in each room a scene from the novel was played out.

Regardless of which of these stages you work in, remember that it is the total theatrical space that is your true working area, not the stage alone. Your adaptation to the positioning of the audience and to the vocal demands of the shape and size of the entire auditorium is essential.

DIRECTIONS ON STAGE

You need to be able to find your way around on stage according to the traditional terms used by directors and playscripts. Though there are many different kinds of stages today, we generally use the nomenclature developed for the proscenium.

Vertical Directions. As we mentioned earlier, the proscenium stage floor was originally sloped upward away from the audience, so we speak of *"up*stage" as being away from the audience, and *"down*stage" as being toward the audience. To stand "level" with another actor is for both of you to stand perpendicular (in profile) to the audience.

Lateral Directions are determined by the actors' view as they face the audience. Thus *stage right* is the same as the audience's left; *downstage right* means toward the audience and to the actor's right (see Figure 6.2).

Turns are described as being either in (toward the center of the stage, whichever side of the stage you are on) or out (again, away from center).

Crossing (that is, moving from one point to another) may be in a straight line, or in a slight arc so that you end facing more in profile to the audience. A cross with an exaggerated arc is called a "circle cross" (or sometimes called a "banana").

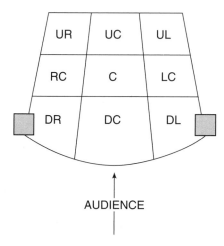

FIGURE 6.2   Locations on a Proscenium Stage

Positions as you pivot relative to the audience are called "one-quarter," "half," and "three-quarters" depending on how far you turn from one side to the other. Thus a director may tell you to "cheat out one-quarter," which means to pivot 45 degrees away from center. This system of directions soon becomes second nature.

Exercise 6.2: Directions on Stage

Have your partner stand in the center of the stage and stand beside them on the stage right side; they will "play director" by giving you the following directions; then reverse positions.

> *Go down right. / Turn out and go up right. / Turn and cheat down one-half. / Take a long cross down left, going upstage of me. / Turn in and do a circle cross up, passing on the downstage side of me and ending level with me on the right. / Cheat out one-quarter. / Now turn in one-quarter. / Go straight down and hold center. / Circle up to the right around me and exit left center.*

THE SCALE OF PERFORMANCE

The type and size of the performance space requires a fundamental adaptation in the size or scale of the performance. Adjusting the scale of performance is a matter of increasing or decreasing its size without distorting the content, just as you might raise or lower the contrast or color level on a television set without changing the content of the picture.

For example, an intimate scene can be played in a large theatre by making an overall increase in its size and volume, as long as the behavior and attitudes of the characters continue to conform to the demands of intimacy in all other respects. Your audience accepts the necessity of the adjustment and by convention reinterprets the scene in their own minds to compensate for it.

In the live theatre, the problem of scale is usually a matter of this sort of enlargement. For certain intimate spaces, however, such as a small full-round stage or an environmental production, you may need to *reduce* scale so as to focus on the minute details of physical and vocal behavior.

The most extreme instance of small-scale work is acting for the camera. Because of its closeness, the camera lens tends literally *to record your thought*; it is usually "too much" for the camera if you do anything more than *think* your way through a scene and allow the rest of your behavior to remain as it would be in life; some actors actually have to suppress their real-life behavior for the camera. Many of the actors who act both on stage and for the camera report the importance of learning to "do nothing" for the camera.

Because small details of behavior are usually beyond the bounds of conscious control, the completeness of your inner work and the intensity of your concentration are at a premium before the camera or in intimate theatrical situations. In general, we can say that *as the external scale of a scene decreases, the level of inner dynamic must increase.*

Scale is determined not only by the size and distance of the audience, but also by the style of the material being performed. Broad comedy and especially farce, for instance, depend on a size, energy, and tempo of performance that is heightened beyond the limits of everyday behavior; on the other hand, the comedic naturalism of Chekhov places behavior "under the microscope" of a nearly scientific scrutiny, and great meaning is attached to even the tiniest details. A more filmic approach is needed here, and indeed Chekhov translates to film far more easily than does Shakespeare.

Your ability to adjust the scale of your performance to fit the needs of your stage and the style of the play is innate: we regularly adapt the size of our behavior to fit different contexts. This automatic and usually unconscious life process is also the way you adjust scale in performance, except that the extremes of largeness or smallness are often far greater when acting than in everyday life.

Especially when doing larger forms of performance, it is important that you do not judge the scale of your performance according to your everyday kinetic sense. I have sometimes videotaped performances requiring large scale (such as an outdoor Shakespeare festival) and when the actors see themselves they invariably say, "I thought I was moving more than that!" Although they had increased the scale of their movement beyond that of everyday life by perhaps 25 percent, so it felt like quite a stretch, an extension of 50 percent or more was actually needed.

THE AUDIENCE AS ENVIRONMENT

When you perform, you join a community dedicated to experiencing the insights and aliveness offered by the drama. You, your fellow actors, and the audience all work together to achieve this experience, and you each have your own task to perform. Sometimes as actors we forget this, and we think our sole job is to please our audience, to "play to" them and to "show them" what our character is feeling and thinking. Such illustrative acting falsifies the character's reality: it says, "Look at me! I'll show you what my character is doing, thinking, feeling!" We call this kind of acting *indicating*. Your job is not to *show* your audience anything:

it is simply to *do* what your character does as completely and accurately as you can, to fulfill your character's dramatic purpose within the play.

Your audience's response is certainly important, and you shape your performance with a desire to make the performance accessible to them; but when you are actually performing, your immediate concentration is on what you, as the character, are doing, *not* on the audience's response to it. Your character's task is the foreground of your awareness, and your audience is the background against which you work.

Think of the audience's presence as part of your stage environment. Accept the audience's presence just as you accept the presence of your fellow actors: even though they are not part of your character's world, and therefore cannot be acknowledged on that level, you have an underlying sense that the other actors and your audience are all your teammates. You do not "play to" your audience, any more than you "play to" your fellow actors; you play "with" them. Your attitude is to invite them to join you in creating the experience of the play; it cannot be complete without them.

SUMMARY

As an actor, you have a special relationship to the environment in which you work; the stage and your fellow actors are your partners in creation. A stage is defined by its relationship to the audience. The four basic types of theatre configurations are proscenium, thrust, arena, and environmental.

We generally use the nomenclature developed for the proscenium: We speak of "downstage" as being toward the audience and "upstage" as being away; lateral directions are determined by the actor's right and left as they face the audience. Turns are described as being either "in" (toward the center of the stage) or "out." Positions as you pivot are called "one-quarter," "half," and "three-quarters" depending on how far you turn.

The type and size of the performance space requires an adaptation in the scale of the performance, increasing or decreasing its size without distorting the content. Your audience accepts the necessity of the adjustment and by convention reinterprets the scene in their own minds.

The most extreme instance of small-scale work is acting for the camera. Because of its closeness, the camera lens tends literally to record your thought, and many actors report the importance of learning to "do nothing" for the camera. In general, as the external scale of a scene decreases, the level of inner dynamic must increase. Scale is determined not only by the size and distance of the audience, but also by the style of the material being performed; do not judge the scale of your performance according to your everyday kinetic sense.

When you perform, you join a community; you, your fellow actors, and the audience all work together. We may forget this, and think our sole job is to please our audience, to "play to" them and to show them what our character is feeling and thinking; this is called *indicating*. Instead of acting *for* the audience, you act *with* them; your character's task is the foreground of your awareness, and your audience is the background against which you work.

Lesson 7

WORKING WITH OTHERS

Whatever else a play may mean, all drama is fundamentally about the interaction of people with one another and with their world, what Aristotle called "people in action." When a dramatic scene flows as it should, an unbroken cycle of shared energy passes between the actors through the chain of action and reaction that moves the scene. Sometimes it is expressed primarily through the words of the dialogue, sometimes as motions and gestures, sometimes as silent looking, but always the energy flows, being given and being received. When the flow of this give and take, this chain of action and reaction, is broken, the scene and the characters die. It follows that drama can be properly performed only by a team of actors working together to achieve the purposes of the play. Even though most dramatic scenes are based on a conflict between the characters, you and your fellow actors remain teammates working together to realize that conflict, and a deep sharing of the energy of the scene produces a more unified and rhythmic result.

As playwright August Strindberg commented a century ago:

No form of art is as dependent as the actor's. He cannot isolate his particular contribution, show it to someone and say, "This is mine." If he does not get the support of his fellow actors, his performance will lack resonance and depth. He will be held in check and lured into wrong inflections and wrong rhythms. He won't make a good impression no matter how hard he tries. Actors must rely on each other. Occasionally one sees an exceptionally egotistic individual who "upstages" a rival, obliterates him, in order that he and he alone can be seen.

That is why rapport among actors is imperative for the success of a play. I don't care whether you rank yourselves higher or lower than each other, or from side to side, or from inside out—as long as you do it together.[1]

Your training as an actor concentrates most on your personal skills, and indeed a team depends on the individual strength of every member; but no matter how strong your individual technique becomes, you must also develop the skill of working effectively within the creative ensemble. The foundation of this collaborative skill is the realization that you are connected to your world and all who inhabit it. Your sense of a separate "I" bounded by the physical body is a limited understanding of your participation in nature. Your ideas of an "inner" and an "outer" world are only different attitudes toward experience; the world is one world, which we merely experience as "inner" and "outer." Your breath itself reveals this, as Mary Caroline Richards points out in her book, *Centering:*

The innerness of the so-called outer world is nowhere so evident as in the life of our body. The air we breathe one moment will be breathed by someone else the next and has been breathed by someone else before. We exist as respiring, pulsating organisms within a sea of life-serving beings. As we become able to hold this more and more steadily in our consciousness, we experience relatedness at an elemental level. We see that it is not a matter of trying to be related, but rather of living consciously into the actuality of being related. As we yield ourselves to the living presence of this relatedness, we find that life begins to possess an ease and a freedom and a naturalness that fill our hearts with joy.[2]

Take a moment to sit quietly and experience your breath in the way Richards describes. This lesson explores the sharing of energy that enables a team of actors to work effectively together.

THE BODILY CENTER AND RELATIONSHIP

Whatever other qualities our relationships may have, our basic attitude toward another person at any given moment is expressed by the way our energy flows toward them (*approach*) or away from them (*avoidance*), even if we don't actually move. There is no relationship where energy is not given or withheld, and there is no way for you to "fake" a relationship if you fail to involve your deepest bodily energy in it. Have you ever seen student actors trying to do a love scene, perhaps even an embrace, while both were actually holding their centers back? Or actors on a proscenium stage standing so "cheated out" that each is facing the audience more than they are facing each other? Neither the actors nor the audience can have a truthful sense of the relationship if either partner fails to commit their bodily center. Try the following experiment, or at least imagine it in your mind's eye.

Exercise 7.1: Bodily Center and Relationship

With two other actors, stand in triangle. Stand so that your pelvis is pointed directly at Partner A, then turn your head (without turning your body) so that your face points at Partner B off to your side. Now, who are you "facing?" That is, with whom do you seem to have the strongest relationship? Can you decide between them, or is the situation ambiguous? Do you see how the ambiguity comes from the fact that your energy is split between them?

Take the experiment further. Turn your face back toward Partner A and speak to them; Partner B interrupts by asking a question, and you turn your head to them and answer; then you turn back to the original partner and continue. Did you feel that your basic relationship with Partner A was only suspended while you spoke to Partner B, so that the side conversation was only a "parenthesis" within the unbroken relationship with Partner A?

Again, speak to Partner A, but this time when Partner B interrupts, turn your pelvis toward them as you answer. Do you feel that you have now established a new relationship with Partner B, and that the original relationship with Partner A has been broken?

The most obvious expression of approach or avoidance is in the way we dispose the weight of our body toward or away from another person. This is particularly important on stage, where the audience sees your entire body and responds strongly to its total condition. Imagine yourself in the first stages of an argument that threatens to become a fight; you are confronting your opponent with your hands raised, and you appear to be ready for combat. In this situation, imagine rocking your pelvis forward, toward the opponent. Do you feel more truly ready to attack? Now rock your pelvis away from the opponent so that your center of gravity shifts backward. Do you feel on the defensive, only pretending to attack? Exercise 7.2 allows you to experience giving your total weight to another.

FIGURE 7.1   Falling Exercise

Exercise 7.2: Falling

Your partner stands in a relaxed alignment, and you stand about three feet behind with one foot thrust back for stability (see Figure 7.1). By mutual agreement and talking to each other the whole time, your partner starts to fall backward with their body straight but not stiff or tense. You catch them almost at once, and gently raise them back up.

They fall only a short way at first, and then gradually farther and farther until you are catching them only a few feet above the floor. If your partner becomes frightened and "breaks" their body on the way down, or remains tense as they fall, encourage and reassure them. Then reverse roles.

CAUTION: Do not attempt this exercise unless you are confident of being able to catch your partner; otherwise serious injury could result.

COMMITMENT, SUPPORT, AND COMMUNICATION

The greatness of a play depends on its unity, the way all of its elements have been synthesized into a single meaningful and dramatic experience. Unity must also be a quality of a good production of that play. It can be achieved only when all the many kinds of theatre artists—director, actors, designers, managers, and technicians—have aligned their efforts toward the common goal of embodying the action of the play within the performance.

When the actors, the designers, and the director have worked as an ensemble in accord with the text, and the audience has likewise given of itself, there occurs one of those rare moments when true theatre lives. All these human energies flow to form one energy that is greater than the sum of its parts; everyone participating in the experience receives more than they have given, and we feel truly moved beyond ourselves.

This communality is the deepest wonder of the theatre, transcending the experience of film and television. It depends entirely on teamwork, and teamwork results from a sense of common purpose and respect. No member of a team needs to sacrifice individuality; rather, each member contributes to the effort of all other members because their work is flowing in the same direction toward the same goal. The ensemble is not a collective in which the individual members have submerged their own identity, but a group of aligned individuals in which each member finds his or her individual power enhanced by membership in the group.

Alignment of effort is achieved within the group when three conditions have been met: first, when each member is genuinely committed to the common purpose; second, when each member supports the others in their particular objectives as members of the group; third, when all agree to maintain the possibility of free and open communication so that any difficulties encountered in the work can be worked out. Let's examine each of these points.

First, *commitment:* it is part of your responsibility as an actor to find a point of personal commitment to your own talent, to each role you play, to each play you perform, to each ensemble of which you are a member, and to the audience you serve through your work. Only when you have committed to your work on all these levels in a deeply personal way can you function at your fullest capacity.

Second, *support for your partners:* we all have different reasons for acting, different reasons for doing particular roles; whatever our reasons, we must support each other's objectives, even if we do not share them.

Finally, *free and open communication:* creating theatre is rarely accomplished without some tension arising between members of the ensemble. No matter how friendly and supportive we may be, we are all bound to encounter differences of opinion, conflicting needs, or problems that are simply hard to solve. All of these problems can become *opportunities for creativity* as long as we can communicate freely about them.

Commitment, support, and communication: these are the cornerstones of teamwork and are equal in importance to all your other acting skills.

Exercise 7.3: Levitations

1. Form groups of seven or nine: one person lies flat, eyes closed, arms folded across the abdomen. The others kneel beside them, three or four on either side, and prepare to lift them (see Figure 7.2).
2. You all begin to breathe in unison. When your rhythm is established, *gently and slowly* lift the person, keeping them perfectly level. The sensation for the person being lifted is one of *floating* or being *levitated*.
3. Float them up as high as the group can reach and still keep them level (see Figure 7.2). Then turn in the direction their head is facing so that you can carry them a short distance, head first, still with the sensation of floating.
4. Slowly come to a halt and begin to float the person down, rocking them gently back and forth along the axis of their body, like a leaf settling to earth.
5. Repeat until each member of the group has been levitated.

TRANSACTION AND TEAMWORK

So far your sense of ensemble has been based on a general sense of trust, respect, and commitment. Of equal importance is your ability to use this foundation to enter into the give and take that actually produces a good scene.

It is the exchange of energy, the chain of action and reaction between the characters, that moves a scene. It is therefore crucial that you and your partners be good at receiving and sending the energy of the scene, because each transaction is a link in the chain that moves the play, and a chain—as we all know—is only as strong as its weakest link. This is why Strindberg said that "actors must rely on each other."

This transfer of energy from actor to actor can be described as a continual process of receiving and sending, leading and following, in which all the actors are both senders and receivers, leaders and followers simultaneously. The next three exercises give you the experience of this simultaneous leading and following.

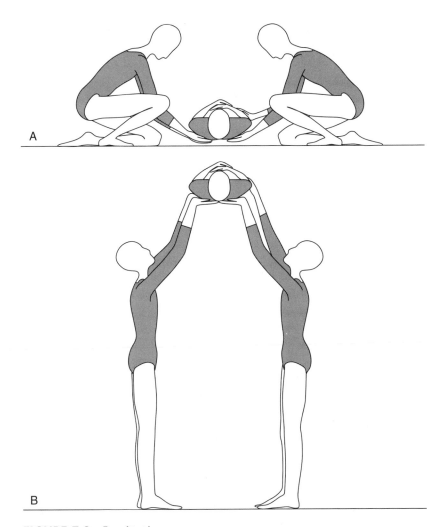

FIGURE 7.2 Levitations

Exercise 7.4: Leading and Following

Blind leading. You and your partner lightly interlace fingertips up to the first joint. Your partner closes their eyes, and you silently lead them around the room. As you gain confidence and control, begin to move faster and extend the range of your travels. Soon you can run. If your situation permits, you can even take a trip to some distant destination. Reverse roles and repeat for the trip back.

Sound leading. Begin as above, but when you are well underway, break physical contact and begin to lead your partner by repeating a single word which they follow by sound alone. Again, extend your range and speed. Run.

CAUTION: Be prepared to grab your partner to prevent a collision.

Review the experience of this exercise: as a follower, did you trust your partner enough to truly commit your weight to your movement, or were you only "pretending" to move while still holding your weight cautiously back? As leader, did you receive your partner's energy and respond to their momentum? Let's continue with another exercise to explore simultaneous leading and following.

Exercise 7.5: Mirrors

1. You and a partner decide who is "A" and who is "B." Stand facing each other; "A" makes slow "underwater" movements that "B" can mirror completely; try to keep the partnership moving in unison. The movements flow in a continually changing stream; avoid repeated patterns. Notice that bigger, more complete, and more continual movements are easier to follow.

2. At a signal, the roles are instantly reversed without a break in the action. "B" is now the leader; "A" is the follower. Continue moving from the deep centers of your bodies; feel yourselves beginning to share a common center through your shared movement; with it comes a common breath. Vocalize the breath and continue to share this common sound, which arises naturally from your movement.

3. The roles are reversed a few more times; each time the leadership role changes, the movement and sound continue without interruption.

4. At last, there is no leader; neither "A" nor "B" leads, but both follow and you continue to move and make sound together. At another signal, both close their eyes for a few moments while continuing to move, then open them again. How well did you stay together?

Watch other partnerships doing this exercise: do you see how intense and connected to each other they seem? Our listening and seeing of each other on stage should always have this kind of literal intensity; you lead and follow each other during a scene just as much as you do in these exercises.

Exercise 7.6: Cookie Search

1. A group of you stands together in a clump at the center of your space and closes your eyes. Then all spin about a few times until you don't know which way you are facing.
2. Without opening your eyes, move slowly in whatever direction you are facing until you reach a wall or other obstacle. Avoid touching anyone else; feel your way with all of your nonvisual senses.
3. When you all have gone as far as you can (and still have not opened your eyes), begin to search for your partner using only the word "cookie."
4. When you find each other, open your eyes and wait in silence for all to finish. Feel the drama of the exercise.

In this exercise you were not led, but had to find your own way toward your partner's sound. Did you feel lonely while searching for your partner and relieved when you found them? Don't be the kind of actor who makes his partners feel lonely during performance.

As you have experienced in these exercises, connectedness depends on how well you see, hear, and feel your partner. As simple as this may seem, such significant seeing and hearing are fairly rare on the stage. Some actors are only superficially aware of their teammates; they are aware instead only of what they themselves are doing, and react only to their premeditated idea of the scene. Although such premeditated and false reactions can sometimes fool an audience, the ensemble effort—and therefore the play as a whole—inevitably suffers.

Now let's use our collaborative skills to create a group scene.

Exercise 7.7: Tug of War

1. Each member of the group "creates" in pantomime a piece of rope about two feet long.
2. Standing in a single long line, each of you "attaches" your rope to those on either side, so the group creates one long rope.
3. Now separate at the center and slide down the rope until two teams are formed.
4. Have a tug of war. At no time can the rope stretch or break. Continue until one team wins.

This exercise is a splendid example of stage reality: the rope ceases to be real if *any* member of the group fails to make their part real and connected to the whole; more important, every individual actor must believe in the *whole* rope, and we must all create the *same* rope. That is why we say "there are no small parts, only small actors."

We'll conclude this sequence on working together with another group exercise.

Exercise 7.8: Group Levitation

1. Stand in one large, perfectly round circle, facing inward. Each of you puts your arms around the waist of the persons on either side (see Figure 7.3).

2. Start to breathe in unison, feeling the breath moving the rib cages of the people you are holding. Bend your knees slightly when exhaling, then lift the person on either side as you breathe in. *Do not lift yourself; lift those you are holding and allow yourself to be lifted by them.*

FIGURE 7.3   Group Levitation

3. As you breathe out, say the word "higher," and try to lift those you are holding higher and higher. Allow the rhythm of the group to accelerate naturally until you all leave the ground.

Do you see how this exercise symbolize the way we work together? *When the energy of every member of the group is aligned on the common goal, the result is greater than the sum of its parts: everyone gets more energy back than they give.* And remember that the audience is part of the team.

SUMMARY

All drama involves the interaction of people with one another, so it can be properly performed only by a team of actors working together. When a dramatic scene is flowing as it should, an unbroken cycle of shared energy passes between the actors. You must therefore develop the skill of working effectively within the creative ensemble. The foundation of this collaborative skill is the realization that you are, by your very nature, connected to your world and all who inhabit it.

What we do with our energy is the most fundamental expression of our relationships with other persons. There is no relationship where energy is not given or taken. Our energy moves either toward or away from the other, and the weight of the body is the most obvious expression of this approach or avoidance.

The greatness of a play depends on its unity, and our production must have the same unity. Our energies must flow together to form one energy. This communality is the deepest wonder of the theatre, transcending the experience of film and television.

The ensemble is not a collective in which the individual members have submerged their identity, but rather a group of *aligned* individuals. Alignment is achieved when three conditions have been met: first, when each member is genuinely committed to the group effort; second, when each member supports the others in their objectives; third, when there is free and open communication.

Each member of the team must be good at receiving and sending the energy of the scene, because each transaction is a link in the chain that moves the play, and a chain—as we all know—is only as strong as its weakest link.

When the energy of every member of the group is aligned on the common goal, the result is greater than the sum of its parts: everyone gets more energy back than they give. And remember that the audience is part of the team.

Lesson 8

ACTION

In Part I you prepared yourself as the "ground" in which the art of acting is to grow. The seed you sow in Part II, the "path" that unlocks your power as an actor, is the concept and technique of *action*. First, however, we must clear up a common confusion about this term, because it is often used in two different ways.

Writing over two thousand years ago, the philosopher Aristotle was the first to describe how plays work. He used the term "dramatic action" to describe the underlying energy that drives a play. For instance, Aristotle might have said that the dramatic action driving Tennessee Williams' *The Glass Menagerie* is the struggle between Tom's sense of obligation to his family as the "man of the house" and his need to live his own life. The events of the play are caused by this underlying conflict between these opposing forces. This action is "universal" because it involves a conflict all of us experience as we grow up and leave home. It is this Aristotelian sense of dramatic action that we mean when we speak of "the action of the play" or "the action in this scene."

ACTION ACCORDING TO STANISLAVSKI

Early in this century the term "action" began to be used in a sense different than Aristotle's when referring to the acting process. The great Russian director, Constantin Stanislavski, was dissatisfied with the bravura acting style of his time. Too often, he felt, the actor's display of emotion and technique became an end in itself and overshadowed the values of the play. He created a new system of acting aimed at economy, greater psychological truthfulness, and above all respect for the ideas of the play.

He based his system on the idea that everything an actor does as the character has to be justified by the character's internal need. As Stanislavski said:

> *There are no physical actions divorced from some desire, some effort in some direction, some objective. . . . Everything that happens on the stage has a definite purpose.*[1]

According to this principle, everything the actor does as the character should grow directly out of the needs of that character; it must be *justified*. The actor can no longer "show off" his or her skills for their own sake, and is obligated to perform in an economical, purposeful way that serves the meaning of the play.

In Stanislavski's terms, the character's needs and desires cause them to do something (which he called their *action*) in an effort to achieve a desired goal (which he called their *objective*, though some schools of acting use the terms *intention* or *task* to mean the same thing). In other words, *need* causes *action* directed toward an *objective*.

Looked at in this way, your job is to put yourself into the character's circumstance, experience the character's needs, experience the objectives they choose in hope of satisfying those needs, then do the things they do in an attempt to achieve those objectives. It is this Stanislavskian sense of action as *a purposeful doing directed toward a specific objective* that we use throughout this book.

ACTION IN LIFE

We began in the very first lesson by saying that you are already an actor. You "act" when you do things to get what you want or need. When what you need is important enough, it commands your whole attention and all your energy flows toward your objective.

You have seen people in this condition of total commitment: an athlete executing a difficult play; people arguing a deeply felt issue; a student studying for a big test; lovers wooing. All these people have one thing in common: they have a *personally significant objective* and as a result they are totally focused on what they are doing. The more important the objective, the more urgent the action and complete the focus, and the more unself-conscious and committed the person becomes. In acting terms, we say that someone who is doing something with this kind of total, unself-conscious commitment is *in action*.

Watching someone in action is an invigorating experience; they seem so "alive" that we feel more alive as we watch them, even if their action is extremely simple. For example, a Canadian mime I once saw began his performance in a striking way: the first spectators to arrive found him sitting alone on the stage, applying his whiteface makeup. He worked simply and without the slightest embellishment, but his concentration and involvement were so complete that the spectators quickly became engrossed in watching him. As more spectators arrived, they too fell silent and watched in rapt attention. As the hall filled, the intensity of the experience grew, as if the spectators were adding their energy and attention to his, and indeed they were. When at last he finished, many minutes after the theatre was full, there was a tremendous ovation. The bond with the audience that his simple but total action had created was unbreakable for the rest of the evening; because our energy had joined with his, we felt that we had come to *know* him.

Indeed, people reveal a great deal about themselves when they are in action, perhaps more than at any other time. As we say, *actions speak louder than words*. When someone is in action, they are so busy *doing* that they have no energy or self-awareness left for deception. As a result, we judge someone who is in action as being authentic and believable.

All these are powerful reasons why being in action, *being fully focused on a personally significant objective*, is the best state for you as an actor. Through this focus, you can achieve unself-consciousness, command of your audience's attention, and believability.

The experience of watching someone in action becomes even more exciting when we add conditions that produce suspense, like an unresolved issue with the outcome in doubt, a deadline, or some other source of urgency. These are the essential elements of drama: *a character pursuing a personally significant objective in an urgent situation with an unknown outcome*. These are the situations that we experience as being the most dramatic in life, as well as on the stage or screen.

You have been in action many times in your life; these experiences can be a foundation for developing the same kind of heightened commitment on stage, though your stage work must be artistically heightened and purified. Think back: in your life you have had experiences during which you were totally "tuned in" to something you were doing, so engrossed in your activity that you became totally unself-conscious, oblivious of passing time or of outside distractions.

Exercise 8.1: Action in Life

For the next few days, notice which people attract your attention: What are they doing? How do they feel about it? What makes them interesting? Notice especially the people in those situations we think of as highly "dramatic": athletes at crucial moments, people in danger, people in the grip of deeply held beliefs, and the like. Record your observations in your journal.

Think about those times when you have been in action. Select one such time and relive it in your imagination. What made it possible for you to achieve this level of complete commitment and focus? Record this in your journal.

INTERNAL AND EXTERNAL ACTION

Action is not just external activity. A jeweler about to split a valuable diamond, hammer raised, is not moving at all; yet we recognize the drama, the sense of "significant doing" in him. This is because dramatic action is felt even *before* it has manifested itself in external activity; it lives even in the *potential* for doing. At such moments, the action is literally living *inside* you, so we can speak of both *internal* and *external* action.

Stanislavski called internal action *spiritual* action, and external action *physical* action:

> The creation of the physical life is half the work on a role because, like us, a role has two natures, physical and spiritual...a role on the stage, more than action in real life, must bring together the two lives— of external and internal action—in mutual effort to achieve a given purpose.[2]

For Stanislavksi it is the *integration* of the internal and external actions—"more than action in real life"—that produces a truthful stage performance, and his acting system is designed to bring about this integration. Best known are his early psychological techniques (such as fantasy and emotional recall), which were designed to work from the internal to the external, from the spiritual to the physical. Later in the development of his method, however, he began to work from the external toward the internal through "the Method of Physical Actions." As he said,

> The spirit cannot but respond to the actions of the body, provided of course that these are genuine, have a purpose, and are productive.... (In this way) a part acquires inner content.[3]

During the first half of our century, the British acting tradition stressed the importance of externals in the acting process, working "from the outside in." Our American tradition, on the other hand, stressed the importance of internals, working "from the inside out." For the past forty years, however, a real effort has been made in both countries to combine these two approaches. Both are essential, as Stanislavski pointed out:

> *External action acquires inner meaning and warmth from inner action, while the latter finds its expression only in physical terms.*[4]

The most useful approach is to avoid thinking of "inner" and "outer" action as being in any way separable. Imagine instead a single *flow* of action that has an inner phase and an outer phase: Something happens to which you respond, and if your response is strong enough, your aroused inner energy then flows outward and becomes external action. When this happens naturally, you experience the inner and outer aspects of the flow as a single action. Unfortunately, actors sometimes disrupt this natural process by being overly self-conscious, by trying to force the inner experience, or trying to manipulate the externals in an artificial way. If your stage action consists only of external movement and speech unconnected to an inner energy, it will seem hollow and lifeless; if it consists only of inner intensity, without skillful outer expression, it will seem vague and self-indulgent.

Exercise 8.2: Internal and External Action

Observe yourself and others to see how action lives in both internal and external forms. What do you notice about the relationship of the two? Which is more suspenseful? Record your observations in your journal.

BELIEVABILITY

Although it is true that we all "act" in everyday life, we do not always act *well:* sometimes our performance is judged to be "insincere" or "unbelievable."

How do we judge the believability of a performance? Social psychologist Erving Goffman points out that our role-playing behavior always sends two kinds of messages: the information we *give* (the impression we are trying to make) and the information we *give off* (the unconscious things we do that reveal how we really feel). In everyday life we intuitively read the information "given off" by watching for traces of unconscious behavior such as "body language" and telltale qualities of the voice; we then unconsciously compare this information with the message being purposely given. When the two are consistent, we judge the performance as believable; but when there are inconsistencies, we feel that the person is faking.

For example, if I am trying to convince you that I am extremely interested in what you are saying but you catch me glancing over your shoulder at the clock, you refuse to believe in my performance. Just so, on the stage, you may see actors glance at the director or audience for approval, or "break" into laughter when the character shouldn't be laughing. Such behaviors that are *inconsistent with the character's reality* make it impossible to believe in the performance.

In life and on stage, the only way to be believable is by being completely committed to your action so that there are no inconsistencies between your conscious and unconscious behavior. Every successful salesman learns this; it is also the idea behind Stanislavski's system of acting.

INDICATING

Besides inconsistent behavior, we have all learned to recognize another symptom of insincerity, and that is *overeffort*. When someone is trying too hard, being too jolly, too sincere, too lovable, we think that, like Cassius, he or she "doth protest too much." Acting students commonly do too much on stage: in addition to (or instead of) doing what their character is doing, they are also trying to *show* us how the character feels, or what kind of a character they are. Their extra effort is saying something like, "Hey, look at how angry I am," or "look at what a victim I am."

In real life we sometimes call this "grandstanding"; on stage we call it *indicating*. You are indicating when you are *showing* us something about your character instead of simply *doing* what the character does.

Actors indicate for various reasons: because it is a way of earning the audience's attention (remember that sense of unworthiness we discussed in Part I); because it is a way of maintaining control over the performance instead of surrendering to the action; or simply because it "feels" like their mistaken notion of acting.

If you recognize indicating and avoid it by committing to a specific action, your action generates and expresses all the emotion and sense of character needed. The essence of good acting is *to do what the character does completely and with the precise qualities required, but without adding anything superfluous.*

Exercise 8.3: A Simple Task

Select a simple physical activity that requires great concentration, such as building a house of cards, or balancing a stick on your nose. Also give yourself a tremendously important reason for doing it: if you can walk all the way across the room balancing the stick on your nose, you will win a million dollars; or if the house of cards falls before you have completed the second level, a loved one will be killed.

As you perform your task, ask your audience to signal by making some sort of noise whenever they feel that you are indicating. Compare their feedback with your own sense of being in action: did you know when you were indicating? How strong is your impulse to "show" instead of "do," or to "do too much?"

SUMMARY

Though Aristotle defined action as the energy driving a play or scene, we use this term in Stanislavski's sense of *a purposeful doing directed toward an objective.* In life, we see people doing things to accomplish important objectives: they are totally committed, unself-conscious, expressive, and believable. We say they are *in action,* and you strive to be in action on stage for the same reasons.

Action exists as a flow of energy both inside you and outside. The internal phase of action gives meaning and believability to the external, while the external gives form and expression to the internal. The two are really different aspects of the same energy, and your character can grow both from the inside out and from the outside in.

In life and on stage, the only way to be believable is by being completely committed to your action so that there are no inconsistencies between your conscious and unconscious behavior. This is one reason why you strive always to be "doing" instead of "showing," which we call *indicating.*

9

ACTION AND THE ACTING PROCESS

The concept of action serves the actor in many ways. In this lesson you will see how it supports your work by enabling you to reduce self-consciousness, to synthesize your actor awareness with your character's awareness, and most important, how it leads to the transformational process by which character is best created.

PUBLIC SOLITUDE

People who are in action are unself-conscious. For example, an athlete making a play in front of millions of spectators is aware only of the play and may "forget" the spectators entirely. This is a state of mind that Stanislavski called *public solitude*.

He discovered it when one of his acting teachers gave him a simple task: he was to go up onto the stage and count the floorboards while the teacher and the class went on with other business. Stanislavski, like most acting students, suffered from stage fright; he became tense and distracted on stage because he was overly aware of being watched. But while he was busy counting the floorboards, he felt at ease because no one was paying any attention to him, and soon he became totally engrossed in his task. When he finished, he discovered that at some point everyone had begun watching him but he had become so caught up in his task that *he had failed to notice.* (The class, by the way, found his "performance" engrossing, just as people had enjoyed watching the mime put on his makeup, described in Lesson 8.)

It was the first time he had ever been on stage without self-consciousness, and the experience was liberating and exhilarating. Stanislavski realized that his total focus on his task had truly allowed him to forget about being watched. He called this state of being "public solitude."

From this experience, Stanislavski developed the concept of the character's objective as a "dramatic task," which, like the task of counting the floorboards, would provide the actor with a point of attention that would reduce self-consciousness and lead to public solitude. The more "in action" you are, the less self-conscious you are.

DUAL CONSCIOUSNESS

It is important that you understand one danger of the concept of public solitude. Many young actors tend to focus so much on the "solitude" that they ignore the "public." Stanislavski would not have approved of you falling into some sort of trance in which you truly forgot that the audience was present: doing so leads to uncraftsmanlike work, which he hated above all.

The question is: can you be completely engrossed in the action and world of your character, while simultaneously being aware of the demands of performance, and making the artistic choices required to express your action in a public form worthy of your audience's attention?

This question is answered by your capacity for *dual consciousness,* the ability to function on more than one level at a time, maintaining artistic choice while simultaneously becoming the character. As the young actor Kostya in Stanislavski's *Building a Character* put it:

> *"I divided myself, as it were, into two personalities. One continued as an actor, the other was an observer. Strangely enough this duality not only did not impede, it actually promoted my creative work. It encouraged and lent impetus to it."*[1]

Dual consciousness is a feature of all acting, though different styles of drama may require more or less emphasis on one level or the other. In some modern plays (Brecht, for instance) we may allow more of the actor awareness to function in the performance, while in highly naturalistic plays we strive to reduce our actor awareness to the minimum. For the camera, it must be completely invisible. No matter how much you reduce it, however, you never lose it completely, for if you did you would lose also the ability to make artistic choice.

Dual consciousness may seem difficult to attain, but it is really a natural ability. When you were a child, the rain puddle became a vast ocean, but it didn't need to stop being a puddle: you hadn't learned yet that something isn't supposed to be two different things at once, and that we aren't supposed to be in two different realities at the same time. To act, you have to allow yourself to rediscover fully this childhood ability.

Exercise 9.1: The Simple Task as Drama

Repeat Exercise 8.3: A Simple Task, but this time give yourself a character and a dramatic situation. If your task was to build a two-story house of cards, perhaps you are a condemned man about to be executed, waiting for the governor to phone with your pardon. See if you can relax enough to allow yourself to "fall into" action while performing this task; can you experience something like public solitude? Are you able to hold the dual awareness of your character's world and your actor's concerns? Again, ask your audience to check you for indicating.

ACTION AND CHARACTER

You now understand that much of your real life is spent "acting" as you present yourself and pursue your objectives, and that your "character" in real life, your personality, develops largely through this interaction with your world.

As an infant, your physical exploration of the world was the main process; as you grew up, your relationships with your parents and eventually with larger social groups shaped you, as did the customs, taboos, and value systems you inherited from your culture. Your personality emerged from this accumulation of experiences and is continually evolving under the influence of new experience. Your personality is not static; you grow and change as your circumstances and experiences change.

Of course, you also received a genetic heritage (your "nature"), which greatly influenced your tendency to respond to your world in certain ways. But it was your interaction with that world, especially in your childhood (your "nurture"), that shaped you within the limits established by your nature.

The characters you play on stage or for the camera develop by this same process; each is a new "me" created from the vast potential of your "I." This is a natural process whereby our behavior in a given circumstance tends to develop in us consistent traits of personality. If we find ourselves stuck in a particular role for a long time, it can even begin to consume us. If, for example, you take a job that forces you to be subservient to a tyrannical boss, you not only *feel* like a victim, but if you stay in that job long enough you will *become* a victim; the victim "me" starts to consume your "I."

In fact, one way of describing mental illness would be to say that someone whose "I" has become so rigid that they can no longer adapt to changing reality is paranoid, whereas someone who has lost their "I" altogether is schizophrenic. But the actor suffers from neither of these disorders: the actor uses a heightened and controlled version of a perfectly natural and healthy process. As you work on a play, your evolving character gradually becomes a new "me," but only within the specific context of rehearsing and performing the play.

All this can be summed up by saying that **character grows out of action.** This is the fundamental principle on which all our work is based, and its importance cannot be stressed enough.

PERSONALIZATION AND THE MAGIC IF

You now understand that the dramatic personality evolves during rehearsal according to the same processes of interaction that formed your personality in life. You don't become the character first and then do things "because that's what my character would do"; instead, you allow yourself to do the things your character does, for the reasons they do them and in the way that they do them, and see who you turn into.

You must feel your character's needs *as if* they were your own needs, select the objectives that can satisfy those needs *as if* they were your own objectives, and then do what the character does to try to win those objectives *as if* they were your own actions. When you have thus put yourself into the character's place, the natural process of transformation begins and a new version of yourself, a new "me," evolves. Stanislavski called this process "the Magic If."

This natural process of transformation, however, works *only* if you allow yourself to fully experience what the character experiences with the same urgency and significance as they do *for yourself*. This is called *personalization,* and it is the necessary companion of the Magic If.

Usually, you can personalize the character's situation and needs sufficiently through your innate ability to "make believe." If you encounter a character whose needs or circumstances are so foreign to your own that you have great difficulty entering into the experience, however, you might try the technique called *substitution.* This involves selecting some existing real need, circumstance, or relationship of your own that is analogous to the character's and *substituting* it in your mind for their need.

This technique is popular with some actors, though it is best used only when an act of the imagination has failed.

You must be aware of a great danger in the process of personalization. If you do not truly reach out into the character's experience, but instead merely drag the character into yourself, then you may end up distorting the character and damaging the play. True, every role suggests some experiences and behaviors similar to those you have had in your life, and you certainly want to use these established connections; but every role also offers the possibility of reaching out into *new* modes of experience. Trust that you possess a vast personal potential; if you can engage your own energy in your character's actions within their world, you find yourself naturally, effortlessly transformed toward a new state of being.

In other words, acting is more self-*expansion* than it is self-*expression*. And this expansion, this exploration of new states of being, is the most exciting aspect of the actor's creative process.

Exercise 9.2: Personalization

Repeat the last exercise, the simple task with character and situation. Find a way to experience fully the need, situation, and action you have invented for the character. If it is difficult for you, try making a substitution. Again, beware of indicating.

Were you able to endow your character's need, situation, and action with personal significance? Did doing so enhance your transformation into the character? Were you able to avoid indicating? Remember, your job as an actor is to create experiences, not to explain behavior.

THE ACTING PROCESS

Though we go on to study much more about the acting process, you now understand its essential elements. We can describe the core of the process as having five steps:

1. You put yourself into the circumstances of your character *as if* it were your own circumstance;
2. You experience the needs of the character *as if* they were your own needs;
3. You allow yourself to form the same objectives the character chooses to satisfy those needs, and to care urgently about them *as if* they were your own objectives;

4. You allow yourself to do the things (the actions) the character does in order to try to achieve those objectives *as if* they were your own actions;

5. If you do all this, simply and completely, you begin to experience a natural process of transformation (the "magic if"). A new version of yourself, a new "me," begins to develop according to the same principles by which your personality developed in life.

These five steps lay the foundation of your work as an actor. Beyond them is a sixth step: through your acting skills, you select, guide, heighten, and purify this evolving self. You constantly check it against the needs of the play, because every character was created to serve a particular purpose within the play. Finally you arrive at the completed characterization, which is an extension of yourself into a new state of being. It is a marriage between who you are now, the life of the character in the play, and who you become when you begin to live that life.

Your characterization must be the result of this process; there are no shortcuts. As your acting skill develops, you are able to work more efficiently and effectively, but no amount of posturing, false voice, or trumped-up emotion can substitute for this natural process of transformation and artistic development.

By following this process with complete conviction you not only create living characters of great value in themselves, you also help to remind your audience of their own potential aliveness. As playwright David Mamet put it,

> Each time we try to subordinate all we do to the necessity of bringing to life simply and completely the intention of the play, we give the audience an experience which enlightens and frees them: the experience of witnessing their fellow human beings saying, "nothing will sway me, nothing will divert me, nothing will dilute my intention of achieving what I have sworn to achieve": in technical terms, "My Objective"; in general terms, my "goal," my "desire," my "responsibility."
>
> If we are true to our ideals we can help to form an ideal society— a society based on an adhering to ethical first principles—not by preaching about it, but by creating it each night in front of the audience—by showing how it works. In action.[2]

SUMMARY

When you can go completely into action, you achieve *public solitude;* your focus on your task is so strong that your consciousness of being in public recedes into the background. Your ability to be in the character's world while simultaneously attending to your actor concerns is *dual consciousness* and can be recaptured from your childhood playfulness.

In life, your personality develops as you interact with your world, and you grow and change as you encounter new circumstances and experiences. The art of acting uses this natural process; your dramatic character evolves in the same way as did the various "me's" that constitute your personality. When you want something in a particular situation and do certain things to get it, your own action changes who you are; character grows naturally out of action.

Your job as an actor, then, is to allow yourself to fully experience the totality of your character's action. You put yourself into the character's circumstances, experience the character's needs, make the choices they make, then do what they do. From this, a natural process of transformation, the "magic if," begins.

Through your artistic skill you guide and heighten this process, working to fulfill the purpose for which the author created your character.

NEEDS, ACTIONS, AND OBJECTIVES

A baseball batter rehearses his stance, grip, swing, and breathing; he studies the opposing pitchers; at the plate, he takes note of the wind and the position of the fielders. As he begins to swing at a pitch, however, he ceases to be consciously aware of all this and focuses his total awareness on the ball. This single objective channels all his energy into his action, the swing. Having this single objective allows the batter to synthesize all his other concerns, and all his rehearsed and intuitive skills, into a single complete action of mind and body. His swing now has *rhythm*, which unifies every aspect of his action.

For you as an actor, the "ball" is your character's *objective*, what he or she is trying to accomplish at any given moment (also sometimes called their intention or task). Your focus on this single objective at the moment of action provides you with the same kind of *rhythmic integration* achieved by the baseball batter. It energizes your action and gives it power, intensity, and control.

In this lesson, you will explore how to define your character's actions and objectives in the most useful way. We begin where the actions and objectives begin, in the needs of the character.

WANTS AND NEEDS

Your character's behavior, like your own behavior in life, is driven by their *wants* and *needs*. There are interesting differences between wants and needs.

First, we may not always want what we need: you may *want* to become a great dancer, but you don't really *want* to spend four hours a day exercising at the barre; you do it because you *need* to. Willy Loman in Miller's *Death of a Salesman* is deeply dissatisfied: he *wants* to be successful, but he doesn't know what he *needs* to do to find success, and his futile search for success drives the entire play.

Second, we usually know what we want, but we may be unconscious of our needs. In *The Glass Menagerie*, Amanda says that she *wants* her children to have independent lives, but unconsciously she *needs* them to remain dependent upon her. As in real life, such unconscious needs are usually stronger than conscious wants. The actress playing Amanda is aware of her character's unconscious needs and builds them into the performance, even though they are not in the character's consciousness—another instance when "dual consciousness" is essential to the acting process.

For convenience, we will hereafter use the term "need" to refer to both needs and wants. Remember, however, that the differences between them can be important.

ACTION AND OBJECTIVES

A character always feels their need as an arousal; they feel like they have to do something, even if they may not immediately know what it is. This arousal can be pleasurable, as in Amanda's expectation of the Gentleman Caller, or painful, as in Willy Loman's dissatisfaction.

As in life, a character may remain aroused for some time without doing anything about it; they may simply be in a condition of expectation or dissatisfaction, as in many of Chekhov's characters, and the unresolved need colors the mood and thinking of the character. The longer a need is suppressed, the stronger it becomes, thus building suspense. Hamlet, for example, spends a great deal of time wondering whether to act upon his need to revenge his father's murder; at last his action explodes in the last scene of the play.

Whether your character acts immediately upon being aroused, or delays action, sooner or later the character must *do* something to try to satisfy their felt need. When your character chooses to act, they form an *objective* that they hope will satisfy the need, and then choose a course of *action* directed toward achieving that objective. In short, **need leads to objective, which leads to action.**

Notice that the need is *internal* while the objective is *external;* the action is a kind of "energy bridge" that goes from the inner need toward the outer objective. Because the need is inside you, it cannot be made observable in a dramatically satisfying way until it surfaces through action. Until it has produced action, we say that a need is not *playable.*

Actors sometimes make the mistake of trying to "play" a need: they try to show us how desperate Willy Loman is, or how lonely Blanche Dubois is, and the result is indicating, *showing* instead of *doing.*

Trust instead that the audience will come to understand your character's inner world by observing your action. The playwright has constructed your character so that what they say and do springs naturally from their needs, and those needs can therefore be deduced by the audience; it is much more satisfying to allow the audience to make this deduction for themselves, rather than for you to "show" them what the needs are.

DEFINING PRODUCTIVE OBJECTIVES

As we said earlier, the purpose of an objective is to *compel your attention,* giving you the kind of focus the batter has on the ball and helping you to be unself-conscious. A useful objective also *energizes* you and leads naturally to stageworthy externals. When an objective does both these things—compel your attention and energize you—it is what Stanislavski called a *productive objective.*

Experience has proven that objectives become more productive when they are directed toward a *single, immediate,* and *personally important* goal. Let's examine each:

1. An objective needs to be *singular* because you wish to focus your energy on one thing rather than diffuse it by trying to do two things at once. Imagine a batter trying to hit two balls simultaneously.
2. The most useful objective is *in the immediate future,* something that can happen right now. The play must move forward and your energy must help propel it; never define your character's objective in a way that moves your energy into the past. Although the character's needs may be rooted in the past, their action is directed toward an objective in the immediate future. Willy Loman's need for success has been with him his whole life, but in our sample scene (see Appendix A) he is trying to persuade his boss to give him a better territory *right now.* The best objective is an *aspiration.*
3. Finally, an objective must be *personally important* to you. As you have already learned, you must define it in a way that enables you to *personalize* it.

We can remember these three requirements as the acronym "SIP": **S**ingular, in the **I**mmediate future, and **P**ersonal.

While you are learning to act, it may help you to form simple verbal descriptions of your needs, objectives, and actions, step by step through a scene. Remember, however, that these verbal descriptions are valuable only insofar as they contribute to your actual experience of playing the scene. The ability to describe something (which comes from the analytical left side of the brain) is no guarantee of the ability to play it (which comes from the intuitive right side of the brain), and the two sometimes get in each other's way.

Let's examine an objective from a scene to see how these principles are applied. In our sample scene from *Death of a Salesman,* Willy Loman wants to be a successful salesman because he has a deeper, lifelong need to be a valuable human being. But he can't be a successful salesman anymore because he's too old to drive all the way to Boston to see his clients; he keeps falling asleep at the wheel. His first boss, who was his friend, has died and his son, Howard, has taken over the business. Willy goes to see Howard; he must get assigned to a territory in town. *Please turn to the Appendix and read the scene now.*

As Willy enters, he sees Howard playing with a new recorder, and his immediate objective is *to get Howard to stop what he is doing and pay attention.* This objective is singular and immediate. It is also supremely important to Willy: if he can't get Howard's attention, he won't be able to get a spot in town, he won't be able to be a successful salesman, and he won't be a valuable human being. His deepest, lifelong needs live in the present moment, giving it all the urgency of a life and death struggle. Continue to examine the scene for yourself to see how each of Willy's objectives are SIP.

Exercise 10.1: A Productive Objective

Repeat Exercise 9.1: The Simple Task as Drama. This time, ask a partner to join you in a passive role: if you are the condemned man waiting for a pardon, they can be a guard or a priest sitting with you in your cell. Form a SIP objective in them: perhaps you want them to call the governor on your behalf because time is running out. Improvise the scene.

CONNECTING ACTION WITH OTHERS

Because plays are about people interacting with one another, you must understand your objectives in ways that not only energize and focus you by being SIP, but also drive your action toward the other characters in the scene. The best way to achieve this is to think of your objective as being *in* another character, to make it something you need *from them.* The most productive kind of objective is therefore *a desired change in the other character.*

For example, in the Willy Loman scene, your overall objective is to get a spot in town, but as you enter and find Howard busy, your immediate objective will be *to get him to stop what he is doing and pay attention to you.* Defining the objective as being "in him" helps to bring you into meaningful *transaction* with him, producing a livelier, more dramatic scene.

We can take this idea further: In life, when we do something to try to make a change in someone else, we watch them to see if what we are doing is working or not; if it's not, we try something else. This should be true on stage as well. Ask yourself, "How would I know I was achieving my objective? What changes might I see in the other character that would encourage me that my approach is working?"

Specific, observable change is what you want to bring about in the other character, and it is the best way to define your objective. The late director Duncan Ross even encouraged his actors to think of this as "a change in the other character's eyes." In the Willy Loman scene, for instance, your first objective might be "to get Howard to look at me with interest." Your full attention is on him, watching to see if your behavior is indeed producing the desired effect, or whether you might have to try a different approach (which you do).

Here are some examples of productive objectives from other plays on our reading list, together with the need that drives them. Can you identify the characters?

1. NEED: To save the King. OBJECTIVE: To convince the King to come inside the hovel.
2. NEED: To end my pain. OBJECTIVE: To trick Peter into picking up the knife so I can kill myself.
3. NEED: To be taken care of. OBJECTIVE: To make Mitch kiss me.

Do you see how each of these conforms to the principles we have discussed?

Exercise 10.2: Observing Objectives in Life

Watch people interacting in life; see what kinds of objectives produce the most interesting interactions. Notice how people read others, and how they deal with failure and success moment by moment. Record your observations and insights in your journal.

SPONTANEITY

What you do on stage should feel spontaneous, "as if for the first time," no matter how many times you have done it before. To achieve this spontaneity, you must keep your awareness on your objective rather than on the mechanics of your external action, just as the batter thinks only about the ball and not about his swing. Otherwise you are just "going through the motions," repeating the external aspects of your performance without re-experiencing the internal needs that drive the externals.

Notice that this spontaneity does *not* mean that your performance is erratic or changeable: during the rehearsal process you gradually refine your external action until it becomes dependable, consistent, stageworthy, and *automatic*, just as the baseball batter has rehearsed all the aspects of his swing until he can do it without thinking. As Stanislavski said,

> . . . *a spontaneous action is one that, through frequent repetition in rehearsal and performance, has become automatic and therefore free.*[1]

Because you are able to perform your action without thinking about it, your mind is free to concentrate fully on the objective and to experience what happens "as if for the first time." In other words, because you could "do it in your sleep," you are able to do it fully awake.

SUMMARY

Having an objective, like the batter's focus on the ball, gives your action power, control, and rhythmic unity. While actually playing a scene, your immediate awareness on the character's objective triggers your well-rehearsed action, just as the batter's focus on the ball synthesizes all his rehearsed skills.

Your character's objective is driven by their wants or needs, conscious or unconscious. You must rediscover these needs and personalize them, experiencing them *for yourself* as strongly as the character does.

A productive objective energizes you and naturally generates stageworthy external action. It also connects you to the other characters in the scene. The most productive objectives are *a change we want to bring about in another character that is SIP: Singular, Immediate, and Personally important.*

While first learning this technique, it may be useful to form verbal descriptions of your need, objective, and action, though eventually this process becomes largely intuitive. Remember, however, that naming something doesn't guarantee that you can play it, and sometimes gets in the way.

By re-experiencing the objective every time you perform the action, you keep your performance spontaneous, even though it is so well-rehearsed as to be automatic and dependable.

PLAYABLE ACTIONS

In the Willy Loman scene, you found a productive objective. As you entered you saw that the boss was busy; your Single, Immediate, and Personally significant task was to get his attention. It was something you wanted from him, a *change you needed to bring about in him*. The question now is, what do you *do* to achieve this objective?

This question is, of course, answered by Arthur Miller: Willy is going to *flatter* Howard as a way of winning his attention. Like any good playwright, Miller has envisioned Willy's inner world and has provided an external action that springs naturally from it. It is therefore possible for you to "work backward" to discover an inner pathway to the given externals, which both serves you as an actor and serves the demands of the play.

As the actor creating Willy, you must recreate this process for yourself. You must go on Willy's inner journey and find your own way to the destination provided by Arthur Miller. This is what Stansilavski called *justifying* the external action by finding the inner need that drives it. Only in this way can you have Willy's experience for yourself, and it is that experience that helps turn you into Willy.

Here is an exercise to explore the sense of objectives and actions. It can be done many times until the experience of action becomes familiar to you.

Exercise 11.1: Simple Action Improvisation

1. Create a need in yourself: loneliness, a need for money, a need to avoid being caught for a crime.

2. Invent an objective growing from this need involving someone in the room: to get them to go out on a date with you, to borrow

money from them, to get them to lie for you. Make it SIP: a single thing, something they can to do right now, and something important to you.

3. Now select an initial strategy that seems likely to succeed with that person, such as "to get Sam to drive me home after class by promising him dinner."

4. Without revealing any of this to anyone, go for it. Watch them to see if your approach is working. If it's not, try a different strategy.

5. Those who are on the receiving end: accept the reality of whatever your partner brings to you; help heighten the drama of the scene by resisting through retreating or counterattacking; make it *difficult but not impossible* for them to earn their objective.

In this exercise you were acting in your own person, inventing your own need, objective, and action. When working on a play, one of your early steps in rehearsal is to discover your character's needs, and each of their objectives and playable actions, step-by-step through the scene. By making this analysis early in the rehearsal process, you can begin to experience the logic and momentum of the scene so that it begins to "play." In this lesson you learn how to analyze the action of a scripted scene.

DEFINING PLAYABLE ACTIONS

We have described how to define productive objectives. Now we consider how to define actions in a way that produces stageworthy externals. These are what actors call *playable* actions.

First, you want the most *active* description possible, so you use *a simple verb phrase* in a *transitive* form: a verb that involves a doing directed toward someone else, such as "to flatter." You avoid forms of the verb "to be," because these are intransitive verbs; they have no external object and their energy turns back upon itself—certainly not a good condition for an actor whose energies must continually flow outward into the scene. You are never interested, for example, in "being angry" or "being a victim" or "being likeable;" these are not playable. Strive instead for *doing*, a transitive condition in which your energy flows toward an object, which, as we have said, is usually a change in another character.

Next, you select a verb that carries a sense of the particular *strategy* employed by the character to achieve the objective. When you choose a course of action in life, you naturally select the one that seems to offer the greatest chance for success in the given circumstances; you ask yourself, "Given what I want, what is the best way to get it in this situation, from this person? What might work?" Characters in plays often do the same.

Let's return to the Willy Loman scene and see how you might describe your action. You have just entered; you desperately need to get a spot in town; you see Howard playing with the recorder. At this moment, you, as Willy, want to get Howard's attention (to get him to look at you), but you want to do it in a way that makes him feel positively toward you. As a salesman, you instinctively appeal to something the "client" is interested in, so you flatter him by praising the recorder and the stupid recording he has made of his family.

Obviously, you have a strong *subtext* here; you seem to be doing one thing, but you are actually doing something else, something that is, for the moment, hidden. But as an actor you *play* the immediate objective (to get him to look at you) through the immediate action (flattery); you trust this immediate action to carry all the hidden pain and hope.

From these principles we see that the most complete description of your action as Willy Loman at this moment is *to flatter Howard by praising the recorder (strategic action) so he will pay attention to me (objective).*

Though you may develop such a description of your action as part of your training or study of a scene, you soon discard verbal descriptions in favor of the actual experience of the scene, moment by moment, and have only as much awareness of all this as the character does (except for that little piece of your actor consciousness that never quite goes away.)

In the last lesson we gave examples of productive objectives from other plays on our reading list, with the needs that drove them; here they are with the actions added:

1. NEED: To save the King. OBJECTIVE: To convince the King to hide inside the hovel. ACTION: To go inside so he will follow.
2. NEED: To end my pain. OBJECTIVE: To trick Peter into picking up the knife so I can kill myself. ACTION: To threaten his manhood so he will defend himself.
3. NEED: To be taken care of. OBJECTIVE: To make Mitch kiss me. ACTION: To tell him what happened that awful night so he will understand why I am the way I am.

Do you see how each of these conforms to the principles we have discussed?

AUTOMATIC ACTIONS

So far we have been describing a process of choice that involves conscious thought. However, a great many things we do in life and on the stage obviously are not necessarily the result of conscious choice. These are sometimes called involuntary responses or conditioned reflexes; Stanislavski called them *automatic* actions.

For example, when riding in a car and presented with sudden danger, you find yourself stepping on the brake, even though you are not driving. Characters on the stage have many responses of a similar kind: when the alarm bell rings, Othello reaches for his sword; when threatened, Laura runs to her menagerie or plays the phonograph. These are habitual actions that serve the needs of these characters on a deep level, and they require little or no conscious thought.

Willy's strategic action is to flatter Howard; he makes this choice "automatically," out of his long experience as a salesman—he is "getting his foot in the door." (We explore the subject of automatic actions and the demands they make on the actor more in Part III.)

UNITS OF ACTION

As we do in life, a dramatic character usually pursues an action until it either succeeds or has been deemed a failure. If it is not working, they shift to a new action, *even though they may not change their objective.* Or they may abandon the first objective, form a new one, and find a new action for it. If, on the other hand, the action is successful and they achieve their objective, they move on to a new objective and form a new action.

Each change in action, whether there is a change of objective or not, can be felt as a change in the rhythm of the scene; each creates what Stanislavski called a new *unit of action,* regardless of which character has made the change. American actors usually call these units of action *beats,* and the moment in which the change of action occurs is called a *beat change.* (One theory about why we say "beat" is that it was originally the word "bit" said with a Russian accent.)

In the scene from *Death of a Salesman,* Willy Loman tries several ways to get a spot in town from Howard, his new boss: by flattery, by appealing for sympathy, by appealing to loyalty, by appealing to honor, by generating guilt, by demanding justice, and finally by begging. Each strategic action is abandoned as it fails, and Willy grows more desperate; each shift in action is a "beat change" and moves the scene in a new direction.

Notice that it is Willy who is "running" the scene at first; he initiates each beat change and Howard only reacts to Willy's shifts in strategy. At the end, however, Howard takes over and makes the final beat change when he fires Willy, forcing Willy to beg.

Though we examine all this in greater detail later, *please read through the scene again now and see if you can feel where the beat changes occur.*

Notice that the sequence of your character's immediate actions and objectives in a scene have a logical flow aimed at larger issues. We discuss this flow in later lessons, but for now be aware that this sequence can carry your through the scene, beat by beat, with a sense of momentum. This sense of logical sequence leading from beat to beat is sometimes called the *scenario* of the scene, though Stanislavski called it the *score.*

It is time, at last, for you to begin work on a scene from a play. Choose carefully, as you will work on this scene repeatedly over several of the following lessons.

Exercise 11.2: Scripted Scene: Action Analysis

With a partner, select a scene (or a logical portion of a scene) no more than five minutes long. Take it from a play you have both read in its entirety, so that you understand how the scene is meant to function within the play as a whole.

Analyze the scene by breaking it into units of action. Define your character's need, action, and objective in each unit.

Read your scene aloud together in front of the class; make no effort to "stage" it. Your aim here is to begin to experience the give and take that moves the scene forward. Afterward, discuss it with the class. Record your insights and problems in your journal.

THE GIVEN CIRCUMSTANCES

In everyday life, you constantly interact with your environment; its physical, psychological, and social aspects profoundly influence your personality, feelings, and thoughts. Just so, a character in a play or film lives in a world created by the author, director, and designers; they are shaped by that world even more than you are shaped by your world, because they and their world have been created specifically to serve one another. Therefore, you work not only on the inner qualities of your character, but also strive to experience the character's world so that your characterization develops in relationship to it.

The specific qualities of the character's world are called the *given circumstances*. These "givens" fall into four categories: who, where, when, and what.

Who refers to the relationship between your character and all the other characters who are important in the scene, whether they are physically present or not. These relationships have two aspects, the *general* relationship (for example, two sisters) and a *specific* relationship (Blanche and Stella as a unique pair of sisters). The general relationship provides a context; in many ways Stella and Blanche are like many other sisters, in that they reminisce about the past, they enjoy going out together for a special occasion, and so on. The specific relationship between Blanche and Stella, however, is fraught with blame and guilt over the past and tension regarding the present. The general relationship, then, provides certain basic considerations that make a relationship similar to others of its kind, while the specific relationship reveals what is unique to this particular case.

Where the scene happens also has two main aspects, the *physical* and the *social*. The physical environment has a tremendous influence on the action. For example, many of Tennessee Williams's plays must take place in the hot, humid climate of the South; think what an air conditioner would do to *A Streetcar Named Desire*. Shakespeare chose to set another play of great passion, *Othello,* in the similar climate of Cyprus, whereas *Hamlet* requires the cold, isolated, and bleak climate of Denmark. Move Hamlet to the tropical climate of Cyprus, and Claudius would be dead by the third act.

Beyond the simple physical influences of climate, the social environment established by the playwright is also of great importance. The society in which Stanley Kowalski moves, for example, is an active part of Stanley's character; we mustn't forget that he was a Marine sergeant, and is still the captain of his bowling team. Think over the plays you have read, and you see how in each case the influences of the immediate locale and society have been carefully chosen, and are indispensable to the specific quality of the action.

When a scene is happening may be equally important, both in terms of the *time of day and year* and also the *historical period,* with all its implications of manners, values, and beliefs. Imagine *The Zoo Story* at night or in the winter, or as an encounter between two Victorians. Or consider the impact of the Elizabethan view of the physical universe on *King Lear.*

Finally, *what* is happening is the most important element of the scene. Consider here also any *antecedent action;* things that we know have happened in the past that affect the present situation, but the playwright has not bothered to actually show us.

Here is a summary list of the givens:

1. Who
   a. General relationship
   b. Specific relationship
2. Where
   a. Physical environment
   b. Social environment
3. When
   a. Time of day and year
   b. Historical time
4. What
   a. The main event of the scene
   b. Any antecedent action that affects this scene

Each of these given circumstances must be evaluated as to its relative importance; don't waste thought and energy on aspects of the character's world that do not contribute to the character's personality or to the action.

Exercise 11.3: The Givens Game

1. One member of the group sits quietly. The rest of you watch this person until he or she reminds you of a real person you have known.
2. Remember this person in a particular real circumstance. Recall all aspects of this real scene: who, where, when, what. Keep this information secret.
3. When you have a clear picture of the givens, get up and join the person on stage. Your task is to let the person know who he or she is and what the givens are by simply relating to the person without indicating. You can't, for example, run up and say, "Hey Dad, can I borrow the car?" Don't try to create a whole event, just be there with the person in the circumstances.
4. Their task is to find out who, where, and when they are, and what is going on. They do this by simply responding to you in various ways until you are both in the same reality. The rest of the group watches and calls "foul" if they see anyone indicating.
5. When you both feel that you are in the same reality, the game is over. Discuss with each other and with the group what you

thought the givens were; compare impressions and notice what produced the strongest and most dramatically satisfying impressions.

Experiencing the givens that most influence the action can be a powerful factor in rehearsing a scene. Consider even working in locations that approximate the conditions of the scene; for example, I have several times held rehearsals for Shakespeare's *A Midsummer Night's Dream* in the woods at night by lantern light, and the "sense memory" of the experience greatly enriched the stage performance.

If the givens of the play are foreign to you, some research is required. The history, architecture, painting, music, and fashion of the time can be very useful. If you are working on *Mother Courage,* you need to know something about the Thirty Years' War; for *The Glass Menagerie,* midwestern city life just before World War II is important.

Exercise 11.4: Scripted Scene: The Givens

1. Working with your partner, analyze the given circumstances of the scene and discuss their influence on your character and on the action.

2. Rehearse the scene in ways that help you to experience the influence of the givens.

3. Read your scene for the class; again, the audience calls foul if they catch you indicating the givens instead of simply experiencing them. Discuss with them the influence of the givens. (By now, you are well on your way to having your scene memorized; subsequent exercises require that you be comfortably "off book.")

SUMMARY

Your character's need generates an objective and an action. Even though the action is provided by the playwright, you must recreate the journey from need to objective to action for yourself so that the character's experience can lead you toward transformation.

Your character chooses an action that seems to have a chance for success in the given circumstances; this is the "strategic" aspect of action. You describe an action with a transitive verb phrase that expresses this strategy. You may also include the object of the verb, which is the other character and the change you want from them. You take note of the sequence of actions and objectives that move your character through the scene; this is called the scenario or *score* of the scene.

An action is pursued until it either succeeds or has failed. In either case, a shift is made to a new action. The shift changes the rhythm of the scene and creates a new unit of action, called a new "beat." The moment at which the new action is formed is called a "beat change." You also consider the circumstances of the scene provided by the playwright to understand how they influence your character and the action.

Armed with your understanding of need, objective, and action, the score of the scene, and the givens, you begin to play the scene. It is here, with the experience of the actual give and take of the living scene, that your true understanding grows and your transformation into the character begins.

Lesson 12

THE FLOW OF DRAMATIC ACTION

You now understand how your character's energy flows from their need toward an objective through their action. In this lesson, we explore how your actions join with the actions of the other characters to create the scene, and how the scene is shaped by the interactions between your characters so as to serve the needs of the play. We begin with a simple exercise that explores how your actions interact with those of others.

Exercise 12.1: Impulse Circle

With your entire class, sit in a large circle, in chairs or on the floor, about eighteen inches apart. Make the circle perfectly round. Each person puts the left hand out palm up, then rests the right hand lightly atop the left hand of the person to their right.

The leader initiates an impulse in the form of a light, clean slap with their right hand. The slap is passed on from person to person around the circle and is allowed to flow continuously, remaining just big enough to be clearly observable. Once the slap is moving well, try the following experiments:

A. Allow your awareness to go to the slap as it moves around the circle. Begin to experience it *as having a life of its own*. Notice any change in its quality as the group begins to experience it as having its own life.

B. Now allow the slap to move as quickly as it can; see what happens when you "get out of its way." Do not force it to go faster, simply remove any resistance to it so that it flows as instantaneously as possible.

C. Now let it slow down; see how slowly it can go *without dying*. Bring it right to the brink of extinction. Keep the external slap sharp and quick, but slow down the impulse as it travels internally. As it moves slowly, see what you need to do to support its life, even while it is not passing directly through you.

Drop your hands, and discuss the many ways in which this exercise is like a scene on stage. Consider these questions:

1. What makes it possible for the slap to flow around the group, and how is it like a scene moving forward?
2. As you experienced it as having a life of its own, how did the nature of the flow change? Did your own experience of it change?
3. Did allowing it to be the focus of your awareness reduce your self-consciousness? Did it affect your body?
4. What are some of the ways the scene can "die"?
5. What are some of the ways we can fail to "pass it on"?
6. What was different about the experience when it was moving slowly? How did it affect your breathing?
7. Did you begin to feel connected to it at all times, not just when it was "your turn"?

Repeat this exercise on subsequent days; it is a good group "warm-up."

ACTION AND REACTION

As you discussed this exercise, you probably agreed that the movement of the slap, like a scene on stage, depended on *cause and effect* as each of you received and sent the slap in turn. Psychologists call it "stimulus and response," and actors call it *reaction and action*. The flow of the slap depended on the ability of every group member to react and act.

In the exercise, you are slapped by the person on your left; you react to the slap by slapping the person on your right; they react by slapping the next person, and so on. For each of you, *reaction produces an action*. Likewise, in a scene, another character says or does something to which you, as your character, react; your reaction becomes an action directed back at them, or toward someone else; this evokes another reaction from them, and so the scene moves through the action–reaction–action–reaction chain of energy passing between the characters.

We might even say that your primary job as an actor at any given moment is to *pass the energy of the scene on in the way most useful to the next actor.* You receive energy, react, and in turn act in a way that moves the scene forward toward its ultimate destination. Each reaction becomes a new action that is a link in the chain of the scene. More simply, we say that *acting is reacting.*

To understand what is required from your action at any given moment, then, you must consider how your individual action fits into the chain of action and reaction that moves the entire scene. This understanding guides you in finding the precise quality of action (and therefore of need and objective leading to that action) that best serves the scene.

THE LIFE OF THE SCENE

During the exercise, when you believed in the impulse as having a life of its own, you became more relaxed and less self-conscious, your awareness opened, your center lowered, your breath became easy, and you stopped judging what you were doing and simply *did* it. Making the slap live became a productive objective, and your focus on that objective took your attention off yourself. You were, in short, *in action.*

When the group related to the slap in this way, you noticed that it began to flow more smoothly and powerfully. When the exercise started, the flow was "chunky," just a sequence of individual actions as each of you waited for your turn, each focused on their own part. When everyone focused their awareness on the whole, however, all the individual parts merged into one flowing event, which did indeed take on a life of its own.

At that moment, the exercise became "easier"; you were no longer *making* it happen, it was making *you* happen. You were receiving more energy from it than you were giving to it, and the whole became greater than the sum of its parts. You also felt that you were part of the whole network through which the impulse flowed all the time, not just when it was "your turn." This is the kind of continuous support and involvement required of everyone in a scene.

These are all ways in which the exercise is like an effective scene on stage. Every actor must be connected to the whole, continuously reacting and acting to contribute to the life of the scene. When this happens, the event begins to take on a life of its own; we say that the scene begins "to play." Your group may wish to repeat the exercise with this awareness.

THE SHAPE OF DRAMA

You may have noticed that there are a number of ways in which this exercise is *not* like a scene on stage. As much fun as it is, it is not particularly dramatic, though it has the *potential* for drama if certain conditions are met. Let's see what the conditions for drama are by trying another simple exercise.

Exercise 12.2: A Dramatic Breath

1. Standing comfortably, try taking a single, complete breath that is as *dramatic* as you can make it. Don't think about it, just do it.
2. Try another; make it even more dramatic.
3. Discuss the things you did to make the breath more dramatic. Did each of these things make it truly more *dramatic* or merely more *theatrical?* If you are in a group, compare notes; was there anything that everyone did?
4. Now discuss situations in life that are naturally dramatic; what qualities do they seem to share? How would your breath be given these same qualities?

When trying this exercise for the first time, most people exaggerate their breath, making it louder and more visible. This, however, serves only to make the breath more "theatrical," not necessarily more dramatic.

Consider for a moment those situations in real life you considered as being naturally dramatic. Let's use a baseball game as an example: what makes for a really dramatic game? The first requirement is that the game must be important to us, either because the outcome affects the team's standing significantly, or team pride needs to be involved, as in a long-standing rivalry with another team. The second requirement is that the outcome must be in doubt; the more evenly matched the teams are, and the closer we get to the last inning with the score tied, the suspense building pitch after pitch, the greater the drama.

This, then, is our definition of a dramatic event: *an urgent situation with the outcome in doubt and building toward a climax.*

How would this apply to a breath? At what moment is the outcome of a breath in doubt? The outcome is most in doubt while the breath is being held, and this is why most people who do this exercise hold their breath for a time before exhaling. They naturally feel the holding of the breath as a moment of *suspense* (which literally means "held up," as in "suspenders").

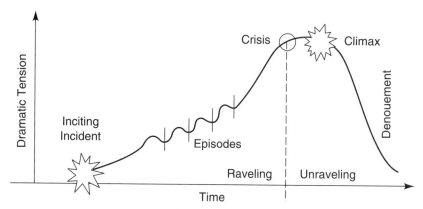

FIGURE 12.1 The Shape of Drama

In a play, as in the baseball game, the sequence of events (the *plot*) moves forward as suspense builds; we begin to wonder "How will this come out?" When the conflict is just on the verge of being resolved, suspense is at its peak. This moment of greatest suspense, just as the outcome hangs in the balance, is called a *crisis* (a "turning point"). The function of everything that happens before the crisis is to lead toward it with *rising* energy, while everything after the crisis flows naturally from it with a *falling* sense of resolution (or *denouement,* which is the French word for "unraveling").

This, then, is the fundamental shape of all dramatic events: a rising conflict, a crisis, and a resolution. (See Figure 12.1.) It is a shape common to all of the performing arts; symphonies and ballets have it. It is the fundamental unit of rhythm, because it is the shape of a muscular contraction and relaxation. It is the fundamental shape of life itself, from birth to death. You can even experience it within a single breath.

Exercise 12.3: A Dramatic Breath Revisited

You can experience the shape of a whole play in a single breath. Start as "empty" as you can: feel the rising energy (inhaling); prolong the crisis (holding the breath), feeling the full strength of the held-back energy; then enjoy a full resolution (exhaling). A single breath can be an exciting event.

In this exercise you heightened the "drama" of the breath in two ways: you extended its dynamic range, which we call its *arc,* by stretching the low and high points of the action farther apart; you also *prolonged the crisis* so as to savor the period of maximum suspense. These same principles apply to the shaping of a play, a scene, and the units of action within a scene.

DRAMA AND CONFLICT

In a baseball game, we wonder which team will win, and the greater the rivalry between the teams, the more dramatic the game. In most plays, suspense is built by the collision between two forces, which we call *conflict*, and it is useful to identify the central conflict driving the play.

In many plays, the central conflict is between two characters, called the hero or *protagonist* and the villain or *antagonist*. In its most simple form this structure tends toward melodrama and is common in popular entertainment like episodic television. The main question generating suspense here is, "Who will win?"

In more complex plays, this two-person conflict can be used to ignite more profound issues: Lear and his daughters, Peter and Jerry, Blanche and Stanley are all examples of protagonist–antagonist conflicts, but the issues involved are far more complex than a mere contest between a "good guy" and a "bad guy," and the question generating suspense may not be simply "Who will win," but a larger issue such as "Will right triumph?"

The central conflict may also live inside the protagonist. While there is a conflict between Hamlet and Claudius in *Hamlet*, for instance, the central conflict of the play really exists within Hamlet himself, between his desire to follow the Ghost's command for vengeance and his moral reticence to commit murder. Such conflicts may not have clear-cut solutions, and many modern characters are trapped in "lose–lose" situations called "double binds." In *The Glass Menagerie*, the central conflict is within Tom: the question is will he stay, sacrificing his own identity, or go, suffering the guilt of having abandoned his family? Either way, he "loses."

A central conflict may also involve a character or characters confronting a difficult situation. In Beckett's *Waiting for Godot*, for example, there is little conflict between the characters: rather, they are in conflict with a situation that forces them to wait for someone (or something) that is unknown and may or may not come. The question here might be "Is this all there is to life?"

Whatever its form, then, all plays are organized around a central conflict between opposing forces. Sensing that conflict, we expect that something is about to happen, and this provides the essential ingredient of suspense. In fact, suspense, the feeling that something *might* happen, is more important than the event itself. This is how contemporary plays with few "events" in the traditional sense can still be dramatically satisfying, like Samuel Beckett's *Waiting for Godot*, Harold Pinter's *The Collection*, or Sam Shepard's *The Buried Child*, to name a few.

When creating a role you must find the connection between your part and the central dramatic conflict of the play, and shape your characterization so as to contribute to that central conflict. For example, if you were playing the next-door neighbor, Charlie, in Miller's *Death of a Salesman*, you would have to see that the central conflict of the play is the choice facing Willy between his brother Ben's way of life (which is based on struggle and material success) and Charlie's way of life (which is based on acceptance and spiritual success). Your main purpose in creating Charlie's character would be to embody this alternative way of life which, if Willy could but choose it, would save his life. We call this your character's *dramatic function*. Your understanding of dramatic function is the necessary basis of all your work as an actor. In Part III we explore this essential concept in greater detail.

SUMMARY

A scene moves through the action–reaction–action–reaction chain of energy being passed between the characters. Your primary job as an actor at any given moment is to receive energy, react, and in turn act in a way that moves the scene forward toward its ultimate destination. More simply, we like to say that *acting is reacting*.

Every actor must be connected to the whole scene, continuously reacting and acting in order to contribute to its life. When this happens, the event begins to take on a life of its own; we say that the scene begins "to play."

Our sense of drama springs from an urgent situation of conflict between opposing forces with the outcome in doubt. This central conflict may be between two characters, within the hero, or between the characters and their situation.

The central conflict generates a sequence of events, called the *plot*; the plot moves forward as the conflict intensifies and suspense builds; suspense is at its peak just as the outcome hangs in the balance, and this is the *crisis*. Everything that happens before the crisis leads toward it with *rising* energy; everything after the crisis flows naturally from it with a *falling* sense of resolution.

This, then, is the fundamental shape of all dramatic events: a rising conflict, a crisis, and a resolution. It is the fundamental shape of life itself, from birth to death. You can even experience it within a single breath.

In most plays, suspense is built by the collision between two forces, which we call the *central conflict,* and it is useful to identify it early on. When creating a role you must find the connection between your part and the central conflict of the play, and shape your characterization so as to contribute to that central conflict. We call this your character's *dramatic function.* Your understanding of dramatic function is the necessary basis of all your work as an actor.

Lesson 13

BEATS AND SCENES

In this lesson you experience how the various elements of the flow of drama—moments, beats, and scenes—work together to create the unified experience of the play. This may be difficult for the mind to comprehend, but it is easily understood by the muscles, so let's begin with a physical exercise.

Exercise 13.1: Shaping Action Phrases

Perform the following sequence of actions, attempting to fully experience the dramatic potential of each. Remember to focus on the crisis in each pattern: treat all that goes before as leading up to the crisis, and all that follows as flowing from it.

1. A single step. Where is the crisis of a step? To intensify the experience, involve your breath by inhaling during the rising action, holding the breath during the crisis, and exhaling during the release.

2. Three steps experienced as one phrase, with the crisis in the third step. The first two steps still have mini-crises of their own, but now they lead up to the main crisis in the third step. Let your breath parallel the larger pattern.

3. Three steps with the crisis in the first step, so that the mini-crises of the second and third steps "follow-through" from the first.

4. Now try a pattern composed of three units of three steps each, with the crisis of the whole pattern in the second unit of three.

5. Invent patterns of your own; add sound.

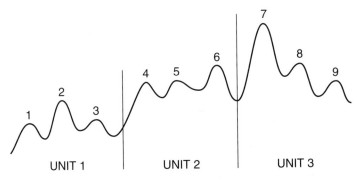

FIGURE 13.1   Compound Rhythms. Here, nine steps shaped as three units combine to produce one large pattern.

In this exercise you experienced how a number of small units of action (like breaths or steps) can be connected into a larger phrase having a shape of its own; likewise, these larger phrases can be connected into still larger patterns, which again have shapes of their own. On all these levels, the fundamental shape of rise, crisis, and release is the same, even though the *proportion* or relationship between the parts may be different. (See Figure 13.1.)

This is how the parts of a play go together to compose the whole play. We begin with the smallest units, the individual transactions between characters, which we call *moments.* Moments work together to form larger units called *beats,* and the beats work together to form *scenes;* the scenes flow toward the *main event* of the play as a whole.

On each level there is one central issue. Take, for example, this transaction from the Willy Loman scene:

Willy: What's that, Howard?

Howard: Didn't you ever see one of these? Wire recorder.

Willy: Oh. Can we talk a minute?

Howard: Records things. Just got delivery yesterday...

This is a single transaction (action and reaction) or *moment* in which Willy tries to get Howard's attention but fails. It is one of several such moments that form the long first *beat* in which Willy tries to get Howard's attention through flattery. A number of beats go together to form this *scene* in which Willy is fired; this scene fits into the flow of the whole so that we see how Willy's being fired eventually leads to his suicide, which is the *main event* of the play.

Each of these levels has the same basic shape of rise and fall, and each has its own mini-crisis. As you work, you develop each part in a way that leads up to, or flows from, the crisis on that level. You explore each moment so that it fits into its beat and creates the *beat crisis;* you develop each beat so that it links with the other beats in the scene to create the *scene crisis;* you develop each scene to achieve the shape of the play, leading to the *main crisis* followed by the *main event.*

Having developed your role in this way, you are free in performance to focus on the most simple and immediate level, playing moment by moment, knowing that each moment serves its beat, the beat serves the scene, and the scene serves the play.

ANALYZING BEATS

You now understand that a beat consists of several transactions between characters, and is the smallest unit of action that has its own complete shape, with a rising action, mini-crisis, and fall. A beat is driven by a very specific, momentary conflict, called the *beat conflict.*

The beat conflict comes from the action of one character encountering the resistance (or even counteraction) of the other. Several transactions may occur as the conflict builds until we reach the *beat crisis.* When the beat crisis is resolved (or produces a stalemate) the *beat change* occurs, because at this moment one of the characters has to shift to a new action, causing the scene to turn and flow in a new direction as a new beat is formed.

This structure is not an arbitrary choice made by the actors: it is built into the scene by the playwright. Every actor in the scene works to recognize the structure provided, and each of them supports the beat changes when they occur, even if they are not initiated by their character.

An analysis of the structure of a scene, beat by beat, is called a *break-down.* As an example of a breakdown, let's again examine the scene from *Death of a Salesman;* follow along in the Appendix, and compare the breakdown that you did on your own in the last lesson.

Beat One: Willy, unable to go on driving as much as his job requires, goes to see his new boss, Howard. Willy enters somewhat hesitantly and finds Howard playing with a new toy, a recorder. Howard wants to avoid this unpleasant confrontation (we learn later that he has already decided to fire Willy and has been putting it off) so he goes on playing with the recorder and forces Willy to listen to inane recordings of his family. Like a good salesman, Willy listens dutifully and even flatters Howard, while trying four times to bring up the reason for his visit. The conflict in this beat is between Willy's action of getting Howard's attention by flattery, versus Howard's counter-objective of avoiding Willy by playing with the recorder. The crisis is finally reached when Howard counterattacks by asking, "Say, aren't you supposed to be in Boston?"

Beat Two: In this short beat, Howard attacks by demanding to know, "What happened? What're you doing here?" Willy reacts weakly, but manages to state his case: "I've come to the decision that I'd rather not travel anymore." He reminds Howard that he had promised to find him "some spot for me here in town," but Howard responds, "Well, I couldn't think of anything for you, Willy." The main conflict of the scene is now on the table: Willy must get off the road, but Howard refuses to help.

Beat Three: This beat might be defined as three mini-beats, three quick thrusts of different strategies by Willy: appealing to sympathy ("I'm just a little tired"), appealing to loyalty ("I was with the firm when your father used to carry you in here in his arms"), and then demanding his right (*"with increasing anger"*); Howard parries each of these thrusts. What unifies this beat, however, is Willy's action of *bargaining,* as he steadily lowers the salary he is willing to accept in return for a spot in town.

Beat Four: Willy tries to make Howard understand by telling him how he decided to become a salesman, and even lowers his price to forty dollars a week, but Howard, who is really the "kid" in this relationship, responds, "Kid, I can't take blood from a stone."

Beat Five: Willy grows desperate and demands justice, reminding Howard of his thirty-four years with the firm and the promises Howard's father had made. Howard simply walks out: "You'll have to excuse me, Willy, I gotta see some people. Pull yourself together."

Beat Six: Willy, now alone, thinks that he sees his old boss sitting in his chair, and is then frightened by accidentally turning on the recorder (which symbolizes Willy's inability to deal with the changes happening in his world). This interlude serves to prolong and heighten the sense of crisis.

Beat Seven: Howard reenters, and Willy, knowing that he has made a terrible mistake, tries to put things back the way they were by saying, "I'll go to Boston." *The scene is now at its main crisis.* Howard fires

Willy: "Willy, you can't go to Boston for us." *This is the main event of the scene.*

Beat Eight: Willy starts to beg, but Howard refuses to take responsibility, and asks, "Where are your sons? Why don't your sons give you a hand?" Of course, the last thing a proud man like Willy could do is accept help from his sons.

As you see, a breakdown greatly simplifies the scene for you. This fairly long scene (some ten minutes' playing time) can be understood as having just six beats leading to its main crisis, followed by one beat of "denouement." As you rehearse, you feel how each beat fits into this overall structure, and you gain a sense of the function of each moment and beat.

Most important, notice that within each beat, each character has a single objective and action. It is this fact that permits you to translate the architecture of the scene into the thoughts and actions of your character. You *as the actor* understand this structure and you design the consciousness of the character so as to contribute to it; then, as you play the scene, you can surrender your immediate awareness *to the character's consciousness* while continuing to ensure that your character's thoughts, words, and actions serve the scene. Again, your ability for dual consciousness comes into play.

If all the actors have worked together to develop a shared understanding of the scenario, the rhythm of the scene is strong and clear. It is as important for actors to agree on the phraseology of their shared action as it is for members of an orchestra to work together to fulfill the phraseology of a piece of music.

Exercise 13.2: Beat Analysis

Working with your partner, answer these questions about the scene from *The Glass Menagerie* in the Appendix, or from the scripted scene you have chosen for yourself.

1. Do a breakdown of the beats of the scene, as in the example above.
2. Select one important beat.
   a. Define its central conflict.
   b. Specify its moment of crisis.
   c. Decide who makes the choice that changes the beat.
   d. See how this beat grows out of the preceding beat and flows into the following beat.

SCENE STRUCTURE

You see now that both beats and scenes are structured like miniature plays: just as a play has an arrangement of scenes (episodes) with a central conflict building to a crisis and climax, so a beat is an arrangement of moments, and a scene is as an arrangement of beats. Each has its own central conflict, its own crisis, and its own main event.

Unlike a beat, however, a scene contains *one major development in the movement of the whole play.* This development may be related to *plot* as a major event, some new piece of information, or a major change in relationship; or it may be a *thematic* development. In either case, every scene contains a "milestone" in the progress of the entire play, and understanding how the scene contributes to the play is crucial to the effectiveness of your rehearsal; it gives your work a sense of priority and direction.

You can identify the scene's function by asking yourself, "What if this scene were cut from the play: what would we lose that would make it impossible for the play to go forward? What would we lose from the meaning of the play?" In the scene between Willy and Howard, for example, the major plot development is that Willy is fired; this event contributes directly to Willy's eventual suicide, which is the main event of the play. Thematically, this scene reveals why Willy became a salesman, and how completely dependent he is on that role for his sense of self-worth. His firing raises the question: Now that he can no longer be a salesman, will he be able to find himself as a human being? Will he be able to find peace by accepting himself, as Charlie has?

Though the author often indicates where each scene begins and ends, short plays like *The Zoo Story* and even some longer plays, like those of Samuel Beckett, may not be divided into scenes at all. In these cases, you can (and should) identify units of scenic action for yourself; the section in *The Zoo Story* in which Jerry takes the bench away from Peter might be thought of as one scene, for example.

SCENE STRUCTURE IN REHEARSAL

Rehearsing a scene is much like making a map of an unknown territory. You and your partners, through trial and error, find for yourselves the pathway of action that the author has hidden beneath the surface of the dialogue. Each beat change is a turning point in the journey; the destination is the scene crisis and the scene's main event. It usually takes some time to explore the beat changes by trial and error, but your exploration may be made more efficient if you agree on the destination—the crisis and main event—as you set out.

The main event is usually obvious; if you have trouble identifying it, ask yourself, "What event in this scene most changes the world of the play? Why couldn't this scene be cut?"

The crisis can then be identified by thinking *backward* from the end of the scene, looking for the moment in which the outcome of the scene most hangs in the balance; this is usually just before the main event. (The same strategy works for the play as a whole.)

The exact placement of the crisis can sometimes be a matter of interpretation: in the *Death of a Salesman* scene, for instance, the crisis is the moment in which Howard finally decides to tell Willy that he is fired. (Notice that moments of crisis are almost always *choices* made by the characters, and so occur "between the lines.") This might happen when Howard leaves Willy saying, "Pull yourself together, I'll be back in a little while," wanting Willy to be better prepared for the bad news; or it might be when Howard comes back in and has to shut off the recorder, realizing that Willy is a hopeless case; or it might be the moment just before he says, "You can't go to Boston for us, Willy." The actors have to find which placement works best for the way *they* are playing the scene.

Though you may analyze the scene's structure by breaking it down intellectually in this way at first, experienced actors usually approach structure intuitively, developing a shared *rhythmic* experience of the rise and fall of the scene's energy as they explore it in rehearsal. However you find it, your sense of scene structure must finally live as a sort of underlying "dance" in the flow of the scene, as we feel the energy building toward the crisis and main event, then flowing naturally away from them.

The sense of the underlying structure of the scene is especially important in film and television when a single camera is used. A section of the scene is usually shot from an overall point of view; this is called the "master." Closer individual shots are then made, called "coverage," which are later to be inserted into the master by the editor. Several "takes" of each are usually required, and the whole process can take many hours. Your performance must be consistent from take to take, your close-ups must "match" the master as to timing, position, and expression. This is made even harder by the fact that scenes, and even coverage within scenes, are often shot out of sequence. The film actor *must* have a firm sense of the structure of the scene, and how every moment fits into it.

In both film and stage work, then, your sense of scene structure is the "map" that traces the energy flow of a scene and permits all the actors to support one another in their journey through it; the map helps you have less fear of becoming lost, making your work more playful and creative; it also helps you to experience the scene as a single, rhythmic event. One symptom that the scene has started to "play" in this way is that it seems shorter to you when you perform it.

Exercise 13.3: Scene Analysis

Working with your partner, answer these questions about the scene from *The Glass Menagerie* in the Appendix, or the scene you have chosen for yourself.

1. What is the major change in the world of the play that occurs in this scene? How does this scene cause the plot to progress? How does it enhance the meaning of the play?
2. What is the central scene conflict?
3. Examine the beat breakdown you made in the previous exercise; which beat contains the crisis of the scene? How do all the previous beats flow toward it, and how do subsequent beats flow from it?
4. Read through the scene aloud on the basis of this analysis. Can you feel the shape of scene action as it flows from beat to beat?
5. Begin to rehearse the scene.

As you rehearse, you explore each *moment* so it fits into its beat and moves toward the *beat crisis;* you develop each beat so that it links with the other beats to create the *scene crisis;* you develop each scene to achieve the shape of the play, leading to the *main crisis* followed by the *main event.*

SUMMARY

This is how the parts of a play go together to compose the whole play: the smallest units, the individual transactions between characters, which we call *moments,* work together to form larger units called *beats,* and the beats work together to form *scenes;* the scenes flow toward the *main event* of the play as a whole.

An analysis of the beat structure is called a *breakdown* of the scene. A breakdown greatly simplifies the scene for you. As you rehearse, you begin to feel how each beat fits into the overall structure of the scene.

Within each beat, each character has a single action or point of reaction. It is this fact that permits you to translate the architecture of the scene into the thoughts and actions of your character.

A scene is an arrangement of beats with its own central conflict, its own crisis, and its own main event. A scene contains *one major development in the movement of the whole play.* This development may be related to *plot* or to *theme.*

Rehearsing a scene is much like making a map of an unknown territory. You and your partners, through trial and error, find for yourselves the pathway of action that the author has hidden beneath the surface of the dialogue. Each beat change is a turning point in the journey; the destination is the scene crisis and main event. This sense of scene structure must finally live as a rhythm as we feel the energy of the scene building toward the crisis and main event, then flowing naturally away from them. If all the actors have worked together to develop a shared understanding of the structure of the scene, the rhythm of the scene in performance is strong and clear.

Lesson 14

THROUGH-LINE AND SUPEROBJECTIVE

THE HIERARCHY OF OBJECTIVES

You now understand that a play is structured on levels: individual trans-actions make up beats, beats make up scenes, and the scenes form the overall shape of rising and falling action that give unity to the whole play.

These levels of action relate directly to the inner life of your character because you have an objective (and therefore an action) on each level. In each transaction you have an *immediate* objective; the sequence of imme-diate objectives leads toward your *beat objective;* the objectives of the beats in sequence lead toward your *scene objective;* and your scene objec-tives can be seen as springing from a deep, overall objective, which is your character's "life goal" or, as it is usually called, your *superobjective.*

For example, consider again the moment from *Death of a Salesman* when Willy finds Howard engrossed in his new recorder. Being a good salesman, Willy tries to get his foot in the door by engaging Howard in conversation and asks, "What's that, Howard?" At this moment, Willy's *immediate objective* is to get Howard's attention by asking about the recorder. Once he accomplishes this, he hopes he can move on toward his *beat objective,* which is to bring up the subject of his work assignment. He would then hope to move toward his *scene objective,* which is to persuade Howard to give him a spot in town. This scene objective is connected directly to his life goal, which we call his *super-objective:* to prove himself a worthy human being by earning money and respect.

You see that Willy's objectives on each level work together in a logical way, his immediate objective leading toward his beat objective, his beat objectives being steps toward his scene objective, and the scene objective as springing directly from his superobjective.

If we were to follow each of Willy's immediate objectives through the play, we could see how he is led from objective to objective in pursuit of his superobjective. The logic of this sequence of objectives striving toward the superobjective is called the *through-line* of the character's action.

> *In a play the whole stream of individual minor objectives, all the imaginative thoughts, feelings and actions of an actor should converge to carry out this superobjective.... Also this impetus toward the superobjective must be continuous throughout the whole play.*[1]

Stanislavski once said that each of your character's actions fit into the through-line like vertebrae in a spine; hence some actors call the through-line the "spine" of the role. Stanislavski elsewhere referred to "the sequence of objectives" as being *the score* of the role, which the actor learns to follow automatically.

Identifying your character's through-line of action as tending toward a superobjective can help you to better understand each of your specific actions, connecting each momentary action to the character's deepest needs and desires. It can also help you to see how the sequence of objectives has a single driving force; thus you can "play through" each moment and achieve both unity and momentum (what we call *pace*) in your performance.

THE SUPEROBJECTIVE

Your character's superobjective may be conscious or (more commonly) unconscious. If the character is unconscious of it, you—the actor—can treat it as you treat everything you know that the character doesn't: you take it fully into account as you work, but you do not let your actor knowledge "contaminate" your character reality. Remember the idea of dual consciousness: what you know as the actor is not the same thing as what your character knows. Lee Strassberg once said the hardest thing about acting "is not knowing what you know."

Either way, the superobjective functions as an underlying principle that affects all of your actions, and establishes your attitude toward life. Notice that it is described according to the same principles as any individual objective.

Willy Loman, for example, is presented with two alternative attitudes toward life. He could, like his brother Ben, strike off on some bold
venture and be the "master of his fate"; or he could, like his neighbor
Charlie, accept his life as it is and find inner peace. Unfortunately, Willy
lacks the courage to follow his brother's example, and lacks also Charlie's
sense of self-identity. Willy has opted instead to try to earn self-esteem
through selling. In the scene with Howard, Willy describes the moment
he formed this superobjective:

> *...I met a salesman in the Parker House. His name was Dave Single-
> man. And he was eighty-four years old, and he'd drummed merchandise
> in thirty-one states. And old Dave, he'd go up to his room, y'understand,
> put on his green velvet slippers—I'll never forget—and pick up his phone
> and call buyers, and without ever leaving his room, at the age of eighty-
> four, he made his living. And when I saw that, I realized that selling
> was the greatest career a man could want.*

Willy has come to confuse success as a salesman with success as a
human being. Like many in our nation's work force, he "is" what he
"does." We would say that his superobjective is "to prove myself worthy
as a human being by earning money and respect through selling." Eventually, however, Willy is no longer able to sell either his products or himself. His last "sale" is his suicide, and the insurance money is the last
paycheck he will "earn." It will give his family the financial indepen-
dence he has so long sought as a measure of his worth.

What drives the entire play is Willy's constant search for the success
that will prove he is a worthy person; his tragedy is that he defines his
success by external measures. Each scene, each beat, each moment of the
role and every aspect of Willy's psychology can be understood as reflecting this superobjective.

Because it is so important to the theme of *Death of a Salesman,* Miller
was explicit about Willy's superobjective; most plays are not so specific,
even in the case of the major character. Most of the time you must *deduce*
your character's superobjective from their behavior in their circumstances. Tom in *The Glass Menagerie,* for example, clearly needs to make
a place for himself in the world, but he cannot do so unless he escapes
his role as the "provider" for his mother and helpless sister. Tom's superobjective therefore translates into the specific need "to leave home without guilt." The through-line of his scene objectives, his beat objectives,
and each of his immediate objectives can be seen as being driven by this
superobjective. His most important single action—bringing home the
gentleman caller—is driven by his hope that Jim will replace him as the
provider for the family.

It is possible for the superobjective of a character to change in the course of the play under the pressure of extraordinary circumstances. King Lear begins his play intent upon retiring from the responsibilities of kingship so that he can enjoy his last days "unburdened" and bask in the love of his family and subjects. In the course of his suffering, however, he learns that he has been ignorant of true love, and he surrenders his self-centered superobjective in favor of a desire for universal justice and the simple, personal love he feels for Cordelia at the end.

It may be difficult to find the superobjective of minor characters, because the playwright has not provided much information; here you can be inventive, so long as your understanding of the character enables you to accurately serve your dramatic function within the play as a whole.

Even more difficult may be those plays in which the internal life of the characters is purposely mysterious, as in plays by Pinter, Beckett, or Shepard. It may be useful to you as an actor to discover some sense of superobjective for such characters, but it would be disastrous if you were to try to reveal your superobjective to the audience. All great plays have some measure of mystery at their heart, and it is a mistake to "pluck it out" by exposing things that the playwright meant to remain obscure.

In fact, it is *never* your aim to reveal your objectives on any level, including the superobjective, to the audience. This would be indicating of the worst sort. The sense of objective is part of your acting process and is *never* intended for audience consumption except through the deductions that the audience may make *for themselves* based on their experience of your behavior.

FINDING AND PERSONALIZING THE SUPEROBJECTIVE

Though you may develop some idea about your character's superobjective before rehearsals start, it is dangerous to become too set in your thinking; these early ideas need to be tested. Ideally, the sense of superobjective emerges gradually from your experience of the specific actions of your character. Let your sense of the superobjective be the result of your rehearsal exploration, not a substitute for it.

Once you have begun to identify the superobjective, you must *personalize* it; you must come to care as deeply about it as your character does. Because the superobjective of most characters is fairly "universal" this is usually not difficult; like Willy Loman, we all want to be thought of as worthy, and we can all "identify" with Willy on this basis, however much we can see that Willy's way of pursuing self-esteem is mistaken.

In some cases, however, the precise manner in which a character manifests the superobjective may be so foreign to you that it presents difficulties. Isabella in Shakespeare's *Measure for Measure,* for example, is faced with a choice between sleeping with the Duke or seeing her brother executed for a trivial crime. Isabella, who is about to become a nun, believes that losing her virginity would damn her, and she fully expects her brother to be willing to die to maintain her virtue, thus winning a place in heaven; when he begs her for his life, she angrily condemns him as a coward.

If you are playing Isabella, it may be difficult for you to identify with such strong and inflexible religious values. In such a case, you may have to find some analogous superobjective that can motivate you as strongly as your character's does her. In this case, you might consider what action is so loathsome to you that you would ask your brother to die before you would do it; then, "substitute" this in your own mind for Isabella's situation.

As we said earler, such substitutions may be useful, but they carry the danger of bringing inappropriate personal material into the performance. It is better, if possible, simply to surrender yourself to your character's situation and belief system. Remember our version of Stanislavski's "magic if": if you were in the character's situation, and if you made the same choices, who would you become? You have a vast personal potential; somewhere in you the religious fanatic, the saint, the mass murderer, the courageous hero, the snivelling coward are all waiting to be realized.

Exercise 14.1: The Superobjective

Working with your partner, answer these questions about the scene from *The Glass Menagerie* in the Appendix, or the scene you have chosen for yourself.

1. Examine your character's actions: can you see a superobjective toward which they are tending, whether the character is conscious of it or not?
2. Define the superobjective using a transitive verb phrase.
3. Look through your script: are there any actual lines that sum up your character's superobjective?
4. Now consider ways of personalizing this superobjective, so that you feel it with the same intensity as does your character.

Now rehearse your scene again and find how the superobjective is expressed in it.

THE THROUGH-LINE OF ACTION

As you work on your role, each moment in your performance begins to "fit" with every other in a harmonious way; moments that may have seemed incomprehensible at first begin to fit into the flow of the whole, like steps in a journey. When finally the whole is in place, each moment of the performance cumulatively supports every other moment, and you move naturally from one to the other by a sense of necessity. This is called the *through-line* of the role. Stanislavski once said that each action fits into the role like vertebrae in a spine, so the through-line is also sometimes called the *spine* of the role.

It is neither easy nor necessary to describe the through-line of a role in words; it is more important to *feel* the sequence and flow of the role, and the "logic" by which one action leads into another, each a step toward a scene objective and through the scene objective to the super-objective. For this reason, the through-line usually emerges gradually as your individual actions are explored and experienced in rehearsal.

In a production of Brecht's *Mother Courage,* for example, the actress playing the role of Kattrin, the mute daughter, needed help with her last scene. In it, Kattrin climbs atop a hut and beats a drum to warn the nearby town of an impending attack. The soldiers coax and threaten her, trying to make her stop drumming, but she refuses and is shot. Obviously, her choice to sacrifice herself to warn the town is the most important choice she makes in the play; it is also the crisis of the entire play. It embodies the play's meaning: we have created a world in which love for your fellow man is suicidal.

The dramatic function of Kattrin's character, then, is to provide one glimmer of selflessness against which we can judge the callousness of a world in which love has been sacrificed to economic necessity. Her super-objective, which we learn in various scenes, is to have a child that she can care for; the fact that there are children in the town is crucial to her, because by sacrificing her life for them she is winning her superobjective in the only way possible in the world of the play.

Knowing all this intellectually, however, didn't help the actress with the playing of her final action. Rehearsal after rehearsal, she tried different ways of climbing the ladder, different ways of drumming, different ways of thinking through the choice. Nothing seemed to work, and she was in despair.

Her mistake was in thinking that the problem was within this climactic scene; her real problem was that she had not yet found the *through-line* that would bring her to this moment properly. She had to go back to the beginning and examine each moment of her role, each of her previous actions and reactions, to see how each contributed to this final action.

Once she understood this, the actress began to go through rehearsals, moment by moment, asking herself, "What do I see going on at this moment that will eventually make me climb that ladder and beat that drum?" Each of her moments, beats, and scenes were quickly understood as contributing to this through-line, and then climaxing in her final choice to warn the town. At once, her final action became not only easy, but unavoidable.

When your character has such a climactic action it must be the "pay-off" resulting from careful preparation. You may reap only what you have previously sown, and this cumulative effect is achieved by sensing the through-line and fitting each action into its proper place in the sequence.

We should note that unlike this example, a character's through-line may not be a "straight line." The character may try one thing, then another; they may need to discover an effective course of action through trial and error. Think of the through-line as the motivational energy driving your character forward toward their superobjective; every time they have to choose what to do, they choose the thing that seems *at that moment and in that circumstance* to move in the desired direction, even if they later discover that they were wrong.

Perhaps the greatest value in experiencing the through-line is that you find how each moment of your performance is driven by your character's deepest energies. In *The Glass Menagerie,* Tom introduces his sister Laura to Jim, the Gentleman Caller. This simple introduction ("Jim, this is Laura; Laura, this is Jim") can be seen as part of Tom's through-line of action moving toward his superobjective:

- *Immediate Objective:* to get Laura and Jim off to a good start;
- *Beat Objective:* to lay the seeds of a relationship between them;
- *Scene Objective:* to bring another man into the house, hopefully permanently;
- *Superobjective:* if there were another man in the house, I could leave home without guilt because Mother and Laura would be "looked after," and I could get out of here and find my own identity.

This is how the through-line of action brings unity and momentum, which we call *pace,* to every moment of your performance. Once you have fit each moment into its place within the structure of the whole during rehearsal, you are then free in performance to give your full attention to playing each moment, secure that it also serves the play as a whole.

Exercise 14.2: The Through-Line

Working with your partner, answer these questions about the scene from *The Glass Menagerie* in the Appendix, or the scene you have chosen for yourself.

1. Examine the sequence of your character's objectives; do you see its logic as a reflection of an underlying movement toward a superobjective?
2. In each transaction, try to feel the connection of the immediate objective to the beat objective, the scene objective, and the superobjective.
3. Run the scene without stopping and feel the momentum of the sequence of objectives.

SUMMARY

Scene structure translates into the thought of your character because in each transaction you have an *immediate* objective; the sequence of immediate objectives leads toward your *beat objective;* the objectives of the beats in sequence lead toward your *scene objective;* and your scene objectives move toward a deep, overall objective, which is your character's "life goal" or, as it is usually called, your *superobjective.*

Once you have begun to identify this superobjective, you must *personalize* it; you must come to care as deeply about it as your character does.

One aim of rehearsal is to feel the "logic" by which one action leads into another as steps tending toward scene objectives and through them to the superobjective. As it becomes clear, each moment in your performance begins to "fit" with every other in a harmonious way; this is the *through-line* of our action.

Lesson 15

THE FUNCTION AND ELEMENTS OF CHARACTER

In Part I you prepared your body, voice, and mind much in the way a gardener prepares the ground before planting a seed. In Part II you developed a way of experiencing action, which is the seed from which the created role springs: as you enter into the actions of your character within the given circumstances "as if" they were your own, the transformational process begins to work and a new "me" begins to emerge. In Part III we explore and extend the fruition of this process, the character.

DRAMATIC FUNCTION

As the play unfolds, it seems as if the things that happen are "caused" by the characters; their needs, the choices they make, the way they interact with one another, all seem to drive the story forward. This is because the playwright, and then the actors, have created characters that can believably perform the actions necessary for the advancement of the plot and meaning of the play; each character is created to do a specific job within the scheme of the play. So although it seems that the characters cause the story to happen, it is actually the needs of the story that have caused the characters to be the way they are.

We call this the *dramatic function* of each character. Your understanding of your character's specific purpose within the play is crucial to the success of your work. Without it, you have no basis for your exploration in rehearsal, and no way to judge the results of that exploration. As Stanislavski put it, the actor's most important task is *to understand how*

*every moment of the performance, and every aspect of characterization, con-
tributes to the reason why the play was written.*

This is a powerful idea, equal in importance to the concepts of action
and transformation. Your sense of function gives action and transformation a purpose, which makes them capable of serving the play.

There are two main ways that your character may serve the play: by
advancing the *plot* through their actions, and by contributing to the
meaning of the play through the values they and their actions express.

In terms of the plot, your character may commit crucial actions that
drive the plot forward; they may serve as a "foil" to frustrate the intentions of another character; or they may simply serve to provide some
essential plot information, like the classical messenger. In terms of the
meaning of the play, your character may represent certain values, or
present a contrast to the values of other characters; they may be the
spokesperson for one of several conflicting points of view; or they may be
an embodiment or extension of the conflict within the main character,
like Ben and Charlie who represent the two life-styles that Willy Loman
must choose between.

Too often actors approach their characters so personally that they
begin to forget the larger purpose for which that character was created.
Without a sense of function, they may create a character who is alive
and believable, but who doesn't fit into the play, doesn't do the job it
was created to do. Even if the audience accepts or is even impressed by
such a performance, the play is damaged, and the actor has failed.

Exercise 15.1: Dramatic Function

Consider the character you have been developing in the previous exercises: what is their dramatic function within their play?

1. If your character were to be cut, what would be missing from
    the plot? What actions would have to be given to another char-
    acter in order for the plot to proceed?
2. How would the meaning of the play suffer if your character were
    cut? Does your character express some value or point of view
    that is essential? Would the meaning of the other characters be
    as clear?

FUNCTIONAL AND LIKENESS TRAITS

In order for your character to serve their purpose within the play believably, the playwright has provided them with certain traits that make the

action required by the play seem "natural" to them; because the story requires that Othello strangle Desdemona, he must be capable of overwhelming jealousy. Aristotle called these *functional traits* because they permit the character to believably fulfill their dramatic function. Whatever other traits of character are suggested by the text, or whatever else you may invent in rehearsal to "round out" the character, you must embody these functional traits first and foremost, and let no other traits obscure or contradict them.

There are other kinds of character traits that do not contribute directly to a character's main dramatic function. These are the traits that help us to recognize the character as a fellow human being, someone we can "know" because he or she is in some way "like" us. Aristotle called these *likeness traits*. Some likeness traits are provided by the playwright, but the actor often contributes personal touches to the role in this area.

Exercise 15.2: Functional and Likeness Traits

Examine again the character you have been developing.

1. What traits must they have to believably perform their function within the play? How has the playwright provided or implied these traits?

2. What additional traits has the playwright provided or implied that help to "round out" your character as a recognizable human being?

CATEGORIES OF CHARACTER TRAITS

Whether they are functional traits or likeness traits, we can classify all characterizational traits in four categories, as outlined here by Oscar Brockett:

The first level of characterization is physical and is concerned only with such basic facts as sex, age, size, and color. Sometimes a dramatist does not supply all of this information, but it is present whenever the play is produced, since actors necessarily give concrete form to the characters. The physical is the simplest level of characterization, however, since it reveals external traits only, many of which may not affect the dramatic action at all.

    The second level is social. It includes a character's economic status, profession or trade, religion, family relationships—all those factors that place him in his environment.

The third level is psychological. It reveals a character's habitual responses, attitudes, desires, motivations, likes and dislikes—the inner workings of the mind, both emotional and intellectual, which precede action. Since habits of feeling, thought and behavior define characters more fully than do physical and social traits, and since drama most often arises from conflicting desires, the psychological is the most essential level of characterization.

The fourth level is moral. Although implied in all plays, it is not always emphasized. It is most apt to be used in serious plays, especially tragedies. Although almost all human action suggests some ethical standard, in many plays the moral implications are ignored, and decisions are made on grounds of expediency. This is typical of comedy, since moral deliberations tend to make any action serious. More nearly than any other kind, moral decisions differentiate characters, since the choices they make when faced with moral crises show whether they are selfish, hypocritical, or persons of integrity. A moral decision usually causes a character to examine his own motives and values, in the process of which his true nature is revealed both to himself and to the audience.[1]

In the following lessons we focus on several of these levels of characterization as they develop through the rehearsal process. First, however, let's look at the information you can get from the play about each of these levels of characterization during your early stages of preparation.

PHYSICAL TRAITS

The first level is physical. It is of primary importance to you because the external traits of body and voice communicate all the other levels of characterization.

The playwright has specified the essential aspects of your character's physical traits. There are four main sources of such information in any text. First, the *stage directions* or *prefaces* by the author. In his preface to *The Zoo Story*, for example, Albee specifies that Jerry is thirty-eight years old; do you see how it isn't the same play if you imagine Jerry as being only twenty-two?

Second, there are traits *described by other characters;* of course, we must evaluate such descriptions and determine if they are accurate, or perhaps distorted by the other character's prejudice. In Shakespeare's *Henry IV, i*, Prince Hal gives an elaborate description of the warlike Hotspur as "a popinjay," but his view is obviously clouded by the jealousy he feels for Hotspur. Aside from such distortions, however, the statements of other characters can be a valuable source of information. "Yon Cassius," in *Julius Caesar*, probably *should* have "a lean and hungry look."

Third, many traits can be deduced from the *style of the play;* a character, after all, lives in the world of the play. Someone in a Restoration comedy had better not slouch around like a Sam Shepard cowboy.

Fourth, and most important, are traits that are *implied by the action;* if you look at the most important actions that your character commits in the play, you see that there are fundamental physical traits required in performing these actions believably. If Stanley Kowalski is going to rape Blanche, for example, he probably should have some of the "gnawing and swilling and hulking" quality that Blanche says he has, even though we can be sure that she is exaggerating.

Exercise 15.3: Physical Traits

Examine the entire play from which your scene comes; find clues to your character's bodily and vocal traits. Check each of the following:

1. The stage directions—what does the playwright specifically tell you about your character's age, body, and so on?
2. Descriptions by other characters—what can you learn from what others say? Are their descriptions accurate, or prejudiced by their point of view?
3. What are the physical implications of the style of the play?
4. Considering the most important actions committed by your character, what physical traits do they need to believably perform these actions?

SOCIAL TRAITS

The second level of characterization is social, and places the character in relation to the others in their world. Just as our personality is greatly influenced by those around us in everyday life, so a dramatic character can be understood only in relationship to the other characters in the play.

It is an automatic and natural process to adjust your behavior to those around you. For instance, whenever we find ourselves in a social group, we tend to "sort ourselves out" by adopting a role in relationship to the others in the group. There are a number of roles that are natural to the psychodynamics of all groups, and we tend to fall into one or another of them whenever we join a group. If the role most natural to us is already taken, we may even adopt an unfamiliar role rather than compete with someone else for a niche of our own. Here is an exercise to explore role-playing within groups.

Exercise 15.4: The Social Repertory Company

Form a group of six or fewer; choose a topic to discuss or a project for the group to plan. Make it something that the group really cares about, like a political issue or planning how to start a theatre.

Below are a list of six roles. Each person in the group plays one of these roles in the group discussion; every two minutes, pass your role to the person on your left; keep the flow of conversation going as the roles are passed, and keep going until everyone has played all the roles.

1. *The Chairman,* who loves to organize everyone and everything, and keep the discussion "on track";
2. *The Victim,* who sees any group action as potentially threatening or unpleasant;
3. *The Philosopher,* who loves to generalize and point out the deeper meanings of things;
4. *The Derailer,* who is forever trying to change the topic;
5. *The Debater,* who loves to argue and doesn't really care what side they are on;
6. *The Red Cross Nurse,* who takes care of anyone and everyone whether they need help or not.

After everyone has played all the parts, share your experiences and perceptions: Why did each of these "characters" behave the way they did? What did they want? How did they present themselves and how did they treat others?

As you played the various roles in this exercise, you probably felt how easy it was to "become" them. Some roles may have been more uncomfortable or unfamiliar than others, but with practice any of them could become part of your social repertoire, a new "me" to be played by your "I." Just so, as you rehearse a play, you allow the actions and experiences of "being" the character to gradually develop into the new "me" we call your characterization, and this happens in specific relationship to the way the other characters are being developed by your fellow actors. In short, *character grows out of action in relationship.*

The play provides basic information about the social traits of a character. This may include their educational and social background, the type of work they do, and their status. The fact that Stanley Kowalski is an ex-Marine sergeant and still dominates his peer group (he is captain of his bowling team) is important to an understanding of his personality.

The most important aspects of social characterization are the general and specific relationships your character has with the other characters in the play. You began to consider these as part of the Given Circumstances, but they must be examined in greater detail, because as in life, we understand a stage character only in relationship.

Consider: If there is a disparity between the way a person wants to be perceived and the way others perceive them, we always believe the evidence of others. If we are walking down the hall, for example, and I am trying to convince you that I am an important person around here, yet the people we pass are ignoring me, what will you think? Think of the difference between the way Amanda in *The Glass Menagerie* wants to be seen, and the actual effect she has on her children.

If you have ever been on stage with someone who failed to relate properly to you, you understand now why it was impossible to overcome the false impression they created of you. In fact, the common idea that the actor creates the character is somewhat erroneous; it would be truer to say that *the actors create each other's characters.* In fact, it is a good idea for you to think less about creating your character and more about *creating the other characters in the play.* If you do that, you find that you inadvertently create yourself.

Sometimes, relationship is the main way a character fulfills their dramatic function. In *Death of a Salesman,* Willy has a relationship with each person in the play: father, husband, lover, neighbor, employee, salesman. We see Willy operating in each of these contexts, and each relationship reveals another aspect of Willy's character. Each relationship penetrates the surface of his behavior and expresses the underlying truth of Willy's character, for his "I" is composed of all of those "me's." Each of the other actors creates a part of Willy through these relationships, and so all the actors must cooperate if Willy is to live fully for the audience.

In short, remember that *you create each other on stage more than you create yourselves.*

Exercise 15.5: Social Traits

Examine the play for information about your character's social background. If no specific information is given, make the best inferences you can.

1. Childhood environment;
2. Educational background;
3. Socioeconomic or class background; and
4. Work experiences.

Consider your relationship to every other character in the play. How does each relationship reveal your needs, desires, and values?

Rehearse your scene with your partner: your aim in this rehearsal is *to create each other.*

PSYCHOLOGICAL TRAITS

With psychological traits, we are concerned with the process of thought that produces your character's action. As Oscar Brockett pointed out, "the psychological is the most important level of characterization" because it *justifies* and *motivates* all the others. Or as Chekhov once said in a letter, "a playwright may invent any reality except one: the psychological." All characters must think before they act.

This is not to say that the psychology of character is always the most important element of the play as a whole. In plays where the external events of the plot are the dominant element, the psychological aspect of character may serve merely to make the action believable. On the other hand, in plays featuring interior action (like those of Chekhov and O'Neill), the psychology of the characters may be the main interest of the play while the plot is secondary.

Just as a character's body has certain qualities, so their mind has certain qualities. Your examination of your character's action has already provided you with the basis for understanding their psychology, and in the following lesson we extend this understanding in considerable detail. For now, ask these basic questions about the character you have been developing.

Exercise 15.6: Psychological Traits

Consider the mental process of the character you are developing. Are they:

1. Simple or complex?
2. Fast or slow?
3. Rigid or flexible?
4. Precise or vague?
5. Rational or intuitive?
6. Global or sequential?

These last two items are qualities of "right brain" or "left brain" dominance; left-brained people tend to be more "rational" whereas right-brained people are more "intuitive." That is, left-brained people tend to reason in a linear way, in verbal and logical terms, but right-brained people tend to think globally, in spatial and emotional terms. If you want to give someone directions to your house, for instance, you should tell a left-brained person to "go three blocks down, turn right, go to the second light, and turn left." A right-brained person, however, has trouble with these verbal, sequential directions; they do better if you draw them a map on which they can see the *shape* of the path to your house.

One of the greatest difficulties in writing this book, by the way, was to translate the global and intuitive skill of acting into a linear, verbal sequence; this is why the physical exercises are so important. Many aspects of the acting process must live more in your body than in your mind, while your mind must provide guidance and judgment to your physical work. Acting is a more "whole brain" activity than any other art form, encompassing as it does all the physical skills of the musician and the dancer, and all the intellectual skills of the poet and critic.

MORAL TRAITS

The moral level of character refers to your character's values. Most important are:

1. Their sense of right and wrong;
2. Their sense of beauty;
3. Their religious beliefs; and
4. Their political convictions.

The moral aspect of character is rarely complex in the case of minor characters, but major characters usually have highly developed and sometimes complex or conflicted moral traits. When the moral aspect of a character is important *it will always relate directly to the thematic content of the play.* The moral choice confronting Willy Loman, for example, carries the whole meaning of Arthur Miller's play: our society tends to erode spiritual values and self-esteem by emphasizing material values as a measure of self-worth.

In the previous lesson you defined your character's superobjective. Without knowing it, you were automatically bringing much of their morality into focus; after all, the superobjective and the means used to achieve it are the active expressions of your character's values. Blanche Dubois, for instance, tries to use sex to achieve sanctuary, but we do not think of her as an immoral character because, unlike Stanley and Mitch, we can understand the level of her desperation, and because we know that her affairs were hollow gestures that did not involve her essential self.

Exercise 15.7: Moral Traits

Speaking as your character, answer the following questions:

1. My religious preference is...
2. I believe that when we die, we...
3. The greatest thing one person can do for another is...
4. The person I admire most is...
5. I would define a good person as someone who...
6. The person I detest most in the world is...
7. The most evil thing I can imagine is...
8. The ugliest thing I ever saw was...
9. The most beautiful thing I ever saw was...
10. The proper role of government is...
11. I am superstitious about...
12. After I die, I want to be remembered as someone who...

ECONOMY OF CHARACTERIZATION

We have examined the four levels of characterization. Each works in relation to the others, though one or more may dominate the others. As Oscar Brockett explains:

> *A playwright may emphasize one or more of these levels. Some writers pay little attention to the physical appearance of their characters, concentrating instead upon psychological and moral traits; other dramatists may describe appearance and social status in detail. In assessing the completeness of a characterization it is not enough merely to make a list of traits and levels of characterization. It is also necessary to ask how the character functions in the play. For example, the audience needs to know little about the maid who only appears to announce dinner; any detailed characterization would be superfluous and distracting. On the other hand, the principal characters need to be drawn in greater depth. The appropriateness and completeness of each characterization, therefore, may be judged only after analyzing its function in each scene and in the play as a whole.[2]*

It is a common impulse of actors to try to treat the maid who announces dinner as if she were Lady Macbeth. This is not to say that the maid should not be fully characterized; she should be as fully character-ized *as she needs to be to fulfill her dramatic function.* Economy of character-ization means giving your character all the traits they need, but no more.

Think of a great athlete; their "style," grace, and power, come from the complete efficiency with which every bit of their energy is focused on the job at hand. They don't "grandstand," that is, they do nothing that does not directly contribute to their purpose; this is *economy of exe-cution* and it produces *beauty.* If your purpose is to be a maid answering the door, any energy directed toward creating qualities beyond those necessary for the fulfillment of this task is wasteful and distracting. An overly detailed performance is as disruptive to the play as an incomplete one.

A CHARACTER CHECKLIST

Here is a checklist that reviews the work of this lesson. Use it as you begin rehearsals to be sure you have gotten from the play the informa-tion you need to begin work; then check again near the end of rehearsals to be sure that you have considered all the possibilities.

Exercise 15.8: A Character Checklist

What are the physical traits that influence your action?

1. Those specified by the playwright;
2. Those reported by other characters;
3. Those that can be inferred from the action.

What are your social traits?

1. Your background and education?
2. Your socioeconomic class?
3. Your attitudes and behavior toward each of the other characters?

What are your psychological traits?

1. Are your mental processes fast or slow;
   a. Rigid or flexible;
   b. Complex or simple?
2. Are you intuitive and global, or analytical and verbal?

What moral, religious, or political values influence your choices?

SUMMARY

Your character was created by the playwright so that your behavior contributes believably to the progress and meaning of the play; you have a specific purpose in relation to the whole. This is your *dramatic function.* No matter how "alive" your character may be, if it does not fulfill your dramatic function, you have failed.

In order that your character may serve their purpose within the play believably, the playwright has provided your character with certain traits that make the behavior and thought required of them by the play "natural;" Aristotle called these the character's "functional traits." Your character also has traits that make them recognizable as a fellow human being; Aristotle called these "likeness traits." In this sense, the story creates the characters more than the characters create the story.

All character traits can be classified on four levels. The first level is *physical,* and it is of primary importance to you because the external traits of body and voice communicate all the other levels of characterization.

The second level is *social,* and places your character in relation to the others in their world. As in life, character on stage is perceived mainly in relationship, so remember that you create each other more than you create yourself.

The third level is the *psychological.* It is the most important because it *justifies* and *motivates* all the others.

The fourth is the *moral* level and refers to your character's values.

A playwright may emphasize one or more of these levels. The appropriateness and completeness of your characterization may be judged only after analyzing its function in each scene and in the play as a whole.

Lesson 16

THE CHARACTER'S MIND

In Lesson 15, we said that your character's dramatic function is to act in certain ways, moment by moment, so as to move the story forward in the proper direction and with the proper qualities of style and meaning. The playwright has created your character so that these required external actions are believable and natural to them. The psychological aspect of characterization results when you have discovered the inner actions that *justify* the external actions required by the plot, meaning, and style of the play. This is what Stanislavski called the actor's most important task: *to understand how every moment of the performance contributes to the reason why the play was written.*

Unlike a novelist, who can take you inside a character's mind to show you the process of their thought, a dramatist can only *imply* it through their actions. As an actor, you learn to understand the psychology of action so that you can recreate your character's mental processes. This is the greatest creative and personal contribution you make to your performance, for it is the foundation of all the other work you do.

Let's begin to examine the psychological aspects of action by setting up a hypothetical situation: imagine that you see a notice on the callboard that I am directing a play that is a favorite of yours. This play has a part that you have been dying to play, and you want to approach me about it. Even though you fear my possible rejection, your need is strong enough that you come to see me. You begin by "buttering me up" with your admiration for my work; you express your love for this particular play; finally, you tell me why you are perfect for the part and ask me to consider casting you; to your delight, I agree.

Let's examine what happened here step-by-step. First, you see the notice and it arouses you: we call this your *stimulus*. This stimulus touches your long-standing desire to play the part, and so your arousal has a particular quality that reflects this need; we call this your *attitude*. You are already beginning to form an *objective* (to get me to give you the part) and so you begin to *consider alternatives,* various ways of satisfying your aroused need: you consider asking a mutual friend to approach me on your behalf, or you think about merely sending a photo and resumé. After surveying your alternatives, you make a *choice* to act in the way you think will work best: see me in person, flatter me, then convince me of your love for the play and rightness for the part. This choice unleashes your *action,* which takes the form of *purposeful activity* to gain your *objective*.

This whole sequence is the mental process by which action is formed: *a stimulus arouses a need expressed by an attitude, which generates a strategic choice, which results in action directed toward an objective.* The steps in this process can be summarized by five key words:

- Stimulus
- Attitude
- Choice
- Action
- Objective

You can see this process represented graphically in Figure 16.1. The large circle represents your skin, the boundary between your "outer" and "inner" worlds. The stimulus sends energy toward you, which enters you through *perception* (seeing, hearing, touching). Once inside you, it arouses a response in you that touches on some *need or desire*; it frightens you, or pleases you, or angers you, and this is your *attitude* toward it.

If the nature of the stimulus and situation is such that it provokes an *automatic* action, your reaction is immediate and involuntary, bypassing conscious thought, and results at once in external action (when the alarm bell rings, Othello reaches for his sword).

If, on the other hand, conscious thought is required, you *deliberate* over alternative ways of proceeding until you make a *strategic choice* about how to proceed. This choice is at the center of the process; it is the moment that unleashes the *action* that you hope wins your *objective*.

Remember the impulse circle exercise: just as in that exercise, this process of action moves the scene forward. Just like the slap you received, another character in the scene does something, or something happens, and this energy enters you as your stimulus; it passes through you in either an automatic or deliberative way, then leaves you through your action directed toward your objective, just like the slap you passed on. Your action becomes a stimulus for the next person, and generates a reac-

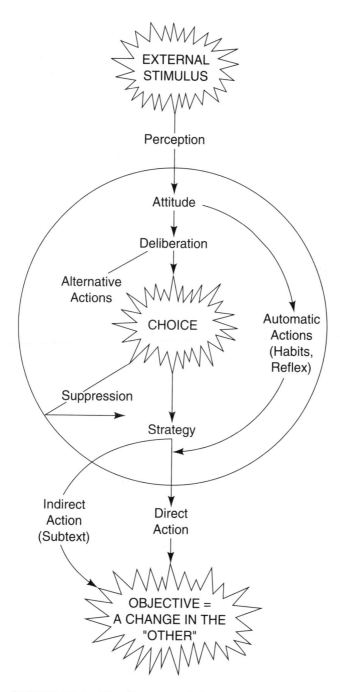

FIGURE 16.1 The Process of Action

tion in them, which in turn generates another action, and so the scene moves. Notice also that the energy leaving you as action is not the same in quality or intensity as the energy that entered you as the stimulus; it has been altered by the nature of your needs, attitudes, and personality.

Here is an example of the process of action from a scene in Brecht's *Mother Courage.* Anna (Mother Courage) and her mute daughter Kattrin receive word of the death of one of Anna's sons; Kattrin stares at her mother, whom she blames for her brother's death, and Anna responds by ordering her to polish some spoons. This seemingly insensitive reaction from the mother can be properly understood only by tracing Anna's inner thought process. Her "stream of consciousness" or *inner monologue* might sound like this:

1. *Stimulus:* "Kattrin is looking at me with blame in her eyes."
2. *Attitude:* "I feel bad enough already; I don't need her blaming me too. Doesn't she understand that I didn't have any choice?"
3. *Alternatives:* "I could ignore her."
4. *Choice:* "No, that won't work. I'll take her mind off it by giving her something to do."
5. *Action:* "Polish the spoons!"
6. *Objective:* To stop her from looking at me and making me feel guilty.

You can see that Anna's needs, values, way of thinking, way of relating to the world—in short, her entire psychology—is involved and expressed in each step of this mental process.

THE INSTROKE OF REACTION

In Figure 16.1, you see the energy coming from your external stimulus flowing inward toward your center through perception, attitude, and deliberation. At center, your choice turns the instroke of reaction into the outstroke of action toward an objective: in other words, *choice is the point at which reaction turns into action.* This entire process provides the compelling momentum of a complete action.

Actors sometimes fail to experience the instroke of reaction fully; they *do* something, but they aren't really receiving the stimulus that is *causing* them to do it. They only pretend to perceive what is said or done to them, preferring the safety of working only out of their own heads, and refusing to allow the actions of others to influence them directly. When faced with this kind of actor, directors often say things like, "You didn't really hear her say that."

Don't let your fear of losing control of the performance turn you into this kind of hermetically sealed, self-stimulating actor. No matter how strong or how long-standing your character's needs are, the stimulus that triggers those needs is always something "out there" in the scene, something that someone else says or does; learn to look for stimuli that are *immediate* and *external*. Remember: acting is not so much doing things as it is allowing yourself to be made to do them. In short, *acting is reacting*.

For example, there is a scene in *A Streetcar Named Desire* in which Blanche tells Mitch what happened years ago on the night that her young fiancé killed himself (see Appendix). Too often, actresses play this scene as if the pain in Blanche is the main stimulus for the telling of the story. Played in this way, Mitch fades into the background and the story becomes a monologue instead of a scene. The actress must find the stimulus for the story not in her own need, but "out there" in Mitch; it is his capacity for understanding that triggers her tremendous need to share, in the hope that he will understand and love her, and therefore take care of her.

Once a stimulus has been received, it is interpreted by your character in relationship to their own needs. Is this a good thing? A threat? A surprise? The evaluation is expressed as an *attitude* toward the stimulus. Directors often help actors to be specific about attitude by asking, "How do you feel about that?" Learn to ask yourself this question as a regular part of your acting process.

You may notice that your character has a typical way of reacting to most stimuli; this can express their attitude toward the world in general. Are they optimistic or pessimistic? Does their attitude reveal any feeling that they may have about themselves? Willy Loman, for example, is quick to sense any criticism from others, and it makes him terribly defensive. This almost paranoid sensitivity reveals his fundamental insecurity and low self-esteem.

Exercise 16.1: The Instroke of Reaction

Working with your partner, answer these questions about one of the scenes from the Appendix, or the scene you have chosen for yourself.

1. In each of your character's actions, identify the external and immediate stimulus.
2. Does your character respond more to some stimuli than to others? How do these sensitivities reflect their needs, values, and personality?

3. Consider what each stimulus means to your character; what is their attitude toward each? Does it trigger any needs already within the character?

4. What attitudes are typical of your character? What does this reveal about the character's attitude toward the world and about themselves?

CHOICE

Because choice is the moment at which reaction turns into action, it is the essence of drama; the most suspenseful moments in plays occur when a character confronts a significant choice. As David Mamet points out, "The only thing we, as audience, care about in the theatre is WHAT HAPPENS NEXT?"[1] From an actor's point of view, this question is really "What is he or she going to do now?"

The suspense is heightened when the choice is difficult, when the character is choosing between equally compelling (or equally unattractive) alternatives. In tragedy, these choices usually take the form of a "double bind" or "lose lose" situation in which there are no "good" alternatives, as when a character must choose between their sense of truth and their life: *Antigone, A Man for All Seasons, Beckett, An Enemy of the People,* and *The Crucible* all center around such a choice. Critic Jan Kott describes it like this:

> ...*A classic situation of tragedy is the necessity of making a choice between opposing values.... The tragedy lies in the very principle of choice by which one of the values must be annihilated. The cruelty of the absolute lies in demanding such a choice and in imposing a situation which excludes the possibility of compromise.*[2]

In comedy, the choices are not so serious; we might instead wonder something like, "How is he going to get away with it this time?"

Those significant choices that affect the progress of the play demand special attention. These are usually *beat changes* at which the choice forms a new action. It makes it easier to define beats, by the way, when you realize that a beat always changes at the moment of a significant choice by one of the characters. Of course, not every choice your character makes is to be given the weight of the significant choices we have been discussing here, but every choice deserves to be fully experienced in each rehearsal or performance.

Choice is the most revealing point in the process of action. In the making of significant choices, your character is responding to needs, to a way of seeing the world, and to relationships, beliefs, and values. If you can experience all the factors influencing your character's significant choices, you will be in touch with everything needed to create the psychological aspect of your characterization.

Perhaps more important, your experience of your character's significant choices is the mechanism by which the Magic If produces transformation. When you have entered into your character's circumstances as if they were your own, felt their needs as if they were your own, and *made the choices they make given those needs in those circumstances,* then action follows naturally and with it transformation.

Choice cannot be fully experienced without real alternatives. Unless you have alternatives to consider, you can only "act out" your character's choice, not relive it. If a choice is especially significant, the playwright structures the situation so that you know what the alternatives are; but most of the time the writer can only imply your character's view of their alternatives, and you have to supply them for yourself.

For this reason, then, you must consider not only what your character *does,* but also what they *choose not to do.* When your character is presented with a significant choice (meaning any choice that affects the progress of the play), you must find for yourself the various alternatives they might consider, and decide how they would feel about each. The creation of these alternatives is a powerful way for you to enter into your character's mind, because they represent an inventory of the way they see the world.

Following is a list of all the factors that may influence any particular choice. These may be either internal in the character's mind, or external in the character's environment.

1. Internal factors influencing choice:

    a. Physiology;
    b. Social background;
    c. Needs and desires;
    d. Psychological processes or "way of thinking";
    e. Ethical values.

2. External factors influencing choice (the Givens):

    a. Relationships with or attitudes toward other characters;
    b. The social environment;
    c. The physical environment;
    d. Specific immediate circumstances.

3. Theatrical concerns requiring adjustment of choice:

    a. The style or genre of the play;

    b. The character's dramatic purpose in the play;

    c. The visual and auditory demands of the performance space.

Although the last three are clearly "actor" concerns rather than "character" concerns, it is part of your job to justify your concerns as a performer as organic aspects of your character's inner world. In this way, the two levels of your "dual consciousness" as actor and character work together toward the same goal, and eventually come together as a single experience.

Exercise 16.2: Choice

As in the previous exercise, consider each of your actions in the scene. Focus on the choice from which each action springs.

1. Decide which are the most significant choices (there are probably only two or three in a scene) and examine each in detail: what factors influence each? (Consider the list of factors provided above.)
2. Rehearse your scene with this awareness; take the time to experience each choice fully.

Once the choice to act in a certain way has been made, your outwardly flowing action becomes a *purposeful activity,* either a doing, a saying, or both, directed toward an objective. As you can see in Figure 16.1, this outstroke can take four forms: it can be an *automatic action* that bypasses conscious choice and flows directly from perception to action; it can be a *direct action* that goes at the objective straightforwardly; it can be an *indirect action* that approaches the objective through some other activity; or it can be a *suppression,* a choice *not* to act. Let's examine each.

AUTOMATIC ACTIONS

As you learned in Lesson 11, characters often act out of impulse without conscious choice; this is what Stanislavski called "automatic" action. It is extremely useful when approaching a part to identify the automatic aspects of your character's behavior as soon as possible, for it is your task to recreate the character's habits in yourself for the purpose of rehearsing and performing the role.

When you consider how much of a character's behavior falls into the area of automatic actions, you see what an important area of concern this is: their voice, their walk, the wearing of their clothes, any special skills (like Othello's swordsmanship) or deformities (like Laura's limp)— these and more must become as natural and habitual to you as they are to your character.

The formation of new habits is accomplished best by regular, spaced repetition over a period of time; you cannot count on rehearsals alone to do the job, nor should you waste the group's time on this sort of personal work. You must develop a program of homework that allows the formation of these habits through short daily exercises. Some psychologists have suggested that it takes three weeks of regular repetition to develop a new habit, so you can't wait very long to start. For instance, if your role involves swords, canes, robes, skirts, or a brace for Laura's leg, you ask for a rehearsal substitute as soon as you can put down your script.

To sum up, follow this general rule: *whatever your character doesn't need to think about, you shouldn't need to think about; whatever your character does need to think about, you must think about each and every time you perform that action.*

And notice that it is neither necessary nor desirable for these habits to invade your real life. We all have many habits that we "turn on and off" to suit the situation, and the habits you develop to play a role can be restricted to rehearsal and performance of that role. Remember that the aim of this personal work is not to "lose yourself" in your character, but to ensure that you don't lose the character in yourself.

Exercise 16.3: Automatic Actions

Again, review your scene with your partner; look for any automatic actions required of your character. Examine them to see what they tell you about your character. What program of homework can you establish to develop these habits in yourself for this role?

DIRECT AND INDIRECT ACTION

We have already discussed how your character selects an action that they think has the best chance for success in the given circumstances. When possible, they probably select a direct action such as persuading, demanding, cajoling, or begging.

However, when there is an obstacle to direct action they choose an indirect approach. Recall the Hostess–Guest scene in Part I: politeness required that the guest and hostess "hide" their real feelings, but these feelings "leaked out" through their body language. In everyday life we often mean one thing while saying or doing another, and this is also common in drama: We call these hidden meanings *subtext*, because in such cases there is a difference between the surface activity (the text) and the submerged attitude or objective (the subtext).

Some schools of acting hold that there is always a subtext, but I argue that subtext is present *only* when there is an obstacle to direct action and the character must choose indirect action instead. The obstacle that makes the subtext necessary may be *external* in the scene, or *internal* in the character's mind.

For example, if I want to tell you that I love you, but I am afraid that you will reject me (internal obstacle) I may choose instead to talk about how lonely I am in this strange town, how dull the people I work with are, how you are the only interesting person I've met here, the only one I feel comfortable with. All this is an indirect way of expressing my love "safely." (This scene is from Chekhov's *The Three Sisters.* Chekhov explored indirect action more than any other playwright.)

Or, if I want to tell you that I love you, but your husband is in the room with us (external obstacle), I may choose instead to talk about our pictures in the photo album, how wonderful you looked at the seashore last summer, what a wonderful time I had because you were there—whatever I think can be said without alerting your husband. (This scene is from Ibsen's *Hedda Gabler.*)

Further, the character may be either *conscious* of the subtext or *unconscious.* For instance, in the moment from *Mother Courage* we examined earlier, Anna's surface activity is to get Kattrin to polish the spoons, but her subtext is to stop Kattrin from making her feel guilty; this is a conscious subtext. In *The Glass Menagerie,* on the other hand, Amanda prepares Laura for her gentleman caller, but she also puts on her own party dress and hangs colored lights to make herself look younger; we realize that Jim is also *her* gentleman caller and that she is reliving her youth through Laura. This is an unconscious subtext.

In all these cases, notice that the author has provided a surface activity through which the subtext may be expressed. You must accept this surface activity as your immediate action; *do not attempt to play the subtext.* When actors make the mistake of bringing the subtext to the surface, it destroys the reality of the scene. For one thing, if the audience can see the subtext, they must wonder why the other characters can't. Iago has a continuous subtextual objective of destroying Othello, but if we can see Iago's villainy and Othello can't, then Othello seems like a fool.

Trust the text and the audience; they will deduce from the situation what is really going on. Your simple awareness of subtext is enough, and often subtext works even if you are unaware of it. Besides, it is part of the fun for the audience to figure these things out for themselves; if you make it obvious, they don't get to play.

Exercise 16.4: Subtext

Work through your scene with your partner; look for any indirectly expressed or hidden objectives.

1. Is the character conscious or unconscious of them?
2. Why can't they be expressed directly?
3. What surface activity has been provided through which they may be expressed?
4. Rehearse your scene with this awareness: avoid playing the subtext.

NOT DOING: SUPPRESSION

There is always at least one alternative available to a character in any situation, and that is the choice *not* to act, to suppress or delay action. Though we often think of "doing nothing" as a passive act, it can actually be a strong form of action because it takes more effort to hold an impulse in than it would to let it out. We call this *suppression*, which literally means "pushing down." Viewed in this way, there are no passive characters on the stage; there are only characters who are aroused but then choose *not* to act, which is itself a positive and playable action.

Supression is common in drama. Stage characters, like people in life, may often be feeling and wanting much more than their overt actions indicate. The plays of Chekhov are especially rich as studies of suppression and prove that holding an impulse down can be more dramatic than its release. Movement therapist Moshe Feldenkrais says this about the process of delaying or inhibiting impulses:

> *The delay between thought process and its translation into action is long enough to make it possible to inhibit it. The possibility of creating the image of an action and then delaying its execution is the basis for imagination and for intellectual judgement. . . .*
>
> *The possibility of a pause between the creation of a thought pattern for any particular action and the execution of that action is the physical basis for self-awareness. . . .*

The possibility of delaying action, prolonging the period between the intention and its execution enables man to know himself.[3]

The decision not to act aids in heightening dramatic tension and suspense. As you noticed in Figure 16.1, when a character chooses to *suppress* an impulse, that unresolved energy is reflected back into them and builds up to become a source of increasing dynamic tension. There are many characters who spend most of their time suppressing; the most famous example is Hamlet, and others are Peter in *The Zoo Story* and Mitch in *A Streetcar Named Desire*.

One good way to use suppression is to devote some private rehearsal time to releasing the inhibited impulses. By strengthening the suppressed impulses in this way, you force yourself to work harder to hold them in when the scene is done in its normal form. It is the effort to suppress the impulse that turns the "not doing" into a "doing" and makes it playable and dramatic.

Exercise 16.5: Not Doings

Work through your scene with your partner.

1. Considering your character in the entire play, do you see a pattern of suppression that may be affecting their choices in this scene?

2. Rehearse allowing any suppressed material to be released, then immediately repeat the scene and hold in those same impulses.

As we said at the beginning of this lesson, recreating your character's thought process is the most important single step toward transformation. One way to check the thoroughness of your psychological preparation is to verbalize your character's stream of consciousness. This technique is called the *inner monologue*. Of course, the inner monologue is only an exercise, and is meant to be done in private; you must *not* carry it into normal rehearsal, and certainly never into performance.

Exercise 16.6: The Inner Monologue

Work through your scene with your partner; each of you softly speaks aloud the inner stream of thought that connects the external things you do and say. Go slowly and allow yourself to experience each step in the flow from stimulus to choice to objective. Your inner monologue might sound something like, "Look at that smug smile! He's not buying it at all. Maybe I could appeal to his vanity...."

SUMMARY

Your character is required to react in a certain way, moment by moment, to move the story forward with the proper qualities of style and meaning. The playwright has created your character so that these reactions and choices are believable and natural to them. The psychological aspect of characterization results when you have discovered the inner process that justifies the external activities and manner of expression required by the plot, meaning, and style of the play.

To recreate your character's mind you must understand the process by which action is formed: a stimulus arouses you, touching a need expressed by an attitude, which generates a strategic choice, which results in action directed toward an objective. The steps in this process can be summarized by five key words: stimulus, attitude, choice, action, objective.

To keep connected to the scene, learn to look for stimuli that are immediate and external. Remember: acting is not so much *doing* things as it is allowing yourself *to be made to do them*. Once the stimulus has been received, your character evaluates it in relationship to their own needs and forms an attitude toward it.

Because choice is the moment at which reaction turns into action, the most suspenseful moments in plays occur when a character confronts a significant choice. Every choice that your character makes that affects the progress of the play (the beat changes) must be well defined and experienced in each rehearsal or performance.

Experiencing choice requires that there be alternatives. Most of the time the writer can only imply your character's alternatives, and you have to supply them for yourself; consider not only what your character *does,* but also what he or she *chooses not to do.*

If you can experience all the factors influencing your character's significant choices, you can be in touch with everything needed to create the psychological aspect of your characterization. These may be either internal to the character, or external in the character's environment.

Only by reliving your character's choices within their given circumstances, as if they were your own, can you enter actively into the world and consciousness of the character. This is what triggers the transformational process, *the magic if.*

Once the choice to act in a certain way has been made, your outwardly flowing action becomes one of four types: it can be an *automatic action* that bypasses conscious choice and flows directly from perception to action. When approaching a part, identify the automatic aspects of your character's behavior as soon as possible and work to establish those habits in yourself. Whatever your character doesn't need to think about, you shouldn't need to think about.

Your action can also be *direct,* which goes at the objective straight-forwardly; or, when there is an obstacle to direct action, the character may choose an *indirect* action; we call these hidden intentions *subtext.* The obstacle that makes the subtext necessary may be external or internal, conscious or unconscious. In any case, the author has provided a surface activity through which the subtext may be expressed; it is disastrous to attempt to play the subtext itself. Finally, your action can be a *suppression,* a choice *not* to act, which is itself a positive and playable action that contributes greatly to suspense.

Lesson 17

THE CHARACTER'S LANGUAGE

In Lesson 16 you explored the character's mind through their action. In this lesson you explore their mind through their speech, which, as you learned in Part I, is a special kind of action.

Unlike a novelist, a playwright cannot describe the character or the character's thought directly, except in a limited way through stage directions. Though the playwright conceives a complete character, the dialogue is all that remains of the fullness of that conception. The words you speak as the character, then, are the *residue* of a complete state of being; it is your job to recreate the fullness of the character by restoring body and consciousness to this residue.

This is made easier by the fact that the playwright, unlike any other writer, knows that their language is going to be spoken aloud; they are writing not for a reader, but for *you*, the actor. Their first concern is the effect the language has on you as you speak it: not only the ideas and associations it generates in your mind, but also what the rhythm of it does to your breathing and your body dynamic, what the sound of it does to your articulatory muscles as you speak it, and the physical sensations its imagery can evoke in you. In a real way, the playwright is reaching deep inside your body and mind through the language of your character.

For example, read aloud this description of death from Shakespeare's *Measure for Measure*. It is spoken by a young man who has just learned that he is going to be executed in a few hours. Feel the physical sensations it evokes, how the rhythm and sound of it can generate his feelings in you.

> *Ay, but to die, and go we know not where,*
> *To lie in cold obstruction and to rot,*

This sensible warm motion to become
A kneaded clod; and the delighted spirit
To bathe in fiery floods, or to reside
In thrilling regions of thick-ribbed ice,
To be imprisoned in the viewless winds
And blown with restless violence round about
The pendant world; or to be worse than worst
Of those that lawless and incertain thought
Imagine howling, 'tis too horrible.

You don't need to be afraid of death in order to say this speech; the speech itself can terrify you.

You can see how a well-trained actor can find in a good text many specific clues about rhythms, inflections, emphases, and all sorts of characteristics needed to create a role. That is why performing the best writers—like Shakespeare—makes you a better actor. But a play is never like a coloring book; acting is not a matter of simply recognizing the playwright's outline and then "filling it in," or of just "saying the words." The creation of a role is always a collaboration between you and the playwright, and also your director, fellow actors, and eventually your audience as well. But the words are where you start, and at the beginning they are all you have.

WORD CHOICE: TEXT AND SUBTEXT

You begin by understanding what the words mean, and why the playwright has chosen to have your character express themselves in precisely the way they do, not only because you have a responsibility to communicate the meaning of your lines accurately, but also because it reveals the way your character thinks and feels.

As we discussed in Lesson 5, a character's speech is the result of a process of verbalization; through a lightning-fast sequence of unconscious choices, the preverbal *germ* of the idea is developed into full verbal form. This process automatically reflects the character's mind and personality, education and social background.

As you relive your character's process of verbalization you begin to participate actively in their mental processes and feelings. You begin by understanding the specifics of the dialogue completely, looking up any unfamiliar words or phrases and considering the effect of historical period on the language. You then ask yourself why your character has chosen to use these particular words instead of some others that might be similar in meaning. What is there about them that is exactly right for the thought and feelings of the character at this moment? This is called the character's word choice or *diction,* in the sense of *diction*ary.

Then you begin to reconstruct the process of thought and feeling from which these particular words spring. Only when you have "worked backward" in this way can you truly speak the character's words as your own; until then, you are merely parroting someone else's words, and you sound mechanical and false. For example, when Blanche Dubois arrives at her sister's apartment she looks around and says,

> *Only Poe, only Mr. Edgar Allan Poe could do it justice.* (She gestures toward street) *Out there, I suppose, is the ghoul-haunted woodland of Weir.*

You might begin with a germinal feeling of revulsion and disappointment: "How awful it is here!" The awfulness of the place reminds Blanche of Poe, the great writer of horror stories, and the visionary painter Weir, whose imagery was fantastic and frightening.

However, this is only a beginning, and you must take the whole context of the character's speech into account. You know that Blanche has arrived here desperate; her life since the grand days on the plantation has become a series of one-night stands in cheap hotels far worse than this place (she calls one of them "The Tarantula Arms"); she depends "on the kindness of strangers." She is clutching at her romantic past, still pretending to be the Southern belle with her trunk of fake jewelry and furs. She must, in her heart, be jealous of Stella who has a home, however poor, and more important, a man, however crude, to take care of her. Blanche has come here as a last resort; it's the end of the streetcar line and the end of her line; the last stop before the asylum.

Understanding this context, you see that Blanche has to denegrate Stella and her home as a way of building herself up; by pretending to be repulsed by Stella's place, she is claiming to be accustomed to much better lodging, and thereby denying her real past. She exaggerates her revulsion by comparing the place to the creations of two famous lunatics, Poe and Weir.

These artistic allusions—quite fashionable at one time—are also intended to put her above Stella as a more "refined" and "cultured" person, an attitude she probably had toward Stella even when they were young (and which may have been one cause for Stella leaving home). She is also reminding Stella that they share a sophisticated educational and social background; back home in the good old days, she is saying, Stella's present circumstances would have been considered the creation of a demented imagination.

Stella bursts Blanche's bubble with her sardonic dismissal, "No, honey, those are the L and M tracks," which really says, "I know it's not much, but it's good enough for me." On a deeper level, she might also be saying "Don't play your old games with me."

What we have done here is to *paraphrase* the character's speech, to put it into our own words in a way that expresses our understanding of both it's surface meaning and its hidden meanings and attitudes, or *subtext*. This is an excellent technique for personalizing your character's speech; it forces you to return to the germinal meaning and recreate it in your own words, just as if you were translating it from some other language.

Exercise 17.1: Paraphrase for Meaning and Subtext

Select a single speech from the scene you have been developing. Write a paraphrase on two levels:

First, a literal translation of the surface meaning into your own words; be sure you understand the meaning of each word and any references that the speech may make (this inevitably sounds stiff and prosaic). Blanche's speech would look like this:

> *Only that drug-crazed writer of horror stories, only Mr. Edgar Allan Poe could describe this place adequately.* (She gestures to-ward street) *The neighborhood looks like one of those terrible, frightening forests full of evil spirits waiting to jump at you, like the ones painted by that insane Mr. Weir.*

Then write a second, more personal paraphrase that expresses the subtext, if any. Again, Blanche's speech:

> *This is awful! The only time I've had contact with a place like this is through the literature and painting of demented artists. How can you stand it? But then, you were always less sensitive than I am.*

Now say all three aloud: the literal paraphrase, the subtextual paraphrase, and finally the original speech. Are you beginning to feel that you "own" the words of the character, that you are speaking real words instead of memorized lines?

RHYTHM

Rhythm is perhaps the single most powerful aspect of stage language. It functions in three primary ways: to support meaning, to express personality, and to express emotion.

Though rhythm is the most physical and least "intellectual" aspect of language, it is closely tied to and supportive of meaning. It functions not only as tempo (fast or slow), but also in the variations of tempo and force that give emphasis to certain words, sounds, images, or other elements of language.

In addition to supporting meaning through emphasis, rhythm is also highly expressive of personality. The blustery, pompous person has a rhythm much different from the thoughtful, introspective person. Even nationality and social background affect rhythm: the Irish, for example, tend to speak each thought on one long exhalation of breath, imparting an unmistakable rhythm to their speech. Good playwrights build these rhythms into the language that their characters speak, so that a character's speech rhythms are appropriate to their personality and social background.

Emotions also have recognizable rhythmic implications. All emotion causes measurable changes in the tension of our muscles, and this has a direct effect on our speech. Take anger as an example: as anger rises in us, the body becomes tense, especially in the deep center where the largest muscles mobilize themselves for action. Tension in the interior muscles is communicated directly to the diaphragm, limiting its movement and forcing us to take shallow breaths. Because we need to oxygenate the muscles for defense purposes, we compensate by taking more short breaths. Tension, spreading to the pharynx, causes an elevation of pitch, and coupled with the increased pressure of the breath stream, this results in a "punching" delivery and increased volume. The vestigial biting and tearing of the jaw related to anger encourages us to emphasize hard consonant sounds, so that our speech may become, in rage, similar to the snapping and growling of an angry animal.

A skillful playwright shapes rhythm carefully, and on several levels at once: syllables, phrases, sentences, and speeches. Let's explore each. The fundamental rhythm of a speech is established by the flow of *accented and unaccented syllables and words*. Look at the following example from Samuel Beckett's *Endgame;* you see that Beckett has used rhythmic patterns of twos and threes; read it aloud for full rhythmic effect; tap your feet.

> *One day you'll be blind, like me. You'll be sitting there, a speck in the void, in the dark, forever, like me. (pause) One day you'll say to yourself, I'm tired. I'll sit down, and you'll go and sit down. Then you'll say, I'm hungry, I'll get up and get something to eat. But you won't get up. You'll say, I shouldn't have sat down, but since I have I'll sit on a little longer, then I'll get up and get something to eat. (pause) But you won't get up and you won't get anything to eat.*

The rhythmic flow of these syllables is as highly developed as any formal poetry ever written.

The next level of rhythm involves *breath phrases*. The evolution of our written language was greatly influenced by the way we speak. A simple sentence can be said on a single breath. If a sentence becomes too complex for one breath, we break it up into phrases and create a compound sentence. Each of these phrases becomes a "sub-breath," a kind of "topping off" of the breath supply, within the main breath of the sentence. These sub-breath phrases are usually marked by commas, semicolons, or colons (in music, the comma is still used as a breath mark). The second sentence in the Beckett quote above is a good example.

You can feel that playwrights use sentence structure to guide you into a pattern of breathing which, as you experienced in Part I, is a powerful factor in the generation of emotion. Try reading the Beckett piece aloud with a small breath at every comma, a full breath at each period, and a large breath at each "(pause)." What emotional experience results?

A still larger pattern of rhythm is developed by the length of sentences, each one of which is usually one main breath. Sentence length is usually our best indicator of tempo; shorter sentences usually indicate a faster tempo, and longer sentences a slower tempo, though this is by no means a hard-and-fast rule.

Finally, sentences are grouped into *speeches*. We get a good impression of the rhythm of a scene by looking at the density of the printed script; a mass of long speeches suggests a different rhythm than the back-and-forth exchange of short lines. You can often see changes in a scene reflected in the speech rhythms; for example, one character might have a number of very long speeches whereas the other has only short replies, until the second "counterattacks" with a long speech, followed by a heated section in which both speak in short lines, often interrupting each other.

By responding sensitively to the rhythms and sounds the playwright has built into your character's speech, and by experiencing them fully in your own muscles, you find them a powerful aid in entering into the consciousness of your character. As Stanislavski said,

> There is an indissoluble interdependence, interaction and bond between tempo-rhythm and feeling.... The correctly established tempo-rhythm of a play or a role, can of itself, intuitively (on occasion automatically) take hold of the feelings of an actor and arouse in him a true sense of living his part.[1]

Exercise 17.2: Rhythm

Using the same speech as in the previous exercise, mark its rhythmic units on each of the levels we have discussed; invent any system of marking that makes sense to you.

Read it aloud to stress each level of rhythm:

1. The flow of stressed and unstressed syllables;
2. The main breath for each sentence and "sub-breath" for any phrases within compound sentences.

Dance it.

Now examine the scene as a whole and see how the rhythm created by the give and take of the dialogue relates to the action and relationship. With your partner, read it aloud to experience this fully.

MELODY

In our everyday life we have an intuitive and highly developed sense of the communicative value of sound and rhythm, which together form the *melody* of speech. It is what gives our speech its color and individual flavor, and helps us to catch implications, sarcasm, and other attitudes. Stanislavski again:

> *Letters, syllables, words—these are the musical notes of speech, out of which to fashion measures, arias, whole symphonies. There is good reason to describe beautiful speech as musical.*[2]

The actor must develop a heightened capacity for the musical aspects of speech. We do this not to produce a beautiful sound, but because we must express extraordinary levels of feeling and experience. As Stanislavski put it,

> *Musical speech opens up endless possibilities of conveying the inner life of a role. . . . What can we express with our ordinary register of five or six notes? . . . We realize how ridiculous we are when we have to express complicated emotions. It is like playing Beethoven on a balalaika.*[3]

A good playwright selects and arranges words not only for meaning, but also for rhythmic and tonal values that support and enhance meaning, character, and emotion. Playwrights often say that their characters begin to "speak" to them as if they had minds and voices of their own. You can rejuvenate these inherent values of tone and rhythm: if you surrender yourself to experience them fully as muscular actions, you can bring them back to life for yourself, and through your experience for your audience.

Scholars have formed various theories about the relationship of sound and meaning in language. One of these was the Roback Voco-Sensory Theory. The psychologist Roback asked experimental subjects to assign meaning to several three-letter nonsense syllables, like *mil* and *mal*. To most people, *mal* seemed to mean something big, and *mil* something little. Roback noticed that saying *mal* requires opening the mouth wide, while *mil* makes the mouth small, so he theorized that the meaning came from this physical association.

The theory went on to suggest that much of language was formed by our association of the physical sensation of pronouncing certain sounds with the meaning of the sounds themselves. Words like "rough" feel rough when spoken, and "smooth" feels smooth, just as *rushing* rushes, and *explode* explodes.

The Voco-Sensory theory can be easily disproved: for example, *small* is made up of "big" sounds, while *big* is made up of "small" sounds. But the general idea is useful to you as an actor: a good playwright selects words that have sounds that generate appropriate sensations when you pronounce them. If you can let these sensations resonate in you, the physical act of pronouncing a speech generates and supports the appropriate feeling. As Stanislavski said,

> *When an actor adds the vivid ornament of sound to the living content of the words, he causes me to glimpse with an inner vision the images he has fashioned out of his own creative imagination.*[4]

On a larger scale, good writers use qualities of sound to help distinguish one character from another, one mood from another, or the changing of emotional states within a role.

You might find, for example, that the sounds of Blanche's speeches are more melodious than Stella's, or that Stanley's are more animalistic (biting, guttural) than Mitch's. You might decide that the dominant sounds in one of these roles suggest a particular pitch range and inflectional pattern. Regional dialect may be important here; O'Casey needs to be delivered in an Irish accent as much as Williams needs the Southern accent.

To sum up, the melody and rhythm of your stage language are powerful sources of a sense of character. Remember the work you did on vocal gesture in Part I and the profound relationship between sound, breath, energy, and character; as we pointed out then, the word *personality* has a root meaning of *per-sona*, "through sound."

Exercise 17.3: Melody

Using the same speech, read it aloud.

    1. What sounds are emphasized?

2. Considering the whole role, is there a pattern of sound, or any kind of sound that is dominant?
3. Are there changes in sound that reflect changes in emotion, action, or relationship?
4. Try singing the speech. What kind of music would best accompany your character?

IMAGERY

Drama is one of the most condensed and intensified forms of literature; what a novelist needs thousands of words to do, a playwright must pack into the dialogue alone. Besides the heightened use of diction, rhythm, and melody, the skillful playwright gets an extra measure of impact and meaning through the potential of language to evoke physical sensation. Stanislavksi reminds us that,

To an actor a word is not just a sound, it is the evocation of images.[5]

In its most literal sense, an *image* is "something imagined." The painting of "word pictures" is the most common kind of imagery, but language may appeal to any of our other senses as well; hearing, smelling, touching, tasting, sense of movement, and general body condition. Try speaking aloud this speech from Peter Barnes' *Red Noses*; in it, a Pope is speaking over the bodies of a troupe of friar–clowns whom he has just had killed:

Wind blow the poppy seeds over them and us, aaaaaawwh.
(He howls softly as the lights fade down)
Heaven is dark and the earth a secret
The cold snaps our bones, we shiver
And dogs sniff round us, licking their paws
Monsters eat our soul
There is no way back
Until God calls us to shadow
So we rage at the wall and howl.
Go down, she said, go down with me.
World go down, dark go down,
Universe and infinity go down,
Go down with me, aaaaaaaawwh.
(The lights are out.)

Good delivery of imagery like this requires that you recreate the sights, sounds, and other sensations in yourself fully; you then find the character's condition generated in you, and through you in the audience as well. Explore each image, recreate it in physical terms either through fantasy or memory of similar experiences, then allow this experience to remain stored in yourself as a specially created "sense memory."

Exercise 17.4: Imagery

Check your speech for any physical sensations it imparts. Dwell on each, recreating it through fantasy or memory. Then read the speech aloud, taking the time to re-experience each sensation as fully as you can.

In all your work on your character's speech, however, remember that your aim is to enhance and support the meaning of your character's *actions*. If your audience is made more aware of your language than of the ideas, feelings, and actions that the language expresses, you have failed.

SUMMARY

The words you speak as the character are the *residue* of a complete state of being; it is your job to recreate the fullness of the character by restoring body and consciousness to this residue. This is made easier by the fact that the playwright's first concern is the effect the language has on you as you speak it: in a real way, the playwright is reaching deep inside your body and mind through the language of your character.

A well-trained actor finds many specific clues about rhythms, inflections, emphases, and all sorts of characteristics needed to create a role in the language, but acting is not a matter of simply recognizing the playwright's outline and then "filling it in." You begin by understanding what your words mean, and why the playwright has chosen to have your character express themselves in precisely this way, not only because you have a responsibility to the meaning of your lines, but also because it reveals the way your character thinks and feels.

You then "work backward" from the words to recreate the thoughts and feelings from which the words spring. As you relive your character's process of verbalization you begin to participate actively in their mental processes and feelings. You must *recreate* your character's words *as your own*, taking into account the whole context of the character's speech. One good way to do this is to *paraphrase* the character's speech, to put it into your own words in a way that expresses your understanding of both its surface meaning and its hidden meanings and attitudes, or *sub-text.*

Rhythm is perhaps the single most powerful aspect of stage language. It functions in three primary ways: to support meaning, express personality, and to express emotion. A skillful playwright shapes rhythm carefully, and on several levels at once: syllables, phrases, sentences, and speeches. You can often see changes in a scene reflected in the speech rhythms.

Sound is a powerful component of emotion. Good writers also use speech melody, sound and rhythm, to help distinguish one character from another, one mood from another, or the changing of emotional states within a role. Remember that the word *personality* has a root meaning of *per-sona,* "through sound."

The skillful playwright gets an extra measure of impact and meaning through the potential of language to evoke physical sensation. The painting of "word pictures" is the most common kind of imagery, but language may appeal to any of our other senses as well; your job is to explore each image, recreate it in physical terms either through fantasy or memory of similar experiences, then allow it to remain stored in yourself as a specially created "sense memory."

In all your work on your character's speech your aim is to enhance and support the meaning of your character's *actions.* If your audience is made more aware of your language than of the ideas, feelings, and actions that the language expresses, you have failed.

Lesson 18

THE CHARACTER'S BODY

In everyday life we can sense the way a person's body reflects their personality and immediate emotion. Your work in Part I began to sensitize you to this "body language." The reading of body language has become an important skill in our culture. Lawyers use it to select jurors, salespersons to determine their strategy toward a customer, interviewers to help evaluate applicants, singles to identify likely partners, and politicians to project desirable qualities of personality. In general, we tend to trust body language as a more trustworthy expression of personality and attitude than spoken language, as we saw in the Hostess–Guest scene in Part I.

The theatre makes special use of this universal physical language. The image of Willy Loman walking with bent back, shuffling through the opening scene of *Death of a Salesman* communicates a vivid sense of Willy's situation to audiences in Chicago or Peking; so, in their own way, do the formal, precise gestures of the Kabuki actor as he employs the conventions of his theatre to express real action and emotion.

PERSONALITY IN THE BODY

As you learned in Part I, many aspects of personality come to be carried within the structure of the body. As we said then, these expressive structural patterns are caused by the cumulative effect of repeated behavioral patterns, especially those in which we suppress or "hold in" certain impulses and reactions. As Alexander Lowen, a psychoanalyst who works in the field he calls "Bioenergetics," puts it:

The muscles can hold back movements as well as execute them. . . .
Consider the case of an individual who is charged with rage and yet
must hold back the impulse to strike. His fists are clenched, his arms
are tense and his shoulders are drawn and held back to restrain the
impulse.[1]

If rage is suppressed in this way often enough, the muscular tension
in the hands, arms, and upper back becomes chronic. Because of this
long-term tension, the muscles and other tissues in these areas eventually harden, losing their flexibility and sensitivity. The rigidity of these
areas eventually affects the person's posture and movement, and a
trained observer can diagnose the precise psychological pattern captured
in this musculature, which is sometimes called the *character armor.*

Even without special training most of us can form fairly accurate
impressions of people who "harbor a lot of resentment," or are "sitting
on a lot of grief," or who "are afraid of their own sexuality," to name a
few examples.

The suppression of emotion is not the only way this kind of structure is created. The influence of heredity, the infant's mimicry of the parents' bodily motions, and patterns of social response (like the teenager's
slouching) can all become "built in" to the body.

Perhaps in your adolescence you were motivated to play the "tough"
by thrusting out your chest, pelvis, or jaw. Years later, even though this
social motivation no longer operates, you may find these earlier muscular patterns still operating, literally "built in" to your body by habit; the
shoulders still pulled back, the pelvis tilted to one side, the chin thrust
forward. These muscular patterns may have become expressive of your
personality and continue to influence the way you confront life. People
you meet may initially think, "Boy, does this person have a chip on his
shoulder!"

THE CHARACTER'S CENTER

You experienced your own bodily center in Part I. Though it may move
in various emotional states (we can be "up" one day and "down" the
next) each of us has a location that is our normal center. The location
of your energy center, and the quality of the energy it contains, can be
a profound expression of your attitude toward life; similarly, in your creation of a dramatic character you work to discover a physiovocal center
that is consistent with the character's attitudes and behavior.

We can suggest five primary character centers that by bodily logic and
cultural tradition are each associated with a different sort of person: head,

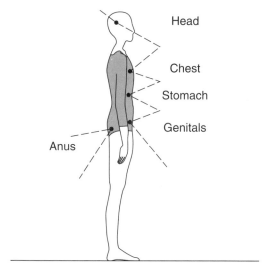

Head

Chest

Stomach

Genitals

Anus

FIGURE 18.1   Primary Body Centers

chest, stomach, genitals, and anus. (See Figure 18.1) Let's look briefly at each.

The *head*-centered person may be thought of as cerebral, "other worldly," flighty, scattered, or off-balance. This sort of person always seems "ahead of themselves." Their energy seems to come out through their eyes or their mouth; if they're passive, they may do a lot of watching; if they're active, they may do a lot of talking or be very aware of oral activity of all sorts, which may be their way of sublimating their sexual energy. ("Chew, chew, chew," are the first words Amanda speaks in *The Glass Menagerie.*)

The *chest*-centered person might have a lot of "heart" and be quite sentimental, or might be the reverse, tough and "militaristic."

The *stomach* person is usually carrying the badge of self-indulgence; they may also be good-natured, easygoing, and nurturing; they often make good parents.

The *genitally* centered person might be sexy, either in a libidinous way, or contrarily in a naive way like the "farmer's daughter."

The *anal* person seems severe, sexually withdrawn, often stingy ("constipated"), dogmatic, and rigid in their behavior.

We have all known people who tend to relate to the world from one of these centers; observe some of your acquaintances from this point of view. Think also of some specific dramatic characters and imagine how this idea of centers would apply to each. What center might Amanda have in *The Glass Menagerie?* Blanche in *A Streetcar Named Desire?* Peter in *The Zoo Story?* Contrast the centers that neighbor Charley and Brother Ben might have in *The Death of a Salesman.*

When we sense that someone is operating from one or another of these bodily centers, we tend to expect them to behave in the ways associated with that center, so the character's center is a powerful tool of characterization. Moreover, if a character undergoes a radical change in the course of the play, it is possible that their center will shift. Think of King Lear; he could be played as a man who is driven out of his mind and into his heart.

The importance of character center is not so much in its influence on an audience; more important by far is its power to affect you as you work on the role, moving you toward transformation. Bringing your own center into conformity with your character's center is perhaps the most fundamental physical characterizational choice.

Exercise 18.1: The Character Center

Examine Figure 18.1; try "putting on" some of these character centers. Experience your impulse as initiating in them; move about and enter into improvised relationships. See what attitudes are evoked in you.

Consider various characters from plays you have read; which center seems right for each? Which center might be right for Jerry in *The Zoo Story?* For Peter? For Charlie in *Death of a Salesman?* For Amanda in *The Glass Menagerie?* Do any of these characters undergo changes that might result in a shift of their center?

THE FLOW OF BODILY ENERGY

As we have said, the body takes on the qualities we associate with various kinds of characters through the repetition of certain responses to life. We now trace the bodily path taken by this process of stimulus and response.

Recall a moment from life, or from the scene you have been rehearsing, when you committed some strong physical action. Take a moment to relax and recall the experience as vividly as you can, so that it feels almost as if you were doing it again right now.

Feel the energy that is in your center; what is your level of arousal? Is it a high charge, or a low charge? We call this its *dynamic.*

Next, follow this energy as it flows away from your center; is it moving predominantly upward or downward, or equally in both directions away from your center?

Notice that the musculature of your body offers two energy pathways running up and down the body. One pathway runs along the back of your body, another along the front. Because the muscles of the back are large and strong, the rear pathway usually carries your aggressive energies; the muscles and tissues in the front of your body are softer and more vulnerable, so that the front pathway usually carries our "tender" feelings. Which pathway are you using now?

Consider whether the energy is impeded or even blocked from flowing through certain areas of your body. Some of the most common points of blockage are the jaw, nape of the neck, small of the back, across the chest, or between the shoulder blades. You can perhaps feel such blockages of this energy within your own body; are the blocks, if any, habitual to you, or did you intuitively create them as part of the character? Finally, become aware of how the energy leaves your body: is there an area or part of the body through which it tends to exit?

You now have traced the pathway by which any motion or sound must begin in a deep center and move through the various energy pathways of the musculature until it erupts into the outer world. When it does, it carries with it the tone, color, and shape of the interior world through which it has passed. Through this process, our physical and vocal expressions become a means by which we "turn ourselves inside out" and make a public expression of our private world.

We have all learned to read these signs, and our everyday language reflects this process: we speak of the happy person as "lighthearted" or "on cloud nine," while the depressed person is a "drag" or a "downer."

Consider the tremendous expressiveness of a person's walk. An insecure person, with a weak sense of self-identity, tends to be unstable, to "walk on eggshells." We speak of such a person as a "pushover," someone who "won't stand on their own two feet." In the opposite extreme is the "pushy" person who carries their weight on the balls of their feet and whose energy flows up the back into the aggressive stance of a fighter, and who walks as if they were punishing the floor and expected everything to get out of their way. It is not surprising that Sir Alec Guiness has said that he knows he has found the essential ingredients of a character when he has found the correct walk.

PHYSIQUE AND PERSONALITY

As we said earlier, repeated patterns of behavior may begin to alter the very structure of the body. We come to hold our energy in a way that affects the contours of our body, so that the body soon comes to announce the nature of the energy that inhabits it. The Elizabethan idea of reading character in the body (e.g., "the bovine man") was crude but entirely accurate in principle. This fact is especially important on stage, where the audience sees the whole body more acutely than we do in real life. We consider, then, how the contours of the body may communicate specific impressions of personality.

We must first, however, distinguish between the way the body is held, which is called *alignment,* and the basic structure of the body itself, which is called *physique.* Certain physiques carry particular associations within our culture: The large-abdomened *endomorph,* for example, is thought of as jolly, easygoing, and a good family type; the thin, wiry *ectomorph,* on the other hand, is expected to be nervous and compulsive, whereas the muscular *mesomorph* is expected to be a lot like Stanley Kowalski.

These body types are of limited importance in the theatre. To be sure, it might be unreasonable to cast an endomorphic actor as the mesomorphic Stanley, but within such broad limits it is possible for almost any physique to capture the psychophysical essence of a role on the stage. Though Lee J. Cobb and Dustin Hoffman have very different physiques, they were each successful in creating the role of Willy Loman.

The camera, on the other hand, has no tolerance for fundamental adjustments of physique which, despite the most skillful makeup and costuming, usually seem false. Insofar as this is true, films and television must be "type cast," at least as far as physique is concerned. Serious film actors sometimes go to extreme lengths in this regard, as did Robert De Niro when he gained sixty pounds to capture the degradation of his character in *Raging Bull.*

BODY ALIGNMENT AND CHARACTER

Bodily alignment, as opposed to physique, can be successfully adjusted both on stage and for the camera. Let's look at the specific qualities that are commonly associated with various bodily alignments. Examine Figure 18.2 and consider the qualities that each body suggests.

The first body, which features rounded shoulders and back, can have two very different qualities. When it is based on a low energy level, it is called the *oral* body. The chest is collapsed, the arms express yearning. The legs are weak, making the body unstable and poorly grounded. Aggressive energies at the rear are blocked, and a great deal of grief is held in the pit of the stomach.

On the other hand, when this structure is based upon a high energy level, it is called *masochistic.* The shoulders are rounded because of the

FIGURE 18.2   Basic Character Alignments

overdevelopment of the muscles in the upper body, giving a gorilla-like hulking aspect. The bound-in aggressions of this type are turned inward upon the self; notice that the energy pathway along the back begins to approach a circle. The second body is sometimes called the "militaristic character" because it resembles the stance of a soldier at attention. It is the most hostile of all alignments. The shoulders are thrown back and an enormous amount of anger is stored in the rigid area between the shoulder blades, the result of a long pattern of inhibited striking. This body is firmly rooted but so rigid in response that it is awkward, even mechanical. Aggressive energies stored in the back dominate, and the tender areas in the front of the body (chest and gut) are made hard. Small wonder that we train soldiers to stand this way and to not think for themselves.

The third body is clearly belly-centered. This "heavy" character responds with great equanimity and could be called the "aw shucks" body. We usually think of such characters as unaggressive (the sway back blocks the aggressive energies of the rear body) but jolly and sentimental (as the preponderance of the frontal energies would indicate).

The last body is called *schizoid*. Here the parts of the body are disassociated so that the person is literally "in pieces" and, as we say, "the right hand doesn't know what the left hand is doing." The head is often cocked in a birdlike way. This body is very unstable and poorly grounded; it lacks grace in movement.

Exercise 18.2: Body Alignment

Try on each of the body alignments described in Figure 18.2. Focus your awareness not on how the body looks from the outside, but on how it feels from the inside. How does energy flow through it? How does it move? Where is it sensitive, where dead?

Do any of these alignments seem right for the character you have been developing? Try rehearsing your scene in this alignment.

CHANGES IN BODILY ALIGNMENT

Although a bodily configuration may be deeply embedded in someone, it is still liable to surprisingly rapid change. I have seen extraordinary and permanent changes occur in people's bodies almost instantaneously as a result of powerful life experiences or through therapy. Likewise, the bodies of dramatic characters who undergo radical changes in the course of their plays would believably change. The Willy Loman we see at the beginning of his play should not be the same Willy we see in his better days during the flashbacks. Likewise, imagine the robust King Lear at the beginning of his play, and again after his ordeal in the storm when his daughter has to help him to walk. Do you see how such changes express not just the character's physical condition but psychological and even spiritual changes?

Remember that the theatre is a bodily place. All its meanings, philosophical or psychological insights, emotions and all that may be communicated by a play, reach the spectator through the physical sensations that you, the actor, generate. The "instrument" that creates the experience, your organism, is identical with the "instrument" that receives the experience, the spectator's organism, and there is an automatic and unconscious process by which your physical condition is imitated in the deep muscles of your audience; whatever your physical condition is doing to you, it also does to them. It is a real power: use it well.

Following is an exercise that reviews all the material we have covered in this lesson. It can help you to apply these principles to the physical life of the character you have been developing. It is important that these physical choices be made *after* you have experienced the character's givens, choices and actions; you must have this foundation to ensure the rightness of your physical work, or it may become mere posturing.

[Lesson 18/The Character's Body]

Exercise 18.3: A Journey into a Character Structure

In this exercise you create the experience of "living inside" the body of the character you have been developing in the previous exercises. You do this by making a series of simple choices as outlined below. Allow at least one hour for this exercise, and do it all in one session. The exercise has three ground rules:

1. Use the full range of everyday movements (walking, sitting, getting up and down) throughout the exercise; do not remain still for too long. Use the voice throughout as well; count, say the alphabet, say your lines, or whatever comes to mind.

2. In each item, make your choices on the basis of what "feels" right; explore the whole range of choice before you settle on what seems to fit your subject. Remember: the basis for the choice is how the energy flow *feels* inside the body, not what "looks" right or what "ought" to be right. Allow your mind to just settle back and witness.

3. The choices are cumulative; stick to the sequence given. After you have made a choice, move on to the next and trust the body to retain the first.

Here are the choices in sequence:

1. *Attitude toward gravity:* As in Exercise 3.4, experiment with your character's "root." Alternate from "plowing" to "floating" to "flying," and the stages between; select the attitude toward gravity that feels right.

2. *Center:* Review your choice of your character's center from the previous exercise; make it more specific.

3. *Dynamic:* Experience the energy flowing from center as a low charge or a high charge and the stages between; listen to the changes in the voice.

4. *Energy pathways:* Determine the way energy flows within this body.
   a. Is it deep in the core or near the surface?
   b. Is it upward or downward from center?
   c. Is it mostly along the front or the back of the body?

5. *Blockages:* Are there places in this body where energy is blocked? Try blocking each of these locations and see if it feels right; if it does, allow the block to remain:
   a. Eyes
   b. Jaw

 c. Head/neck
 d. Space between the shoulder blades
 e. Space between the breasts
 f. Pit of the stomach
 g. Small of the back
 h. Genitals (how are they held?)
 6. *Bodily alignment:* Try on each of the four alignments discussed:
 a. Oral
 b. Masochistic
 c. Militaristic
 d. "Aw shucks"
 e. Schizoid

Now, allowing the body to hold whatever it retains of these choices, stand with your partner or, better, in groups of four or five. Speak directly to each of these persons with the following phrases, and allow a new spontaneous ending to erupt each time you repeat the phrase as you go around the group. If a spontaneous ending does not arise, simply say "pass."

When I wake up in the morning...
Ever since I was a child...
When I look in the mirror...
I can remember...
The child in me...
I need...
I hate...
Strength to me means...
Weakness to me means...
Right now I am aware...
Sometimes I want to cry out to people...
Pain to me is...
I love...
If I could be free to do what I want to do...
My body...
If you could hear the music in me...[2]

At the conclusion of the exercise, watch yourself for a time in a mirror if possible. Then use the Phasic Relaxation exercise to "erase" the character structure you have created.

Share your experiences of this exercise. What did you learn about your character that you never knew before? What did your body teach you? Learn to treat the body as a source of discovery; there is much about acting that can be found only in physical experience.

SUMMARY

Many aspects of personality come to be carried within the body. These expressive structural patterns are caused by the cumulative effect of repeated behavioral patterns, as well as heredity, the infant's mimicry of the parents, and patterns of social response. Some therapists call such semi-permanent alterations in the body's structure the *character armor.*

Bringing your own center into conformity with your character's center is perhaps the most fundamental physical characterizational choice. There are five primary character centers that by bodily logic and cultural tradition are associated with different sorts of people: the *head*-centered person may be thought of as cerebral; the *chest*-centered person might have a lot of "heart," or the reverse and be "militaristic"; the *stomach* person is usually good-natured and easygoing; the *genital* person is either libidinous or naive; the *anal* person seems severe and rigid in their behavior.

We must distinguish between the way the body is held, which is called *alignment,* and the basic structure of the body itself, which is called *physique.* Certain physiques carry particular associations within our culture: The large-abdomened *endomorph* is jolly, whereas the wiry *ectomorph* is nervous and compulsive, and the muscular *mesomorph* is a lot like Stanley Kowalski. Within broad limits it is possible for almost any physique to capture the psychophysical essence of a role on the stage. The camera, on the other hand, has little tolerance for fundamental adjustments of physique.

Bodily alignment, as opposed to physique, can be successfully adjusted both on stage and for the camera. The oral body has a collapsed chest; the masochistic body has a gorilla-like hulking aspect. The militaristic body resembles the stance of a soldier at attention. The "aw shucks" body is unaggressive but sentimental. The schizoid body has its parts disassociated so that it is literally "in pieces."

Although a bodily configuration may be deeply embedded, it is still liable to surprisingly rapid change; the bodies of dramatic characters who undergo radical changes in the course of their plays would believably change.

Remember that the theatre is a bodily place; whatever your physical condition is doing to you, it also does to your audience. Use this power well.

THE CHARACTER'S EMOTION

What is emotion? The root meaning of the word is *an outward movement*. It is any activity that expresses the immediate condition of our organism and is directed toward the outside world, arising automatically out of our efforts to relate to life. Emotion is not primarily for purposes of communication: though there are times when you want to make your feelings known to others, the feelings themselves arise in the course of your interaction with the world.

In everyday life emotion serves several purposes, some of them essential to survival. Of special interest to you as an actor is the function emotion serves as a *value judgment* that you pass on your actions. When you try to attain an objective and are successful, you become happy; when you try to attain an objective and fail due to your own actions, you are sad; when you try to attain an objective and are prevented by circumstance or by someone else's actions, you become angry; when you try to attain an objective and fail, and don't know why, you become afraid.

Thus emotion is tied inextricably to action; it arises *automatically* from any significant effort to interact with the world. So it is on stage: *as an actor, you do not create emotion; rather, emotion arises of its own accord out of your action.*

FROM ACTION TO EMOTION: WORKING FROM THE OUTSIDE IN

Near the turn of the century two psychologists, Fritz Lange and William James, developed a theory of emotion of special interest to the actor. (Stanislavski was familiar with it.) This theory holds that what we call emotion is our recognition of a bodily condition that is itself a response to some external situation; or, put another way, that *the emotion* is *the physical condition.*

Let's say you are stepping off a curb when, out of the corner of your eye, you see a car rushing toward you. Immediately you leap back out of danger. You are afraid, but you did not jump because you were afraid: you didn't have time to become afraid first, you had to react directly to the sign of danger; in acting terms it was an "automatic action." Your body prepared for "flight or fight," as the psychologists say, and only after you had jumped clear, with your heart pounding, adrenalin flowing, your breath short, did you recognize your own condition and call it "fear." *Your emotion did not cause your action, your action caused your emotion.*

In *Death of a Salesman,* Miller describes Willy's first entrance:

> *From the right, Willy Loman, the Salesman, enters, carrying two large sample cases . . . He is past sixty years of age, dressed quietly. Even as he crosses the stage to the doorway of the house, his exhaustion is apparent. He unlocks the door, comes into the kitchen, and thankfully lets his burden down, feeling the soreness of his palms. A word-sigh escapes his lips—it might be "Oh, boy, oh, boy."*

This physical pattern by itself is powerful enough to generate an emotional state in you if you perform it with full participation of body and mind. As Plato noted two thousand years ago, the actor mimicking the gestures of an angry person tends to become angry. Or, as some directors say today, "Do the act, and the feeling will follow."

However, Willy's action is more than the physical pattern described in this stage direction. What we are seeing is the final phase of a larger action, in which Willy tried once again to be a successful salesman by driving to Boston to see clients, but he has failed. As he says to Linda when she comes into the kitchen:

Willy: I suddenly couldn't drive any more. The car kept going off onto the shoulder, y'know?

Linda, helpfully: Oh. Maybe it was the steering again. I don't think Angelo knows the Studebaker.

Willy: No, it's me, it's me. Suddenly I realize I'm goin' sixty miles an hour and I don't remember the last five minutes. I'm—I can't seem to—keep my mind to it.

His emotion is his evaluation of his action: he has failed in his objective, and it is his own fault, so he is sad. His emotion has arisen from his action, and the physical condition in which we see him has resulted. As the James–Lange Theory suggests, his emotion *is* his physical condition.

This process aids you in rehearsal. As you try various things—movements, line readings, business—your own emotional response to what you are doing serves to guide you in checking the correctness of your action. This is what the experienced actor means when they try something, but "It didn't feel right"; it is an evaluation of the action itself through its resultant emotion. When you have found the *correct* act, then the *correct* feeling follows, and it coincides with the implied physical conditions embodied in the rhythms, sounds, and sensations of your text.

All this is meant to persuade you that you needn't be concerned with emotional behavior as such; if you are able to pursue your character's action with full involvement, the emotion *arises automatically* and it *is communicated* to your audience. Emotions are states of being, not actions; you are *never* concerned with playing emotion.

A note about stage directions: some acting teachers encourage students to disregard stage directions because they want the actor to discover the external form of the performance for themselves. This might make sense when you are dealing with an acting version of a play in which the stage directions have been inserted by a stage manager to describe what particular actors did in a particular production. But when the stage directions come from the playwright, they should be taken into account in the same way that a musician would note the markings for tempo and volume in a musical score. You must consider the internal state that the playwright meant for them to imply. When Chekhov says that Natasha stamps her foot, the actor who ignores this stage direction does so only at her peril.

Exercise 19.1: Working from the Outside In

Examine your scene again, paying special attention to the external actions (words, gestures, movements) and the physical condition suggested for your character. Rehearse it so as to involve yourself in these externals as fully as possible; surrender to the experience that they produce in you.

FROM THOUGHT TO EMOTION: WORKING FROM THE INSIDE OUT

We began by saying that emotion arises out of your attempts to cope with the world, and is your way of evaluating these attempts; in this sense, emotion arises from action. But there is another way that emotion is also generated, and that is by your thoughts, expectations, and attitudes. The school of psychotherapy called "cognitive therapy" is based on this fact:

> *The first principle of cognitive therapy is that all your moods are created by your cognitions, or thoughts. A cognition refers to the way you look at things—your perceptions, mental attitudes, and beliefs. It includes the way you interpret things—what you say about something or someone to yourself. You feel the way you do right now because of the thoughts you are thinking at this moment....*
>
> *...The moment you have a certain thought and believe it, you will experience an immediate emotional response. Your thought actually creates the emotion.*[1]

For example, suppose you want to become an actor and are reading this, thinking, "Hey, that sounds good; Benedetti's approach could really help me!" This positive thought makes you feel good. If, on the other hand, you are thinking, "This is too hard, I could never do it," then your feeling is negative and sad.

Psychologists who treat depression have noticed that depressed people are seldom less "successful" in objective terms than many who are not depressed; the difference lies more in the way they subjectively view themselves and their lives. They "send themselves messages" that are negative, and every hint of failure confirms this negative self-attitude.

Some people hold a view of themselves as being unworthy: like Willy Loman, they can't accept praise or success that they don't feel they've "earned" through great effort, and they often can't accept the love that others offer them; this too must be "earned" because they don't feel worth loving.

Of course, cheerful and optimistic people are also sending themselves messages; they tend to evaluate their transactions with the world in more positive terms, such as "I'm getting better at it," or "What I do makes a difference." If depressed people can identify their negative self-messages and replace them with such realistically positive ones, they can change the way they feel.

In developing the emotional life of a character, it may be useful to examine the character's attitude toward themselves. Willy Loman is no less successful in objective terms than is his neighbor, Charlie, but he feels like a failure whereas Charlie feels like a success. Willy is constantly sending himself the message that he has to earn the respect of others and even the love of his own sons; he tries to do this by "selling" himself. He refuses to admit, as Charlie urges him to do, that he is a worthwhile human being. Willy has accepted the materialistic attitude of his society, and measures his personal worth in external terms: when the size of his paycheck and the smiles of his clients diminish, he is diminished.

The messages that someone sends themselves express a dominant attitude toward life that is clearly reflected in that person's superobjective. Willy's superobjective is "to prove myself worthy by earning money and respect"; the underlying assumption is that he is *un*worthy. He has created an unconscious attitude toward himself, which is his *self-image*.

We tend to become strongly attached to our self-image, even when it is negative. Much of Willy Loman's behavior seems perversely dedicated to proving his own unworthiness, just as Blanche Dubois behaves in ways that prove that she needs "to depend on the kindness of strangers." This kind of repeated pattern of behavior based on the self-image often makes the self-image a self-fulfilling prophecy.

To sum up: Character superobjectives are related to their self-image, which is in turn reflected in the choices they make in "acting out" their lives. Let's apply these ideas to your scene.

Exercise 19.2: Self-Image: Working from the Inside Out

What is your character's dominant self-image? What messages do they send themselves? Enter into your character's frame of mind and complete these phrases:

1. The most beautiful part of my body is...
2. Happiness to me is...
3. The thing I most want to do before I die is...
4. The most embarrassed I ever was...
5. The ugliest part of my body is...
6. The thing I like best about myself is...
7. Pain to me is...
8. The most secret thing about me is...
9. I can hear my father's voice speaking through my own when I tell myself...
10. Love to me is...
11. The thing I am most proud of is...
12. If you could hear the music in me...
13. I want my epitaph to be...

Immediately enter into the scene and allow these feelings to affect what you do.

As you have seen in the last two exercises, it is possible to work *either* from the inside out *or* from the outside in. Emotion arises automatically out of your involvement in *both* the actions *and* thoughts of your character. Though you may find one approach more powerful for you than the other, most actors work both ways simultaneously.

EMOTIONAL RECALL AND SUBSTITUTION

As you begin to participate fully in the actions and thoughts of your character, you begin to have associations or memories of past situations in your own life that were similar. Connecting this personal material with the character's situation can enrich the performance.

Stanislavski experimented with the idea that the actor could develop a wealth of emotional memories as a resource for the acting process, much as a painter learns to mix colors:

> *The broader your emotion memory, the richer your material for inner creativeness.... Our creative experiences are vivid and full in direct proportion to the power, keenness and exactness of our memory.... Sometimes memories continue to live in us, grow and become deeper. They even stimulate new processes and either fill out unfinished details or suggest altogether new ones.*[2]

Stanislavski worked in the theatre at a time when psychology was emerging as a specialized field, and he was deeply interested in it. (Pavlov was a friend who contributed to his thinking.) One idea from early Russian psychology that appealed to him was the notion that every cell in the body had a capacity for memory, so that the recall of emotional states had the potential to energize the actor in much more than a merely mental way.

We would not entirely disagree with this idea today, though we have other ways of understanding the function of memory. One contemporary school of thought, called "Psychocybernetics," describes the operation of memory as serving the needs of survival. Your mind tends to record events that, for various reasons, might be useful as a basis for future action. They remain "on file," ready for recall should a similar situation occur, when we can repeat (or avoid) actions that were in the past successful (or unsuccessful).

For example, you probably suffered some physical injury, discomfort, or severe psychological distress at some time in your childhood, and you have probably "filed" certain prominent details of the event. These details, or things that merely remind you of them, may continue to evoke feelings when they recur, even when the new situation is quite different from the original, or when the original has been lost to consciousness. In this way, some events and details continue to evoke strong responses even when there is no longer a direct link to the original situation. (Smells are especially powerful in this regard.)

There are several techniques by which stored memories may be evoked. Common to all of them is the crucial ingredient of *relaxation;* when we relax, the storehouse of memory and subconscious material becomes more accessible.

One of the easiest of these techniques is *visualization.* By relaxing deeply and entering into a visualization of your character's situation, you can invite associations from your store of memories. These associations, or "recalls," automatically become attached to the character's actions and situation; it is neither necessary nor desirable to "play" them; they are simply allowed to "be there."

Another recall technique that may be useful in certain situations involves making a mental *substitution* of someone from your own life for one of the other characters in the scene. If you are supposed to be terribly afraid of another character, it might be useful to recall someone frightening from your own life and substitute them for that character. Such a substitution is a special kind of emotional recall, and often arises naturally as you work. Recalls and substitutions needn't be rooted in real events; *fantasies* sometimes supply more powerful material than real events.

A word of caution: as useful as emotional recall and substitution may sometimes be, there are dangers connected with their use. First, although recalls may be useful for opening an initial connection into the character's experience, you must go beyond this initial connection into the *specific* experience of the character within his or her given circumstances; if you do not, your response may be merely personal without being appropriate to the demands of the character or style of the play.

Second, memories can be very powerful, and those that have not yet been fully mastered can easily overwhelm artistic control. If you fall into your personal memory and emotion too fully, you may lose your necessary dual consciousness. Lee Strasberg claimed that seven years was sufficient time for a memory to have come within the province of artistic control, and he discouraged the use of younger ones. However, as Stanislavski pointed out, some memories grow stronger with age, so there is no guarantee that time alone will provide mastery over them.

Third, recalls and substitutions can become obstacles between you and your scene partners. It is awful to be on stage with someone who is looking at you but "seeing" someone else. How much better to find the necessary qualities in the actor who is actually playing the role.

Last and most dangerous, the emotional power of recalls may distract you from your focus on your objective and action, and lure you into playing an emotional state.

For all these reasons, though recalls and substitutions may be useful as training devices, they are of limited use in rehearsal, and absolutely *not* intended for use in performance. Stanislavski himself eventually abandoned the technique. Because memories and associations arise naturally in the course of preparing a role, not much is gained by using them in a premeditated way, and much can be lost. David Mamet said it best:

> *The laws of attention which are true off stage are true* on *stage. The self-concerned person is a bore and the self-concerned* actor *is a bore. And whether the actor is saying, "I must play this scene in order to be well thought of," or, "I must remember and recreate the time my puppy died in order to recreate this scene well," makes no difference. In both cases his attention is self-centered, and in both cases his performance will tell us nothing we couldn't have learned more enjoyably in a library.*
>
> *Acting, as any art, must be generous; the attention of the artist must be focused outward—not on what he is feeling, but on what he is trying to accomplish.*[3]

Exercise 19.3: Emotional Recalls and Substitutions

Place yourself comfortably at rest and do the Phasic Relaxation exercise.

Now go through your scene mentally; picture the entire circumstance and live through your character's actions as if you were actually doing them in those circumstances. Let your body respond freely.

As you live through the scene, notice the emotional associations that arise. Do you remember events from your past? Do the other characters remind you of people you have known? Avoid internal censorship; release into these memories fully.

Now examine the most significant of these recalls. Ask yourself the following questions about this memory:

1. Where in my body is it located?
2. What is it like? How big is it, what color is it, how much does it weigh, is it hot or cold?
3. How does it make me feel about myself? About the other people in this memory?

4. Are there ideas, attitudes, or beliefs connected with this memory?

5. Do I recall making any choices at this time, even unconsciously, that have affected me since?

6. Are there images from even earlier times contained in this memory? If so, experience these: continue to allow such images to flood up and take you back further and further in time.

Review this exercise and evaluate any connections that were made; are they useful to the scene? Do they need to be specified or altered to meet the exact demands of the scene or style of the play?

Rehearse your scene and simply allow these associations to "be there."

THE ROLE OF EMOTION IN PERFORMANCE

Finally, we must say something about the way in which you will experience your character's emotion in performance. Young actors sometimes think that they must recreate the character's emotion in order to generate each performance "truthfully," but this is an exhausting and unreliable way of working. Because emotion arises from action and thought, you need only *do* what your character does and *think* the thoughts involved in the action; the performance itself gives you the emotion.

We may sometimes be tempted to admire the emotionality of the actor who loses control and is overwhelmed on stage, but the display of emotion for its own sake is never our true purpose. The great actor aspires to use emotional technique to realize the truth of the character according to the demands of the play; the ultimate test of a performance is not only its emotional power, but the completeness with which it contributes to the whole play as a work of art; emotion is a means to this end, never an end in itself.

This was the position to which Stanislavski had come by the time of his last book, *Building a Character,* in which he said,

> Our art . . . requires that an actor experience the agony of his role, and weep his heart out at home or in rehearsals, that he then calm himself, get rid of every sentiment alien or obstructive to his part. He then comes out on the stage to convey to the audience in clear, pregnant, deeply felt, intelligible and eloquent terms what he has been through. At this point the spectators will be more affected than the actor, and he will conserve all his forces in order to direct them where he needs

them most of all: in reproducing the inner life of the character he is portraying.[4]

The important idea here is that in performance, *the spectators will be more affected than the actor.* This is necessary for several reasons. First, strong emotion interferes with your craftsmanship; as Stanislavski put it, "a person in the midst of experiencing a poignant emotional drama is incapable of speaking of it coherently."[5] Second, it is unreliable to depend on emotion to generate a performance that must be done repeatedly and on schedule. Stanislavski used the example of the opera singer who, at the moment the music requires a certain note with a certain feeling, cannot say to the conductor, "I'm not feeling it yet, give me four more measures." Finally, and most important, your aim is the creation of a *transparent* performance, one through which we get a clear view of the events, characters, and ideas of the play. If your performance calls undue attention to itself, you have failed. As an audience member I am not here to watch *you* weep; I am here to weep *myself.*

SUMMARY

An emotion is any activity that expresses our immediate condition and is directed toward the outside world. In everyday life emotion serves several purposes; the one of greatest interest to us is as a *value judgment* that we pass on our actions. In this way, emotion arises automatically from any significant effort to interact with the world. It should be so on stage as well: *you do not create emotion; rather, emotion arises of its own accord out of your action.*

The James–Lange theory holds that what we call emotion is our recognition of a bodily condition that is itself a response to some external situation; or, put another way, *the emotion is the physical condition.* As some say, "Do the act, and the feeling will follow." When you have found the correct act, the correct feeling follows, and it coincides with the implied physical conditions embodied in the rhythms, sounds, and sensations of your text.

It follows that you needn't be concerned with emotional behavior as such; if you are able to pursue your character's action with full involvement, the emotion *arises automatically* and it *is communicated* to your audience. You are *never* concerned with playing emotion.

Although it is true that emotion arises from action, it can also be generated by your thoughts, especially the messages you send yourself about yourself. This is the first principle of cognitive therapy. In developing the emotional life of a character, it may be useful to examine the character's attitude toward themselves. A character's superobjective is related to their self-image, which is in turn reflected in the choices they make in "acting out" their lives.

You see that it is possible to work either from the inside out or from the outside in. Emotion arises automatically out of your involvement in *both* the actions and thoughts of your character. Though you may find one approach more powerful for you than the other, most actors work both ways simultaneously.

As emotion arises in rehearsal, it often brings with it associations or memories of past situations in your own life. Stanislavski experimented with the idea that the actor could develop a wealth of emotional memories as a resource for the acting process. There are several techniques by which stored memories may be evoked; one of the easiest is *visualization*. Another involves making a mental *substitution* of someone from your own life for one of the other characters in the scene. Recalls and substitutions needn't be rooted in real events; *fantasies* sometimes supply more powerful material.

As useful as emotional recall and substitution may sometimes be, there are dangers connected with their use. Because memories and associations arise naturally in the course of preparing a role, not much is gained by using this process in a premeditated way, and much can be lost.

Young actors sometimes think that they must recreate the character's emotion in each performance in order to be "truthful," but because emotion arises from action and thought, you need only *do* what your character does and *think* the thoughts involved in their action; the performance itself gives you the emotion.

Emotion in performance must be held at a reduced level for three reasons: First, strong emotion interferes with your craftsmanship; second, it is unreliable; finally, and most important, your aim is the creation of a *transparent* performance.

THE REHEARSAL PROCESS I: FINDING THE CONTENT

You auditioned for a role, were cast, and now rehearsals begin. At last you are truly at work.

Though there are various ways in which directors may choose to structure the rehearsal process, the typical sequence has ten steps:

1. Auditions;
2. Preparation and homework;
3. Early readings;
4. Getting up and off book;
5. Exploring the action;
6. Establishing the score;
7. Pacing the performance;
8. Polishing the performance;
9. Technical and dress rehearsals;
10. Growth after opening.

The first five are the early period of exploration when the *content* of the performance is being developed; we discuss them in this lesson. The last five are devoted to establishing the *form* of the performance; these are discussed in Lesson 21.

AUDITIONS

Though not usually thought of as part of the rehearsal process, auditions are in fact a time when you may form an initial approach to a role, which can greatly influence your later work.

Auditions are a nerve-wracking but necessary part of the actor's life. If it is any consolation to you, directors are under even more pressure during auditions than are actors. The casting of a play is the most important single decision the director makes, and yet they often have to make it with only minimal knowledge of the actors.

In general we can divide auditions into two types, the "general" and the "specific." Most general auditions, sometimes called "cattle calls," are used for preliminary screening for a role, or for membership in a company. Most often, you are asked to present two monologues of different types, such as modern and classical. You should develop a repertoire of at least three or four carefully chosen and prepared monologues, including comedy and tragedy, poetic and modern styles. About two minutes is a good length for each, though some might be as short as one minute, others as long as three. Beware of going on too long; actors often go on long enough to reveal their weaknesses. It is much better to make a strong initial impression and leave the auditioners hungry for more.

Introduce yourself and your selections clearly and in a businesslike way. Dress neatly and appropriately to the material you are going to perform, but not in a "costume." Take time to prepare yourself and the space, but work efficiently. Your focus should be on the work itself; let your appetite for acting motivate you.

Provide a well-organized and attractive resumé, and an eight-by-ten black-and-white photo. This "head shot" assists the auditioners in remembering you; it should be current and "neutral;" that is, it should look like you, and not limit the impression it provides of you to one quality like "sexy," "likeable," or "dangerous." Shape each speech to have a smooth, logical progression; this requires some judicious editing, and internal cutting is allowable. In monologues where another character is assumed to be present, be careful to "create" the other person by the way you relate to them; place them (in your mind) somewhere just off center (not off to one side) a bit closer to you than the auditioners. Do not look directly at the auditioners unless the speech is intended by the author as direct address.

Make sure each piece has a satisfying ending, even if that is not how it would be performed in context. This shows the auditioners that you have a desire to satisfy an audience.

Your repertoire of speeches should be chosen to demonstrate your abilities to the best advantage, but most important, they should be material that you love; it is a tremendous advantage to you if your positive feelings for your material outweigh your negative feelings about auditioning.

When auditions are for specific roles, various techniques are used. Most directors have developed their own auditioning style, some of which can be rather disarming, but usually you are asked to read a scene from the play. In the live theatre, you are usually able to read the entire play in advance and prepare a selection from the role. In film and television, you are often given only a few pages from the script and only a short time for preparation (though it is a union rule that an entire script must be made available if you ask to see it). Don't hesitate to ask questions about the character's given circumstances, about the contribution the character is expected to make to the show, or about the approach the director intends to take.

If you have limited time to prepare for an audition, your immediate job is to find a productive objective and playable action in the material, and to make that objective important to you through some kind of personalization. Use the principles you learned in Part II.

Some actors can give good cold readings with only a few moments' work, but theatre directors are sometimes suspicious of this; many times these slick cold-readers fail to develop much beyond their initial reading. In television, however, quick results are required; here, casting is often done by producers who are even more result oriented than are directors; they want to see exactly what you can do on the set.

Perhaps the greatest challenge in an audition is to allow yourself to really be in the here and now. Usually, you come away from an audition with only a vague sense of what happened or who was there; you are so threatened that you retreat into the back of your mind and become rigid or manic. Take a moment at the beginning to breathe, to see where you are and who is there; don't make a big thing of it, just treat it like a social situation in which you are glad to be present.

Then, as you perform, go for it. Make the event live. Don't be tied to your script (but don't ignore it completely). It is better to be a bit rough but alive, than to be technically correct but mechanical. Most important, make contact with the person you are reading with, whether that is an imaginary character, a stage manager, or a casting director. As in any other acting situation, the scene can live only *between* you. Put your objective into them, try to affect them.

In film and television auditions, don't try to create a character or some special emotional state: just let yourself say and do what the character does with your own voice and your own body. They don't want a character, they want you.

Auditions are much more enjoyable if you approach them without a sense of competitiveness. Think of them not as a contest with other actors but as an opportunity to communicate your potential to a director or producer. Take the long view and remember that the opinion formed of you at an audition may be important at some future time; it is therefore important that you honestly present your best abilities and avoid falsifying yourself for the sake of the particular instance. The question young actors most often ask about an audition is, "What do they want?" A much better question would be, "How can I best show them what kind of actor I am?"

Above all, do not take auditions personally. It usually requires many auditions before you land a part. (In film and TV about twenty seems to be an average, in live theatre it varies tremendously.) You can't take every rejection as a reflection on your talent. Auditions do not test your artistry so much as they test your usefulness for the specific role at hand. True, you have to deliver the goods, but first you have to be in the right place at the right time.

Exercise 20.1: Auditions

Set up a general audition situation in your class. Each of you is to present two monologues, one modern and one classical. They should be no more than a total of four minutes: a timekeeper will stop you when your time is up. After each audition, the class critiques the work.

PREPARATION AND HOMEWORK

Now that you have been cast in your role, you must do some important preparation before rehearsals begin. Analysis, private experimentation, beginning to learn the lines, and private rehearsal of special skills must be accomplished outside the rehearsal hall. Never should you waste the time of your fellow actors and director by failing to do your homework.

Remember that homework is a *preparation* for rehearsal, not a *substitute* for it. Your pre-rehearsal work identifies the possibilities that are then explored in rehearsal with your fellow actors; it does *not* determine the form of the finished product. Unfortunately, some actors are so insecure that they prepare for rehearsal as if it were performance, creating a rigidly premeditated form; the director then must be a "referee," mediating between the various actors' ideas of how to play their roles. Remember that rehearsal is a time for *mutual* exploration through trial and error.

Depending on the demands of the play, your preparation may take various forms. Certainly you study the play as a whole, and develop a preliminary sense of your character's dramatic function. You also examine each of your scenes and do a preliminary breakdown of your action, looking for your beat and scene objectives, and beginning to form a sense of your superobjective.

There may be technical demands on your voice or body related to the specific character; Laurence Olivier devoted a full year to his vocal preparation for *Othello;* Robert De Niro did extensive physical preparation for his role as a prizefighter in *Raging Bull.* As we said in Lesson 18, many of the physical and vocal aspects of character, and the character's habits, have to be practiced almost daily throughout the rehearsal period, and it is never too early to start.

Besides technical preparations of vocal and physical skills related to the external behavior of the character, you also want to prepare yourself to enter their mind as well. For this purpose you may need to do research into the intellectual world from which the character comes. You are most interested in those things that established the character's psychological and moral qualities, such as the religious and philosophical beliefs of the time, the educational experiences of the character, the quality of home life, the work environment, the system of government and justice, and so on.

You might also need to develop certain technical skills related to the style of the production, such as fencing, dancing, tumbling, the use of canes, fans, large skirts, or robes. For period plays especially, you may want to do some research into the fashions of the time, the ideas of grace and beauty, and social behavior. Experiencing the music, painting, and architecture of the time is valuable; documents such as diaries, letters, and newspapers can also be helpful. Review your list of the Given Circumstances; be sure you have considered all the possibilities.

The social backgrounds of plays as recent as *The Glass Menagerie* or *Death of a Salesman* are different enough from our own to require you to learn about life in the Great Depression and World War II, and about the popularity of "The American Dream" through such self-help methods as the Dale Carnegie books. Our credit-card culture, for example, cannot fully appreciate the importance to Willy Loman of "weathering a twenty-year mortgage," or the humiliation for Amanda Wingfield of having to ask Garfinkle's Delicatessen for credit.

Two good ways to focus your research into the character's inner and outer worlds are by writing an autobiography and a diary entry for them.

Exercise 20.2: Autobiography and Diary

Imagine that as your character, you have been asked to write a short autobiographical sketch of yourself. Limit yourself to two pages and include only those things that were most influential in your life; title your essay, "The Things That Made Me Who I Am."

Imagine also that you keep a diary. Select an important day within the time frame of the play and write the diary entry for that day. Check your list of Given Circumstances and be sure you have covered all the operative elements.

As valuable as it is to do this sort of personal and psychological research on your character, you must also remember that your character is a creature of the theatre; it is useful for you to understand the theatrical world in which they were created. Reading other plays by your author and their contemporaries can help; so can study of the physical and social environment of the theatre of the time. For instance, the open-air, thrust quality of the Elizabethan playhouse with its pit in which the "ground-lings" stood throughout the performance is important to an understanding of Shakespeare's plays. Just so, it is revealing to learn that the Moscow Art Theatre in which Chekhov's plays were first presented sat 1,200 persons, so that the scale of the performances must have been somewhat larger than we usually think.

Likewise, coming to understand the literary conventions that influenced the playwright may help you to understand your character. It is revealing to learn of Chekhov's passion for the writing of the French Naturalists and their "scientific" approach to personality and behavior; this is even more illuminating when we consider his training as a doctor and the fact that he wrote his four great plays after learning that he was dying of tuberculosis.

In the same way, understanding the playwright's psychological and moral values can be revealing. It is helpful to know that Bertolt Brecht was an ambulance driver in World War I and was permanently affected by the carnage and misery he experienced then.

In all, remember that good plays are written out of a deep need to communicate some important insight into the human condition, and that you must approach your work with the same sense of purpose. This requires commitment, preparation, and homework beyond the confines of the rehearsal hall.

Exercise 20.3: The Theatrical Life of the Play

Imagine that you are someone attending the very first performance of the play in which your character appears. Write an account of coming to the theatre and watching the performance, or simply relive it in your mind.

Pretend you are the author of your play, and that you have just begun to write it. Write a letter to a friend and try to explain how you feel about this new play, why you are writing it, and what you hope to achieve with it.

EARLY READ-THROUGHS

Now rehearsals begin and you are meeting for the first time with your fellow cast members. Your director may greet you in a variety of ways: some outline their interpretation and approach to the play; some lead a discussion about it; some may do exercises to "break the ice" and to establish a working rapport in the ensemble; many dispense with any such preliminaries and begin at once to read the play.

These early readings are your first forays into the heart of the material. Begin to work at once on the play as a whole; listen to it in the living voices of your fellow actors and begin to discover how it lives within this particular group of people.

Above all, read *in relationship,* with a spirit of give and take, reaction and action; get your awareness and your eyes out of your book as much as you can and contact the other characters in your scenes. Begin to search for the action that lives only in the specific transactions between the characters. Read also with deep muscle involvement, so that you involve your whole self; you may find that a wealth of associations and ideas well up.

These early rehearsals are exploration, but never indiscriminate exploration. Any meaningful exploration has a sense of goal that prevents it from degenerating into blind groping. There is usually in the vision of a play as communicated by the director some sense of the direction in which your exploration must go.

Not all of your rehearsal discoveries result from purposeful experimentation, of course; the accidental is an important part of all creative processes. You must have the courage to be playful, to invite the *happy accident* to happen, and to benefit from it. Such spontaneous discovery grows best from the receptiveness and responsiveness of each cast member to each other and to the moment. In these early stages of rehearsal, as rapport is being established within the company, it is especially important that each actor make an act of faith to work together toward the defining of goals with respect, trust, good humor, and a generous heart.

GETTING UP AND OFF BOOK

As soon as possible, begin to put your book aside so that you can explore the action on your feet. This, of course, requires learning the lines. You have to find your own best method for line memorization. Some actors like to have a friend read the other parts (cue them); some make a tape recording of their lines to listen to at night; some even write out their lines. Many find it useful to begin working in paraphrase, finding the ideas behind the lines in their own words first.

However you work, be sure to learn the *action* as well as the lines; that is, learn the words in the context of the give and take of the scene, paying considerable attention to what the other character is saying. This is not only an easier way of learning lines, it also makes learning them a useful first step in your exploration of the action.

The transitional rehearsal period during which you are putting the book down can be a frustrating one. When you were still reading your lines, the information that your eyes received from the text passed directly the short distance to the brain; now you are beginning to recreate the whole process of action, which requires a longer, deeper neurological pathway of response within your body. You are literally translating the play from a "literary" form into the complete psychophysical form of the live performance.

During this period you must not waste rehearsals by stopping the flow of the emerging action, even if you must call for lines; it is expected that you will call for lines, so don't waste time apologizing, and above all *keep the action going while you call for lines in character.*

This is the time to get your rehearsal clothing and props and start using them regularly. Pay special attention to the effect of the character's clothing on your body, and be sure to wear the correct type of shoes to rehearsal so as to establish the correct relationship to gravity.

EXPLORING THE ACTION

Now that you are off book, you and your partners are beginning to shape and specify the transactions of action–reaction that form, link by link, the chain that binds the scenes and the play together. Your preliminary breakdown of the role is being tested and refined, moment by moment, beat by beat, and scene by scene. The rightness of each of your actions is being determined by the way it fits into the cause–effect chain of inter-actions between characters, which in turn moves the play. As you *feel* the connectedness of every moment with every other moment, your through-line begins to emerge.

As the correct sequence of actions begins to form, your scenes begin to play, to flow "under their own power." You no longer have to *make* things happen, you can *let* them happen, and your scenes begin to feel simpler and shorter.

The many choices you must make during rehearsal cannot be pre-judged: you must actually do a thing in order to know whether it is right. One of the most common expressions you should hear during rehearsal is "Let's try it." Each choice you make reveals more about the whole play, and in turn each of these revelations of the larger pattern helps you to find the rightness of each detail.

Exercise 20.4: Making Connections

Work through your scene with your partner; either of you may stop the rehearsal at any point when you do not feel connected to the flow of the action, when you are not being "made" to do what you must do next. At each point of difficulty, examine the moments that lead up to it; what can your partner supply to correct the problem? What do you need to be getting from your partner in order to be *made* to do what you do next? Work it out between you until every moment of the scene grows organically out of the flow of action and reaction.

Note: You do *not* tell your partner what to do, you only tell them what you need from them; you might say something like "I need to be more threatened by that," but you leave it entirely to your partner to determine how best to accomplish this.

This exercise can help you to realize that a difficulty at one point in a scene is often caused by problems earlier in the scene, or even earlier in the play. Don't always try to fix a problem by making an immediate adjustment; trace back and see if you can clear it up by adjusting some earlier action, value, or relationship.

SUMMARY

As nerve-wracking as they are, auditions are a time when you can form an initial approach to a role. For general auditions you should develop a repertoire of three or four prepared audition pieces chosen to demonstrate your abilities to the best advantage, preferably material that you love.

When auditioning for specific roles, your immediate job is to find a productive objective and playable action in the material, and to make the objective important to you. In the audition itself, allow yourself to be in the here and now; make the event live. Make contact with the person you are performing with (even if imaginary) and try to affect them.

Take the long view and remember that the opinion formed of you at an audition may be important at some future time. Think "How can I best show them what kind of actor I am?"

Once cast, you begin your preparation: analysis, beginning to learn the lines, and private rehearsal of special skills must be accomplished outside the rehearsal hall. Remember that homework is a *preparation* for rehearsal, not a *substitute* for it.

At first readings begin at once to search for the action that lives in the transactions between the characters; read *in relationship,* with a spirit of give and take. As soon as possible, put your book aside so that you can explore the action on your feet. Keep the action going while you call for lines in character without apology. This is the time to start using your rehearsal clothing and props regularly.

The breakdown of the scene now begins to emerge. The rightness of each action is determined by the way it fits into the action–reaction chain between characters; this binds you to the other actors, and them to you. Each of you has the right to receive, and the obligation to give, what best serves the common purpose.

Lesson 21

THE REHEARSAL PROCESS II: DEVELOPING THE FORM

Having found much of the content of your performance, you now begin to develop a form that is expressive and reliable. During much of the rehearsal to this point, you and your fellow actors have been exploring the individual connections that form the chain of action and reaction that move the play "under its own power." Now it is time to begin "setting" this sequence of actions and their objectives, which Stanislavski called the *score* of the role. This is the "map" of your performance, which you will follow each time you take the journey.

ESTABLISHING THE SCORE

You come to understand the score partly through analysis, but mostly through trial and error in rehearsal. As the score emerges from the actual experience of action and reaction, stimulus and response between you and your partners, you begin naturally to assimilate it until it becomes part of you, an "inner model" that guides you through the scene.

The score eventually becomes habitual; you absorb it so totally that you can begin to experience the scene fully, moment by moment. This is the point at which your actor's awareness begins to give way more and more to the character's awareness; when the score is completely automatic, then you can give yourself fully to each moment with complete attention to "the here and now," confident in the knowledge that the scene can move toward its proper conclusion. In a way, you must be able to do the scene "in your sleep" in order to be able to do it fully awake.

In *Creating a Role,* Stanislavski describes the operation of the score like this:

> *With time and frequent repetition, in rehearsal and performance, this score becomes habitual. An actor becomes so accustomed to all his objectives and their sequence that he cannot conceive of approaching his role otherwise than along the line of the steps fixed in the score. Habit plays a great part in creativeness: it establishes in a firm way the accomplishments of creativeness. In the familiar words of Volkonski it makes what is difficult habitual, what is habitual easy, and what is easy beautiful. Habit creates second nature, which is second reality. The score automatically stirs the actor to physical action.*[1]

In *Stanislavski Directs,* Gorchakov quotes him as saying:

> *The law of theatrical art decrees: discover the correct conception in the scenic action, in your role, and in the beats of the play; and then make the correct habitual and the habitual beautiful.*[2]

At what point do you commit to a choice and allow a particular element of the score to become habitual? Some actors wait a long time before making their final choices and approach their roles warily in early rehearsals, gradually filling in the full performance. Others work at performance levels right off, though they maintain enough flexibility to avoid making final choices too soon.

You have to determine your own best approach in relation to the disposition of the director, your fellow actors, the nature of the play, and the length of the rehearsal period. To lie back and play the waiting game is usually unfair to your coworkers because they depend upon you for their reactions, but neither should you make final choices too soon, committing yourself to insufficiently tested actions.

As the score emerges, your through-line of action, and the full experience of your superobjective emerges with it, and provides unity and momentum to the performance.

BLOCKING

The patterned use of space in a stage performance is called *blocking.* Good stage blocking is much more than the creation of pleasing spatial arrangements; it must also reflect the nature and relationships of the characters, and most of all the underlying action of the scene. Who is dominant at this moment in the scene? What space do they control?

Who is on their side? Who is on the attack? Who is retreating? When do they counterattack? These are the things that determine good blocking.

Although the sense of spatial relationship is artistically heightened on the stage, it is based on our sense of blocking in everyday life. Remember the Hostess–Guest scene: do you see how the prolonged encounter at the door, the guest's unwillingness to cross the threshold and enter the hostess's territory, expressed the situation? Once inside, the guest refused to surrender his coat as a symbol that he was only a temporary visitor, that he "didn't belong." How would you imagine him moving in that room? How would he sit in a chair? Where would he sit? How would he eat?

Exercise 21.1: Blocking in Life

Spend a few days watching the "blocking" of everyday life. Notice how attitude, relationship, and action are expressed in the way people place themselves in a room and in relationship to each other. Record your observations in your journal.

DEVELOPING THE BLOCKING

Blocking evolves in the course of rehearsal in a variety of ways, depending on the approach of the director. Some directors will preplan the blocking in detail and lay it out for the actors at an early stage of rehearsal (this may be especially necessary in shows with large casts or with highly stylized material). Most directors, however, prefer that the actors provide the basic movement impulses that generate the blocking, with the director then editing the pattern as needed. Some directors do no blocking at all, waiting for the actors to find the spatial patterns that best express the action of the scene as it unfolds during the rehearsal process.

No matter how the director works, it is your ability to experience the way in which your movements are organic to the action of the scene that makes blocking truly alive and expressive. Even without a director's help, you should be able to utilize your stage environment to create spacially logical patterns that express the action of your scene and your relationship to other characters.

Blocking for film and television is an even more critical matter. Here your movements are expressed not in feet but in inches. Once a shot has been established by the director and cameraman, strips of colored tape are placed on the floor to mark the exact position of each actor's feet; if there are movements within the shot, each interim destination is marked in the same way. As you do the scene, you must "hit your marks" exactly, without looking down. It can even matter which foot your weight is on, because the composition of the shot and the focus of the camera may require your head to be in a precise location at a precise time.

The nature of film also requires that your eye movements be "blocked;" that is, you must look in precisely the right place at the right time, because the apparent location of the other character must be exactly the right distance away from the lens. If the "eye line" isn't consistent in the various shots of a scene, it can't be edited together.

Eye movements are also one of the major factors that determine when an edit is made, so you may have to provide "a look" to a precise point at a precise moment in a scene in order to motivate a cut to another character. When the camera is seeing only one character in a scene, the other actors usually stand off camera to provide the correct eye lines.

As difficult as all this sounds, even this kind of critical positioning becomes second nature after a time. As you develop your performance, be it for the camera or for the stage, the blocking emerges and is incorporated as a natural part of your total action. By concentrating on what your character is doing, you naturally make the correct movements to the correct locations without thinking.

JUSTIFYING THE BLOCKING

Blocking is "dead" movement until it is endowed with meaning by the way you motivate it as an expression of your character's action. For example, if the director suggests that you move upstage of the sofa while you say, "I don't want to hear this," that movement may be desirable for spatial or pictorial considerations: the director may, for instance, want you to move there so that focus is thrown to a doorway through which someone is about to enter (this is called "setting up" an entrance).

At first, this movement may feel awkward and unnatural to you, and probably would appear that way to an audience as well. There is a marked difference between the way we move when we are responding to the external commands of another person, and when we are responding to an internal need of our own. The audience unconsciously senses that difference when you move to the sofa; in acting terminology, you have not yet *justified* the cross.

Your task now is to justify the movement as a believable action performed by your character at this particular moment in the scene out of a real need. You might, in this example, find that your character needs to protect themselves from what the other person is saying at this moment, and so goes to "hide" behind the sofa.

By justifying your movement and your spatial relationship to the setting and the other actors in this way, your blocking comes to life as believable movement. You also find that justified blocking is easy to remember; because it has become a natural expression of your character's action at a particular moment, you need only concentrate on what your character is doing and the blocking "happens on its own."

You also find that the *timing* of lines and crosses makes a critical difference in the process of justifying a line or a cross. Deciding whether you should say "I don't want to hear this" before, during, or after the move can change the psychological meaning of the line; it can feel right one way, and quite wrong another.

All these decisions are usually made by trial and error, and that is one of the main functions of rehearsal. As you gain experience, your ability to justify movement or dialogue, or to determine the timing of a move or line, eventually becomes almost intuitive and almost instantaneous. For now, here is an exercise to explore these matters.

Exercise 21.2: A Blocking Scene

Here again is the blocking pattern you learned in Exercise 6.2, Directions on Stage. This time, we are adding dialogue; the blocking appears as stage directions.

Your partner remains at center stage throughout this scene, though they may turn to face you as you move.

You: I've had enough of this. *(Go down right.)*

Partner: I'm really sorry.

You: (Turn out and go up right as you say) That's what you said the last time.

Partner: This time I really mean it.

You: (Stop, turn, and cheat down one-half) I'm not falling for it this time. *(Take a long, slow cross down left, going upstage of partner, as you say)* Every time this happens, I end up taking the blame, but not this time. *(Turn in and do a circle cross up, passing on the downstage side of partner and ending level with them on the right)* This time, you are going to have to take your share of the responsibility! *(Cheat out one-quarter)* And don't look at me like that. *(Turn in one-quarter)* I know you think I'll probably give in eventually. *(Go straight down and hold center and speak to audience)* And you know, I probably will. *(Circle up to the right around partner and stop at left center, turning to them)* But at least not for a while! *(Turn away and exit)*.

Justify these movements by entering into the situation: feel what the relationship might be. Experiment with the timing of crosses and lines: should a particular line come before, during, or after the cross? You may alter my stage directions to find the timing that works best for you.

THE GROUNDPLAN AND SETTING

The shaping of the stage space and the placement of entrances is a decision made with particular care by the director and scenic designer; we call this the creation of the *groundplan*. When directors and designers discuss groundplan and setting, for instance, they often pay special attention to "territoriality": To whom does the space belong? Whose taste does it reflect? Are there areas within it that belong to certain persons? Do the entrances and exits reflect status or relationship (for example, strangers use the front door, whereas family and friends always come in through the kitchen)?

When the groundplan has been correctly established, you find that your character moves within it naturally as the action unfolds; the room itself provides the reason for moving here or there as different needs are felt. For this reason, some directors say that "the groundplan really blocks the show."

Usually, the scenic design has been completed before rehearsals begin, and a picture or model of the set is shown to you early on. As soon as you put the show "up on its feet" the groundplan is usually taped out on the floor of the rehearsal hall and you must visualize the space as it will eventually look in the completed set. You can then rehearse within the groundplan so you are ready to move onto the real set with a minimum of disruption.

Work with your stage manager to select rehearsal props and costumes with care as accurate substitutes for the real things. Take full advantage of costume fittings to get the feel of your clothes, making all the movements your part may require (and to alert the costumer to any problems of motion). Once the set is in place, make it part of your homework to spend some time in it, walking your part or simply getting the feel of the environment.

Although all aspects of the physical set, costumes and props—the period, decor, color, and so on—are usually determined by the director and the various designers, only *you*, the actor, can endow the space with life by justifying every aspect of it. No amount of scenery, costuming, and lighting can compensate for your failure to "live" in the character's world. Remember: an elaborate production can feel like a dead museum tableau, but a skillful actor can create a whole world on an empty stage.

Exercise 21.3: Blocking Your Scene

Together with your partner, decide on what type of stage (full round, thrust, proscenium) you would like to perform the scene you have been preparing. Design a groundplan for the scene and set up your own rehearsal hall, arranging furniture as needed. Rehearse the scene and allow the blocking to emerge, then work to justify the blocking. Perform the scene in class and discuss.

SUMMARY

Having developed the content of your performance, you now develop its form. The basis is the sequence of actions that Stanislavski called the *score* of the role. The score eventually becomes habitual; you must be able to do the scene "in your sleep" in order to be able to do it fully awake. This is also the time that your *superobjective* starts to come into focus.

At what point do you commit to a choice? You have to determine your own best approach; to play the waiting game is unfair to your co-workers because they depend upon you for their reactions, but neither should you make final choices too soon.

The patterned use of space in a stage performance is called "blocking." Good stage blocking must reflect the nature of the characters, the character relationships, and most of all the underlying action of the scene. Most directors prefer the actors to provide the basic movement impulses that generate the blocking, with the director then editing the pattern as needed. Blocking for film and television is a critical matter; once a shot has been established, strips of colored tape are placed on the floor to mark the exact position of each actor's feet; you must "hit your marks" exactly, without looking down. The camera may even require that your eye movements be blocked.

But no matter the situation, it is your ability to experience the way in which your movements are organic to the action of the scene that makes blocking truly alive and expressive. Blocking is "dead" movement until you *justify* it as a believable action performed by your character out of a real need. Justified blocking (and dialogue) is easy to remember because it has become a natural expression of your character's action.

The timing of lines and crosses makes a critical difference in the process of justification. These decisions are best made by trial and error in rehearsal.

The shape of the environment in which the play occurs is the *ground-plan*. When the groundplan has been correctly established, the room itself provides the reason for moving here or there; some directors say that "the groundplan really blocks the show."

The groundplan is taped out on the floor of the rehearsal hall; learn to visualize the space as it will eventually look. Only you can endow the space with life by justifying it; an elaborate production can feel like a dead museum tableau, but a skillful actor can create a whole world on an empty stage.

Lesson **22**

THE REHEARSAL PROCESS III: PREPARING TO OPEN

Your score and the blocking having been more or less established, you move into the final phase of rehearsal in which the performance is given its final form prior to opening. One of the major developments in this final phase is the perfecting of the show's rhythm, which lives in its shape and pace.

SHAPING AND PACING THE PERFORMANCE

When you and your fellow actors established the score, you began to experience how each of your individual actions and objectives contributed to the flow through each beat change, leading to each scene crisis, and each scene moving toward the crisis of the entire play. This *shape* is now to be perfected as you set the temporhythms of the performance. Each beat change, each scene crisis, and the momentum toward the major crisis of the play is brought into sharp focus, and the flow of action that connects these milestones is established and smoothed to provide momentum, a sense of drive, urgency, significance, and rising dramatic tension, which we call good *pace;* by contrast, a performance lacking in pace feels "flat" and fails to compel our attention. Note that "pace" refers to the momentum of the action, regardless of its "tempo," which refers to its speed.

When a performance lacks pace, there is a temptation to speed up or artificially "hype" the action; this is always a mistake. Good pace results only from the natural flow of the action when each transaction of reaction and action between the characters is real and complete.

Rushing or forcing the scene only blurs these connections and harms the pace. Paradoxically, poor pace is usually best corrected by taking the time to reestablish the connections within the scene.

The best source of pace is the underlying conflict of the play itself as it lives in each scene. Whatever form the conflict has been given, it provides momentum by driving the conflicting forces against one another as the need for a resolution grows. If you can experience the conflict in this way, scene by scene, it can provide momentum as part of the intrinsic reality of the play, thus avoiding an artificial heightening of energy by rushing or forcing your action.

The given circumstances may also supply a sense of urgency: there may be an *external deadline* that requires that an objective be achieved as quickly as possible, such as someone about to enter, or the fear of discovery. More commonly there is an *internal deadline,* such as the need to do something before you lose your nerve, to say something before breaking into tears, and so on.

In some cases, because no playwright is always perfect, it may be necessary for the actors and director to invent some external or internal source of momentum for a scene. This might involve redefining the given circumstances to provide urgency. Another strategy is to invent some surface activity, such as sewing, smoking, drinking, eating, or playing cards, that might help you to channel your energy outward and thereby move the scene forward.

On the other hand, it may be that at moments of great tension or emotion, *containment* and *stillness* produce better pace than activity. Remember that activity "spends" energy and that you must invest your stage energy with great discrimination; it is often true that "less is more," *if* it is the right "less."

One important element of good pace is *cueing,* the way in which one character begins to speak after another has finished. In real life, if you and I are discussing something, I listen to you in order to understand the idea you are trying to express. When I have grasped that idea, I form my response and am usually ready to begin answering *before* you have actually finished your sentence. Listen to real-life conversations; do you hear how we actually overlap one another's speeches slightly, or at least are *ready* to respond before the other person has stopped talking? This is good "cueing."

Sometimes pace is harmed by the actors doing "too much," engaging in extraneous business, unnecessary pauses for thought, or emotional displays. Any action, any piece of business, any emotion, or any character trait that impedes the pace of the scene should be discarded. As Stanislavski was fond of saying, "Cut 80 percent!"

Exercise 22.1: Shaping and Pacing the Scene

Examine your scene with your partner; is each beat change and the scene crisis fully realized? Can you feel these as changes in the scene's rhythmic shape?

Look together for those aspects of the situation that provide urgency or a sense of deadline and thereby contribute to the scene's momentum:

1. The physical environment: time, place, and so forth.
2. The social environment: customs, the presence of others.
3. The situation: internal or external factors that create urgency or tension.
4. The conflict between you.

Practice your listening and responding skills to produce good cueing.

After rehearsing your scene to achieve good shape and pace, perform it for your class. Ask them to signal whenever they feel the shape of the action becoming vague, or the pace dropping.

MAKING FINAL ADJUSTMENTS

Having laid the foundation of your score and characterization, having set the basic form of the blocking, and having established good shape and pace, your production is ready to add the final technical elements in the last days of the rehearsal process. During this period you have to make many final *adjustments*.

Of course, you have been making adjustments throughout your rehearsal process, and your ability to make complete adjustments quickly is one of your most fundamental and useful acting skills. An adjustment is any alteration in the form of your performance made to meet some external need, such as a blocking problem, a lighting or scenic concern, the need of a fellow actor for support in a particular moment, and the like. The adjustments you make in this final stage of rehearsal, however, are more demanding because the form being adjusted is more fully set, and the anxiety you feel as opening approaches makes you less flexible.

Although the adjustment is in the external form of your performance, it must be *justified* by being the result of some change in the inner phase of your action. If you alter only the external form of your activity without adjusting the process of thought from which it springs, the results seem forced, unnatural, and incomplete. For instance, if the director yells, "Louder!" you do not merely say the line more loudly: You instantaneously review the process of inner action from which the line springs and adjust something in the perception, attitude, or choice so that the line *must* be said more loudly.

Although almost all adjustments can be made in your inner phase of action, you can also make adjustments by redefining the given circumstances. Because your stimulus is almost always the action of another character, you can even make adjustments by asking your fellow actor to provide you with a stimulus that can move you more readily toward the desired goal.

Exercise 22.2: Justifying Adjustments

Select a section from your scene for this experiment in making adjustments. Justify each of the following adjustments first within some phase of your inner action; experiment also with adjustments in the stimuli you and your partner are giving one another.

1. Explore adjustments that might be demanded by style:
   a. Do the scene as if it were a Classical tragedy;
   b. As if it were a romantic comedy;
   c. As if it were a farce;
   d. As if it were modern realism.
2. Explore adjustments that might be demanded by the theatre space in which you perform:
   a. Do the scene for a huge auditorium;
   b. For an arena stage;
   c. For a film.
3. If possible, work with someone as director, and practice justifying changes in blocking, tempo, volume, etc., as requested by the director.

TECHNICAL AND DRESS REHEARSALS

The final phase of the rehearsal period is devoted to incorporating the physical production elements: makeup, props, costumes, set, lights, and sound. Ideally, this is a time of completion and crystallization of your performance; many actors do not feel that their work comes fully to life until all the physical production elements are in place. Stanislavski spoke of completing a characterization only when, in full makeup and costume, he would rehearse before a mirror to be sure that his external appearance was correct.

In most American theatres, only the final week of rehearsal is devoted to the assimilation of all the completed technical elements. This can be a period of tremendous frustration and distraction for you if you have not prepared yourself for it in the earlier stages of rehearsal.

Above all, avoid the temptation to "freeze" your work during this final phase of rehearsal. Many fine performances wither on the vine before opening because the outer form becomes the focus of the actor's attention and the inner phase of action ceases to live and grow. Use the addition of the technical elements as an opportunity to extend and specify the score of your role, and to explore further the life of the character within a more complete environment.

There are two main ways in which you must be prepared for this final phase: first, to have a solid score—your "energy map" or "sequence of actions"—which helps you to keep your focus on the action without being distracted by all the new technical elements; second, to have used good rehearsal substitutes for props, costumes, and groundplan.

During this period, you probably have less rehearsal time available to you as the energies of the production are taken up with technical matters. It is important that you continue to work on your own to prepare yourself for the coming of the audience. One way to do this is to *visualize* the performance as it will be under audience conditions. Visualization is an excellent form of private rehearsal; it is most effective when used during periods of relaxation when your deep muscles actually participate. Here is an exercise in the technique called Visuo-Motor Behavior Rehearsal, which was first developed for the 1980 Winter Olympics, and used by athletes like Jean-Claude Killy with great effectiveness.

Exercise 22.3: Visuo-Motor Behavior Rehearsal

Using the Phasic Relaxation, put yourself into deep muscle relaxation and mental restful alertness.

Now visualize the following: you are about to open in the play from which your scene comes; the theatre is ready, you hear the buzz of the audience in the house, and you are standing in your costume with your fellow actors ready to take your places.

Go into the set and take your opening positions; feel the stage lights shining on you, smell the makeup, feel your clothing, see your fellow actors and the set.

The scene begins; live through it totally; let your deep muscles respond to the experience; feel the props and all the business.

Tests have shown that this form of rehearsal can be just as effective as ordinary rehearsal, and sometimes more so.

GROWTH AFTER OPENING

The opening of the show is never the completion of your work, but only the start of a new phase of the growth process. The audience contributes in many ways, perhaps most by providing the responses that complete the rhythmic shaping of the work. These responses take many forms, from the overt (such as laughter or sobs) to the covert (such as rapt still-ness or restlessness, or just the "feeling" inside the auditorium). Whatever their form, the audience's responses are an important element in the rhythm of the scene. So far, you have been guessing what those responses may be, and your director has been substituting for them as "an ideal audience of one," but now you have the real thing, and you can fine-tune the shape and flow of your action accordingly. This is the business of "preview" performances, or invited audiences at dress rehearsals, if you are lucky enough to have them.

The audience's presence may also cause a shift in context, a change in the way you experience your own work; there may be many discover-ies for you to make from this altered point of view. Some things you thought would work well may turn out to be too personal or obscure, whereas other things that you hadn't really noticed turn out to be powerful or worth developing further. At last you have a sure basis for judgment.

This sure basis for judgment naturally causes you to begin economiz-ing. You find after a time that you expended more energy during rehears-als than you do in performance, and that you generally expend less and less energy as the run continues. This is not because you begin doing your part mechanically, without thought or feeling, but because you pen-etrate deeper and deeper to its essence; as this happens, unessential detail begins to fall away. Your performance is made more effective by distilling it to its essentials in this way; you are doing more with less.

SUMMARY

This *shape* is now to be perfected as you set the temporhythms of the per-formance. Each beat change, each scene crisis, and the momentum toward the major crisis of the play is brought into sharp focus, and the flow of action that connects these milestones is established and smoothed to provide momentum, a sense of drive, urgency, significance, and rising dramatic tension, which we call good *pace*. One important element of good pace is *cueing,* the way in which one character begins to speak after another has finished.

By now your production is ready to add the final technical elements in the last days of the rehearsal process. During this period you have to make many final adjustments in form to meet external needs. These adjustments must be *justified* by being the result of some change in your inner phase of the action. Technical and dress rehearsals can be a period of tremendous distraction for you if you have not prepared yourself properly with a strong score, and effective use of the rehearsal ground-plan, props, and costume pieces.

The opening of the show is never the completion of your work, but only the start of a new phase of the growth process. At last you have a sure basis for judgment and you can penetrate deeper and deeper to its essence; as this happens, unessential detail begins to fall away. Your performance is made more effective by distilling it to its essentials; you are doing more with less.

Lesson 23

THE ACTOR AT WORK

Underlying all the techniques and principles you have studied so far are your attitudes and values as an actor. These are reflections of the motivations that brought you to acting, your personal beliefs, your relationship to your world, and your hopes for your future as an actor. These values and hopes profoundly affect the way you work, though their influence is often unconscious. If you can develop productive attitudes as the foundation of your working process, you will be able to take charge of your own growth as an actor.

An effective work process depends on three things: good communication skills, a creative attitude, and a clear sense of purpose. We end our study by exploring these fundamental attitudes.

SUPPORTING EACH OTHER

The interactive nature of drama means that your individual creation cannot be separated from the work of all the other actors and the director. Your attitude toward your fellow workers is as important as your attitude toward your own work. Remember this observation by playwright August Strindberg quoted in Part I:

> *No form of art is as dependent as the actor's. He cannot isolate his particular contribution, show it to someone and say, "This is mine." If he does not get the support of his fellow actors, his performance will lack resonance and depth.... He won't make a good impression no matter how hard he tries. Actors must rely on each other.... That is why rapport among actors is imperative for the success of a play. I*

don't care whether you rank yourselves higher or lower than each other,
or from side to side, or from inside out—as long as you do it together.[1]

Your working relationships are most effective when they are based upon three principles: first, mutual commitment to the relationship and to the work itself; second, mutual support for one another's individual objectives and methods; third, free and open communication so that problems can be thrashed out and thereby become opportunities for creative interaction. Let's examine each.

First, you are *committed* to the working relationship because it enables you to do better work as an individual. Friendship results from most of your working relationships; there is a wonderfully warm sense of kinship among theatre people. Often you meet someone for the first time and because of your mutual friends you know at once that you are family. But commitment to the working relationship is not necessarily the same thing as being "friends," and it is possible to work effectively with people you don't particularly like.

Although group membership requires generosity, good humor, and a spirit of reasonable compromise, it should *not* involve either the sacrifice of self-esteem or the surrender of personal standards; the need to be "nice" should never cause you to falsify your values or discipline. Remember: the group doesn't make good work because it is a good group; it becomes a good group because it creates good work.

Second, your *support* for one another's objectives and methods is the basis of respect. You might not share another actor's reasons for doing what they do, nor work the same way, but you respect their motives and their right to work in their own way, just as you expect respect for your motives and methods. If your different ways of working cause a problem (as they sometimes do), negotiate compromises on both sides, which, as much as possible, meet everyone's needs equally.

Finally, the possibility of free and open *communication* is critical. Problems arise in any creative process and they must be worked through and negotiated; only good communication makes that possible. This topic is important enough to be considered separately.

FREE AND OPEN COMMUNICATION

Free and open communication does not mean that we say everything that's on our mind in the name of "honesty"; some things are best left unsaid—as Falstaff says, "discretion is the better part of valor"—but the *possibility* of discussing problems needs to be felt by everyone. Otherwise an atmosphere of repression develops and tensions mount, perhaps to a boiling point.

In addition to the group's need for good communication, you have an individual need for it. We have already discussed how actors depend on feedback more than most other artists; the notes you get from your teachers, directors, and fellow actors are tremendously important in guiding your growth. Actors therefore have a solemn responsibility to provide accurate and useful feedback to one another. The most effective feedback we can give each other is based upon a few basic principles:

Most important, say *what you see* and *how it makes you feel.* Don't say, "Why are you hiding from us," say, "I noticed that you rarely looked at your partner during this scene, and that made me feel as if you were hiding from us. What was going on?" Do you see the difference between these two statements?

In the first statement, you *interpreted* the reason for what you saw, then reported your interpretation as if it were true. If the other person doesn't feel that they were "hiding," they have to reject your input, and they lose an opportunity for improvement. In the second statement you reported your specific observation, then reported the feeling it engendered in you. Both these statements must be true because neither involves interpretation: you saw what you saw, and it made you feel a certain way. Now you can go on to discuss the situation profitably.

Having an effective message to send, consider some effective ways of sending it:

1. Be *clear* about your message before you deliver it.
2. Be *specific, simple,* and *direct;* use examples.
3. Pick an *appropriate time* to communicate.
4. *Check* to see if your message was received accurately.

Here is an exercise to practice these communication skills.

Exercise 23.1: Attractions and Reservations, Agonies and Ecstasies

Join with one of your fellow workers to share impressions of your own and each other's work. Take turns completing the following statements, and in each case say what you saw and how it made you feel; be specific and direct; supply examples.

1. My greatest agony about my own work just now is . . .
2. The greatest reservation I have about your work is . . .
3. The thing I feel best about in my own work is . . .
4. The thing that attracts me most about your work is . . .

Compare your feelings about praise and criticism. Which do you take more seriously? Did you learn equally from each? Are you benefiting from the feedback of others enough? Or are you *too* dependent on them?

Unfortunately, despite the nature of their work, most actors have no better communication skills than butchers or bankers. Here is an exercise to help you to avoid the most common pitfalls in good communication.

Exercise 23.2: Communication Disorders

With your partner, think back over your working experiences. Have either of you suffered from or been guilty of any of the following communication disorders?

1. *Fogging:* Using generalities without referring to specifics. Example: "You need to work on your voice."
2. *Mind-raping:* Assuming you know what someone is thinking without bothering to check. Example: "Why are you hiding from us in this scene?"
3. *Defusing:* Excessive self-criticism that makes it impossible for anyone else to criticize you. Example: "I just couldn't concentrate at all today; I know the scene was terrible, but what did you think?"
4. *Dumping:* Using criticism as an emotional release or as a weapon.
5. *Gunnysacking:* Saving up grievances until an explosion becomes likely.
6. *No trespassing:* When unstated rules exist within a group that certain people or certain issues may not be criticized.
7. *Holier-than-thou:* Criticism of others for the purpose of avoiding criticism of self.
8. *Doomsaying:* Feedback that emphasizes only the negative without acknowledging the positive.

YOU AND YOUR DIRECTOR

The relationship between actor and director deserves special attention. Because the director is the focus of the group's working process, your ability to work effectively together is critical. It helps if you have a clear sense of what each of your functions, rights, and responsibilities are.

The director has three main functions: to guide the development of an overall interpretation for the production, to align the efforts of all the different artists contributing to the production, and to provide feedback during rehearsals by being an ideal audience of one. The interpretive function makes the director a "central intelligence" for the production, establishing its point of view. The director either provides this focus at the outset, or guides the cast in discovering it during rehearsals.

Your performance, like every other element of the production, must be aligned toward this central interpretation. Even if your personal preference might be for a different interpretation or emphasis, once you have accepted the role it is your job to work effectively within the director's production concept.

Perhaps the most destructive attitude is that of the actor who becomes an apologist for their character, arguing from the character's point of view as if every scene "belonged to them." Group interpretation can be ruined by actors who insist upon adopting their character's point of view at the expense of the play as an artistic whole.

On the other hand, we do a great disservice to our director, our fellow actors, and ourselves if, out of our desire to avoid conflict, we fail to express ourselves honestly. An actor who is too pliable is as destructive as one who is too rigid. Your ideas are appreciated if they are presented in a reasoned, timely, and respectful fashion. Although a show has only one director, everyone connected with it must feel responsible for the whole production, and provide any ideas that may be of value.

There are many ways in which the responsibilities of director and actor can overlap and where compromise is necessary. The actor, intimately involved with the life of the character, possesses insights into the life of that character that are denied to the director. At the same time, the director has an objective overview unavailable to the actor. In an effective working relationship, each respects and values the insights of the other and seeks to join their points of view to the best possible advantage.

Even in the best situations there are times when insoluble disagreements occur; when this happens, ties go to the director. The director has assumed public responsibility for the interpretation of the play, whereas you have assumed public responsibility only for the portrayal of your character within the context established by that interpretation. Once the director's interpretation has been clarified, it is your responsibility to find the best possible means of implementing it; if this proves to be impossible, the relationship must be severed for the sake of the play. Unless you have become a major star, this means that you get fired.

Besides interpretation, another important function of the director is to establish a common approach in the conduct of rehearsals. Each director has a characteristic way of working, and it is easier for the actors to adapt to the director's method than for the director to adopt an individual approach to each of the actors. It is therefore part of your job to adapt, as much as is reasonable, to the director's approach, and to help the director develop the most effective channel of communication with you.

To sum up, you and your director are coworkers, not master and slave. Though you share many responsibilities, you have essentially different functions that are interdependent and equal. The director's first responsibility is to the overall patterning of the play as a theatrical experience; your responsibility is to bring your role to life so as to best contribute to that pattern. Therefore, it is ultimately the director's function to evaluate *what* the actor does, and the actor's job is to find *how* best to do it.

THE FEAR OF FAILURE

The fundamental drive for most actors, like most people, is the desire for success and its flip side, the fear of failure. Everyone has both, of course, though one may be said to be dominant over the other in many individuals. Each is a powerful source of energy, but the differences between them are important.

At the 1984 Olympics in Los Angeles, the champion athletes were tested to see which were driven primarily by a desire for success, and which were motivated primarily by the fear of failure; it was found that over 70 percent were driven by the desire for success, whereas less than 30 percent were motivated by the fear of failure. Although the study was not specific about the differences between these two groups of athletes, I would suspect that those motivated by fear of failure tended to be technically precise but cautious, whereas the larger group would include more "inspired" athletes who were greater risk-takers. The fear of failure encourages safe and conservative choices, but the desire for success can generate energetic though sometimes risky choices.

No one has ever tested a group of actors in this way, but I suspect that a larger proportion of actors would be found to be driven by the fear of failure. There are many unsuccessful or marginal actors, perhaps 80 percent, who hang on in the business for year after undistinguished year, whose work is competent but uninspired, who deliver reliable but cautious performances, and who simply don't "go for it." Their motto seems to be "nothing ventured, nothing lost."

The fear of failure encourages the attitude that "I must do it exactly right," producing, at best, technical skill, precision, and consistency. These are qualities which, in athletics, are rewarded for their own sake, but when you reach the top levels of competition the absence of creative inspiration is damaging; you can't win on technical points alone, you have to have the style points as well. In acting, the situation is even clearer: technical skill, although valued, never entirely compensates for a lack of creativity. For the actor, technical skill is only the means toward the expression of an artistic vision.

An excessive fear of failure can cause you to censor creative impulses, fearing that "I'll look foolish." When you censor an impulse, you must literally "hold it in," and this causes muscular tension. It is no accident that we tell overly cautious people to "loosen up."

Finally, and most important, the fear of failure may cause you to continually judge your own performance to see if you are "doing it right," and this judgmental attitude encourages self-consciousness. As George C. Scott once observed in an interview:

> *I think you have to be schizoid three different ways to be an actor. You've got to be three different people: you have to be a human being, then you have to be the character you're playing, and on top of that, you've got to be the guy sitting out there in row 10, watching yourself and judging yourself. That's why most of us are crazy to start with or go nuts once we get into it. I mean, don't you think it's a pretty spooky way to earn a living?*[2]

Exercise 23.3: The Fear of Failure

Think back to your most recent work in an audition, rehearsal, or performance: do you remember censoring yourself? Were you sending yourself messages like, "This isn't going to work," or "This might make me look stupid." What physical tensions resulted from "holding in" your impulses?

Next time you work, notice these moments of self-censorship as they occur: simply release the tension, take a breath, and get back to work.

THE DESIRE FOR SUCCESS

A working actor needs the drive, courage, and long-term tenacity that a strong desire for success can provide. Each of us must define success for ourselves: what constitutes true success for you?

There are really two ways of measuring success: in purely internal terms, such as pride, sense of accomplishment, and feelings of growth; and by external measurements such as reviews, grades, and the response of the audience. Obviously, all actors are, and should be, concerned with both. What we need is perspective and balance between the two.

Most actors err on the side of emphasizing external measures of success over internal. Even if they have a sense of their own worth, they usually don't trust it, and they feel so dependent on the opinions of others that a negative response from anyone damages their self-esteem.

Of course, it hurts any actor when their work is not received well. But the serious actor strives to balance the healthy desire for immediate success with the equally important long-range demands of artistic development. You should approach each new role, each rehearsal, and each performance, with a desire not only to please others but also a desire to *learn and grow* for yourself. When evaluating the experience, you must not only ask "Did I do the job well," but also "Am I now a better actor for having done it?"

Winning parts, applause, and good reviews, as important as these things are, is not enough. I know some actors, especially in film and television, who are wildly successful in commercial terms but who derive little personal satisfaction from their careers. The "business" demands that they use the same skills, play the same sort of character in the same type of material, role after role; no matter how highly developed these skills may become, they can bring only limited artistic satisfaction.

Serious actors insist on continuing to develop and extend their abilities with disciplined regularity throughout their lifetime. There is no real substitute for meeting the day-to-day demands of rehearsal and performance; this is why the actor in a repertory company, preparing a continual variety of roles, may develop much faster than the actor who works in long runs, or repeatedly plays the same kinds of roles.

Most difficult is the situation of film–TV actors who, unless they are among the 6 percent who work regularly, work only a few weeks out of every year. Classes, workshops, and little theatre roles are the only chance such actors have to maintain and extend their skills. In the waiting room at a TV audition I heard one actor tell the others this joke:

> *Three actors were complaining about being out of work. "Heck," said the first actor, "I haven't had a part for four months." "That's nothing," said the second actor, "I haven't even had a decent audition for a year!" "I've got you both beat," the third actor said, "I haven't had a part for six years. It's gotten so bad, I'm thinking of leaving the business."*

Exercise 23.4: Measuring Success

Think back to your most recent performance; did you have your own independent evaluation of it? Did you trust that evaluation? How did the comments of others affect you? Did you distinguish between the short-term measurement of your success in the role, and the long-term benefits of the work to you as a developing artist?

YOUR SENSE OF PURPOSE

We use the word "professional" to describe a high level of skill, reliability, and commitment in many fields, but it means something special among actors. When actors want to pay someone a real compliment, they say they're "a real pro." But what is it that defines a professional?

In athletics, we distinguish between professional and amateur on the basis of money: the professional is paid, whereas the amateur (from the root *amat,* "to love") participates only for the love of the sport itself. But in acting, "professional" seems to mean much more than the fact that someone receives money; the term carries an implication of integrity, reliability, high standards, and most of all *commitment.*

The root of the word comes from an old French verb, *profes,* which meant "to make a solemn vow," as in joining a religious order. In our culture, professionals have special knowledge or skills that give them power over other people: doctors, lawyers, clergymen, and others of the "professional class" are responsible for the well-being of their clients. Society has placed a special trust in them, and in return they are expected to use their special powers only for the benefit of those they serve. Thus a professional is *someone who has taken a solemn vow (professed) an ethical standard.* They have accepted personal responsibility for work that affects the lives of others.

As an actor, you have special power over others. We don't usually take acting as seriously as that, but it is true. With this power comes a public responsibility for the well-being of those whose lives you affect, and this demands an enormous commitment.

This commitment operates on three levels simultaneously: first, you must be committed to *your own development as an artist.* Without this commitment to yourself, you cannot offer to others all of which you are capable.

Second, you must be committed to *your work;* If you are merely using your work to advance yourself, you obscure its value to others.

Third, you must be committed *to the world you serve through your work.* Acceptance of this social responsibility gives you a sense of purpose to something greater than yourself, and this can lead you to extraordinary accomplishments. As the director Eugenio Barba said in a letter to one of his actors:

Whatever hidden, personal motives led you to the theatre, now that you have entered that profession you must find there a sense which goes beyond your proper person and fixes you socially in the sight of others.... If the fact of being an actor means all that to you, then a new theatre will be born.[3]

The philosopher Descartes said that reading good books was like conversing with the greatest minds of history, minds that had distilled their experience and wisdom in their art. We who perform good plays go a step further: we actively participate in the experience of peoples, places, and times that have been shaped and condensed by the artistic consciousness of great playwrights. Theatre is the most human of all the arts, and we can preserve and expand our humanity through our art in ways denied us by everyday life. As the American playwright David Mamet says,

What can be preserved? What can be communicated from one generation to the next?

Philosophy. Morality. Aesthetics.

These can be expressed in technique, in those skills which enable the artist to respond truthfully, fully, lovingly to whatever he or she wishes to express.

This is what can and must be passed from one generation to the next. Technique—a knowledge of how to translate inchoate desire into clean action—into action capable of communicating itself to the audience.

This technique, this care, this love of precision, of cleanliness, this love of the theatre, is the best way, for it is love of the audience—of *that which* unites *the actor and the house; a desire to share something which they know to be true.[4]*

The desire of which Mamet speaks, this *need to express the truth within the techniques of art,* is not merely personal. It involves a sense of service to something greater than ourselves, and as such it is the deepest and most lasting motivation of the actor. As he says,

Our workers in the theatre—actors, writers, directors, teachers—are drawn to it not out of intellectual predilection, but from necessity. *We are driven into the theatre by our need to express—our need to answer the question of our lives—the questions of the time in which we live. Of this moment.[5]*

This need "to answer the question of our lives" demands both the highest artistry and the deepest humanity. Again, Mamet:

Who is going to speak up? Who is going to speak for the American spirit? For the human spirit?
    Who is capable of being heard? Of being accepted? Of being believed? Only that person who speaks without ulterior motives, without hope of gain, without even the desire to change, with only the desire to create: The artist. The actor. The strong, trained actor dedicated to the idea that the theatre is the place we go to hear the truth, and equipped with the technical capacity to speak simply and clearly.[6]

This sentiment, expressed recently by one of our leading playwrights, harkens back to the original impulses of the founders of our modern school of acting when, more than eighty years ago, Stanislavski and Nemirovich-Danchenko debated the requirements for actors to be taken into the company of the Moscow Art Theatre:

"Take actor A," we would test each other. "Do you consider him talented?"
    "To a high degree."
    "Will you take him into the troupe?"
    "No."
    "Why?"
    "Because he has adapted himself to his career, his talents to the demands of the public, his character to the caprices of the manager, and all of himself to theatrical cheapness. A man who is so poisoned cannot be cured."
    "And what do you say about Actress B?"
    "She is a good actress, but not for us."
    "Why?"
    "She does not love art, but herself in art."
    "And actress C?"
    "She won't do. She is incurably given to hokum."
    "What about actor D?"
    "We should bear him in mind."
    "Why?"
    "He has ideals for which he is fighting. He is not at peace with present conditions. He is a man of ideas."
    "I am of the same opinion. With your permission I shall enter his name in the list of candidates."[7]

It is important, then, for you to consider how you may serve through acting. Traditionally, artists have announced their specific commitment through the publication of a *manifesto;* this was their way of taking the same kind of public vow that lawyers and doctors take when they are licensed. A manifesto is a brief, passionate, and personal statement of belief and purpose. It requires considerable thought, and should be as simple and direct as possible.

Exercise 23.5: Your Manifesto

Write your own manifesto for the art of acting. Make yours just two paragraphs long:

1. What you want to do for the world through your acting: how do you want to make a difference?
2. What techniques and process are necessary to achieve your purpose? What skills and capabilities must *you* develop to empower yourself to achieve your purpose?

When you are satisfied with it, publish it in some public forum; read it in class, or put it up on the wall.

Afterword

TRANSFORMATION

Your sense of purpose grows from your respect for your own talent, your love for the specific material you are performing, and your desire to use both to serve your audience. It is this drive to be *at service* through your art that finally overcomes the self-consciousness of your ego and carries you beyond yourself, giving you a transcendent purpose from which comes dignity, fulfillment, and ongoing artistic vitality.

Stanislavsky called this ongoing artistic vitality "theatrical youthfulness." Near the end of his life he addressed a group of young actors who were entering the Moscow Art Theatre with these words:

> *The first essential to retain a youthful performance is to keep the idea of the play alive. That is why the dramatist wrote it and that is why you decided to produce it. One should not be on the stage, one should not put on a play for the sake of acting or producing only. Yes, you must be excited about your profession. You must love it devotedly and passionately, but not for itself, not for its laurels, not for the pleasure and delight it brings to you as artists. You must love your chosen profession because it gives you the opportunity to communicate ideas that are important and necessary to your audience. Because it gives you the opportunity, through the ideas that you dramatize on the stage and through your characterizations, to educate your audience and to make them better, finer, wiser, and more useful members of society....*
>
> *You must keep the idea alive and be inspired by it at each performance. This is the only way to retain youthfulness in performance and your own youthfulness as actors. The true recreation of the play's idea—I emphasize the word true—demands from the artist wide and varied knowledge, constant self-discipline, the subordination of his*

personal tastes and habits to the demands of the idea, and sometimes even definite sacrifices.[1]

The art of acting has always had a very special service to render, one that has become increasingly important today: it is rooted in the actor's ability to transform, to become "someone else." At a time when mass culture, big business, and bigger government make us, as individuals, feel more and more insignificant and impotent, the actor's ability to be "in charge" of personal reality can be a source of hope and inspiration to others.

The actor's ability to undergo transformation is itself a kind of potency, a kind of power over the future. Although a play may teach us something about who we are, it is the actor's ability to be transformed that teaches us something about whom we may *become*. The actor's ability to redefine personal reality before our very eyes reminds us of our own spiritual capacity for self-definition, and thus the theatre becomes a celebration of our vitality and of the ongoing flow of life.

Sensing the capacity of the theatre to help enrich our spiritual lives at a time when we have a great need of spiritual revivification, we have begun to explore more than ever the full richness of the experience that may pass between actor and spectator, and the way in which the theatrical moment can affect our lives long after the curtain has fallen.

The actor's horizons are thus being continually broadened, and the art of acting has begun to encompass not only an expanding range of performance techniques and possibilities, but a renewed sense of ethical and spiritual purpose as well. It is a wonderful time to be an actor.

Appendix A

SAMPLE SCENES

FROM *DEATH OF A SALESMAN* BY ARTHUR MILLER[1]

[Howard Wagner, thirty-six . . . is intent on threading the (recording) machine and only glances over his shoulder as Willy appears]

Willy: Pst! Pst!

Howard: Hello, Willy, come in.

Willy: Like to have a little talk with you, Howard.

Howard: Sorry to keep you waiting. I'll be with you in a minute.

Willy: What's that, Howard?

Howard: Didn't you ever see one of these? Wire recorder.

Willy: Oh. Can we talk a minute?

Howard: Records things. Just got delivery yesterday. Been driving me crazy, the most terrific machine I ever saw in my life. I was up all night with it.

Willy: What do you do with it?

Howard: I bought it for dictation, but you can do anything with it. Listen to this. I had it home last night. Listen to what I picked up. The first one is my daughter. Get this. *[He flicks the switch and "Roll out the Barrel!" is heard being whistled]* Listen to that kid whistle.

Willy: Ts, ts. Like to ask a little favor of you . . .

[The whistling breaks off, and the voice of Howard's daughter is heard]

His Daughter: "Now you, Daddy."

Howard: She's crazy for me! *[Again the same song is whistled]* That's me! Ha! *[He winks]*

Willy: You're very good!

[The whistling breaks off again. The machine runs silent for a moment]

Howard: Sh! Get this now, this is my son.

His Son: "The capital of Alabama is Montgomery; the capital of Arizona is Phoenix; the capital of Arkansas is Little Rock; the capital of California is Sacramento..." *[and on, and on]*

Howard [Holding up five fingers]: Five years old, Willy!

Willy: He'll make an announcer some day!

His Son [Continuing]: "The capital..."

Howard: Get that—alphabetical order! *[The machine breaks off suddenly]* Wait a minute. The maid kicked the plug out.

Willy: It certainly is a—

Howard: Sh, for God's sake!

His Son: "It's nine o'clock, Bulova watch time. So I have to go to sleep."

Willy: That really is—

Howard: Wait a minute! The next is my wife. *[They wait]*

Howard's Voice: "Go on, say something." *[Pause]* "Well, you gonna talk?"

His Wife [shyly, beaten]: "Hello." *[Silence]* "Oh, Howard, I can't talk into this..."

Howard [snapping the machine off]: That was my wife.

Willy: That is a wonderful machine. Can we—

Howard: I tell you, Willy, I'm gonna take my camera, and my bandsaw, and all my hobbies, and out they go. This is the most fascinating relaxation I ever found.

Willy: I think I'll get one myself.

Howard: Sure, they're only a hundred and a half. You can't do without it. Supposing you wanna hear Jack Benny, see? But you can't be at home at that hour. So you tell the maid to turn the radio on when Jack Benny comes on, and this automatically goes on with the radio...

Willy: And when you come home you...

Howard: You can come home twelve o'clock, one o'clock, any time you like, and you get yourself a Coke and sit yourself down, throw the switch, and there's Jack Benny's program in the middle of the night!

Willy: I'm definitely going to get one. Because lots of time I'm on the road, and I think to myself, what I must be missing on the radio!

Howard: Don't you have a radio in the car?

Willy: Well, yeah, but who ever thinks of turning it on?

Howard: Say, aren't you supposed to be in Boston?

Willy: That's what I want to talk to you about, Howard. You got a minute? [*He draws a chair in from the wing*]

Howard: What happened? What're you doing here?

Willy: Well...

Howard: You didn't crack up again, did you?

Willy: Oh, no. No...

Howard: Geez, you had me worried there for a minute. What's the trouble?

Willy: Well, tell you the truth, Howard. I've come to the decision that I'd rather not travel any more.

Howard: Not travel! Well, what'll you do?

Willy: Remember, Christmas time, when you had the party here? You said you'd try to think of some spot for me here in town.

Howard: With us?

Willy: Well, sure.

Howard: Oh, yeah, yeah. I remember. Well, I couldn't think of anything for you, Willy.

Willy: I tell ya, Howard. The kids are all grown up, y'know. I don't need much any more. If I could take home—well, sixty-five dollars a week, I could swing it.

Howard: Yeah, but Willy, see I—

Willy: I tell ya why, Howard. Speaking frankly and between the two of us, y'know—I'm just a little tired.

Howard: Oh, I could understand that, Willy. But you're a road man, Willy, and we do a road business. We've only got a half-dozen salesmen on the floor here.

Willy: God knows, Howard, I never asked a favor of any man. But I was with the firm when your father used to carry you in here in his arms.

Howard: I know that, Willy, but—

Willy: Your father came to me the day you were born and asked me what I thought of the name Howard, may he rest in peace.

Howard: I appreciate that, Willy, but there just is no spot here for you. If I had a spot I'd slam you right in, but I just don't have a single solitary spot.

[*He looks for his lighter. Willy has picked it up and gives it to him. Pause*]

Willy [*with increasing anger*]: Howard, all I need to set my table is fifty dollars a week.

Howard: But where am I going to put you, kid?

Willy: Look, it isn't a question of whether I can sell merchandise, is it?

Howard: No, but it's a business, kid, and everybody's gotta pull his own weight.

Willy [*Desperately*]: Just let me tell you a story, Howard—

Howard: 'Cause you gotta admit, business is business.

Willy [*Angrily*]: Business is definitely business, but just listen for a minute. You don't understand this. When I was a boy—eighteen, nineteen—I was already on the road. And there was a question in my mind as to whether selling had a future for me. Because in those days I had a yearning to go to Alaska. See, there were three gold strikes in one month in Alaska, and I felt like going out. Just for the ride you might say.

Howard [*Barely interested*]: Don't say.

Willy: Oh, yeah, my father lived many years in Alaska. He was an adventurous man. We've got quite a little streak of self-reliance in our family. I thought I'd go out with my older brother and try to locate him, and maybe settle in the North with the old man. And I was almost decided to go, when I met a salesman in the Parker House. His name was Dave Singleman. And he was eighty-four years old, and he'd drummed merchandise in thirty-one states. And old Dave, he'd go up to his room, y'understand, put on his green velvet slippers—I'll never forget—and pick up his phone and call the buyers, and without ever leaving his room, at the age of eighty-four, he made his living. And when I saw that, I realized that selling was the greatest career a man could want. 'Cause what could be more satisfying than to be able to go, at the age of eighty-four, into twenty or thirty different cities, and pick up a phone, and be remembered and loved and helped by so many different people? Do you know? when he died—and by the way he died the death of a salesman, in his green velvet slippers in the smoker of the New York, New Haven and Hartford, going into Boston—when he died, hundreds of salesmen and buyers were at his funeral. Things were sad on a lotta trains for months after that. [*He stands up. Howard has not looked at him*] In those days there was personality in it, Howard. There was respect, and comradeship, and gratitude in it. Today, it's all cut and dried, and there's no chance for bringing friendship to bear—or personality. You see what I mean? They don't know me anymore.

Howard [*Moving away, to the right*]: That's just the thing, Willy.

Willy: If I had forty dollars a week—that's all I'd need. Forty dollars, Howard.

Howard: Kid, I can't take blood from a stone, I—

Willy [*Desperation is on him now*]: Howard, the year Al Smith was nominated, your father came to me and—

Howard [*Starting to go off*]: I've got to see some people, kid.

Willy [*Stopping him*]: I'm talking about your father! There were promises made across this desk! You mustn't tell me you've got people to see—I put thirty-four years into this firm, Howard, and now I can't pay my insurance! You can't eat the orange and throw the peel away—a man is not a piece of fruit! [*After a pause*]: Now pay attention. Your father—in 1928 I had a big year. I averaged a hundred and seventy dollars a week in commissions.

Howard [*Impatiently*]: Now, Willy, you never averaged—

Willy: [*Banging his hand on the desk*]: I averaged a hundred and seventy dollars a week in the year of 1928! And your father came to me—or rather, I was in the office here—it was right over this desk—and he put his hand on my shoulder—

Howard: [*Getting up*]: You'll have to excuse me, Willy, I gotta see some people. Pull yourself together. [*Going out*]: I'll be back in a little while.

[On Howard's exit, the light on his chair grows very bright and strange]

Willy: Pull myself together! What the hell did I say to him? My God, I was yelling at him! How could I! *[Willy breaks off, staring at the light, which occupies the chair, animating it. He approaches this chair, standing across the desk from it]* Frank, Frank, don't you remember what you told me that time? How you put your hand on my shoulder, and Frank... *[He leans on the desk and as he speaks the dead man's name he accidentally switches on the recorder, and instantly]*

Howard's Son: "...of New York is Albany. The capital of Ohio is Cincinnati, the capital of Rhode Island is..." *[The recitation continues]*

Willy: *[Leaping away with fright, shouting]*: Ha! Howard! Howard! Howard!

Howard: *[Rushing in]*: What happened?

Willy: *[Pointing at the machine, which continues nasally, childishly, with the capital cities]*: Shut it off! Shut it off!

Howard: *[Pulling the plug out]*: Look, Willy...

Willy *[Pressing his hands to his eyes]*: I gotta get myself some coffee. I'll get some coffee...

[Willy starts to walk out. Howard stops him]

Howard: *[Rolling up the chord]*: Willy, look...

Willy: I'll go to Boston.

Howard: Willy, you can't go to Boston for us.

Willy: Why can't I go?

Howard: I don't want you to represent us. I've been meaning to tell you for a long time now.

Willy: Howard, are you firing me?

Howard: I think you need a good long rest, Willy.

Willy: Howard—

Howard: And when you feel better, come back, and we'll see if we can work something out.

Willy: But I gotta earn some money, Howard. I'm in no position to—

Howard: Where are your sons? Why don't your sons give you a hand?

Willy: They're working on a very big deal.

Howard: This is no time for false pride, Willy. You go to your sons and you tell them that you're tired. You've got two great boys, haven't you?

Willy: Oh, no question, no question, but in the meantime . . .

Howard: Then that's that, heh?

Willy: All right, I'll go to Boston tomorrow.

Howard: No, no.

Willy: I can't throw myself on my sons. I'm not a cripple!

Howard: Look, kid, I'm busy this morning.

Willy: [*Grasping Howard's arm*]: Howard, you've got to let me go to Boston!

Howard: [*Hard, keeping himself under control*]: I've got a line of people to see this morning. Sit down, take five minutes, and pull yourself together, and then go home, will ya? I need the office, Willy. [*He starts to go, turns, remembering the recorder, starts to push off the table holding the recorder*] Oh, yeah. Whenever you can this week, stop by and drop off the samples. You'll feel better, Willy, and then come back and we'll talk. Pull yourself together, kid, there's people outside.

FROM *THE GLASS MENAGERIE* BY TENNESSEE WILLAMS[2]

[*Laura is seated in the delicate ivory chair at the small claw-foot table. . . . She is washing and polishing her collection of glass. Amanda appears on the fire-escape steps. . . . Before entering she looks through the door. She purses her lips, opens her eyes very wide, rolls them upward and shakes her head. Then she slowly lets herself in the door. Seeing her mother's expression Laura touches her lips with a nervous gesture*]

Laura: Hello, Mother, I was— [*She makes a nervous gesture toward the chart on the wall. Amanda leans against the shut door and stares at Laura with a martyred look*]

Amanda: Deception? Deception? [*She slowly removes her hat and gloves, continuing the sweet suffering stare. She lets the hat and gloves fall on the floor —a bit of acting*]

Laura [*Shakily*]: How was the D.A.R. meeting? [*Amanda slowly opens her purse and removes a dainty white handkerchief which she shakes out delicately and delicately touches to her lips and nostrils*] Didn't you go to the D.A.R. meeting, Mother?

Amanda [*Faintly, almost inaudibly*]: —No.—No. [*then more forcibly*] I did not have the strength—to go to the D.A.R. In fact, I did not have the courage! I wanted to find a hole in the ground and hide myself in it forever! [*She crosses slowly to the wall and removes the diagram of the typewriter keyboard. She holds it in front of her for a second, staring at it sweetly and sorrowfully—then bites her lips and tears it in two pieces*]

Laura [*Faintly*]: Why did you do that, Mother? [*Amanda repeats the same procedure with the chart of the Gregg Alphabet*] Why are you—

Amanda: Why? Why? How old are you, Laura?

Laura: Mother, you know my age.

Amanda: I thought that you were an adult; it seems that I was mistaken. [*She crosses slowly to the sofa and sinks down and stares at Laura*]

Laura: Please don't stare at me, Mother.

[*Amanda closes her eyes and lowers her head. Count ten*]

Amanda: What are we going to do, what is going to become of us, what is the future? [*Count ten*]

Laura: Has something happened, Mother? [*Amanda draws a long breath and takes out the handkerchief again. Dabbing process*] Mother, has—something happened?

Amanda: I'll be all right in a minute, I'm just bewildered— [*Count five*] —by life....

Laura: Mother, I wish that you would tell me what's happened!

Amanda: As you know, I was supposed to be inducted into my office at the D.A.R. this afternoon. [*Screen image: A swarm of typewriters*] But I stopped off at Rubicam's Business College to speak to your teachers about your having a cold and ask them what progress they thought you were making down there.

Laura: Oh...

Amanda: I went to the typing instructor and introduced myself as your mother. She didn't know who you were. "Wingfield," she said. "We don't have any such student enrolled at the school!"

I assured her she did, that you had been going to classes since early in January. "I wonder," she said, "if you could be talking about that terribly shy little girl who dropped out of school after only a few days' attendance?"

"No," I said, "Laura, my daughter, has been going to school every day for the past six weeks!"

"Excuse me," she said. She took the attendance book out and there was your name, unmistakably printed, and all the dates you were absent until they decided that you had dropped out of school.

I still said, "No, there must have been some mistake! There must have been some mix-up in the records!"

And she said, "No—I remember her perfectly now. Her hands shook so that she couldn't hit the right keys! The first time we gave a speed-test, she broke down completely—was sick at the stomach and almost had to be carried into the wash-room! After that morning she never showed up any more. We phoned the house but never got any answer"—While I was working at Famous and Barr, I suppose, demonstrating those— [*She indicates a brassiere with her hands*] Oh!

I felt so weak I could barely keep on my feet! I had to sit down while they got me a glass of water!

Fifty dollars' tuition, all of our plans—my hopes and ambitions for you—just gone up the spout, just gone up the spout like that. [*Laura draws a long breath and gets awkwardly to her feet. She crosses to the Victrola and winds it up*] What are you doing?

Laura: Oh! [*She releases the handle and returns to her seat*]

Amanda: Laura where have you been going when you've gone out pretending that you were going to business college?

Laura: I've just been going out walking.

Amanda: That's not true.

Laura: It is. I just went walking.

Amanda: Walking? Walking? In winter? Deliberately courting pneumonia in that light coat? Where did you walk to, Laura?

Laura: All sorts of places—mostly in the park.

Amanda: Even after you'd started catching that cold?

Laura: It was the lesser of two evils, Mother. [*Screen image: Winter scene in a park*] I couldn't go back there. I—threw up—on the floor!

Amanda: From half past seven till after five every day you mean to tell me you walked around in the park, because you wanted to make me think that you were still going to Rubicam's Business College?

Laura: It wasn't as bad as it sounds. I went inside places to get warmed up.

Amanda: Inside where?

Laura: I went in the art museum and the birdhouses at the Zoo. I visited the penguins every day! Sometimes I did without lunch and went to the movies. Lately I've been spending most of my afternoons in the Jewel-box, that big glass house where they raise the tropical flowers.

Amanda: You did all this to deceive me, just for deception? [*Laura looks down*] Why?

Laura: Mother, when you're disappointed, you get that awful suffering look on your face, like the picture of Jesus' mother in the museum!

Amanda: Hush!

Laura: I couldn't face it.

[*Pause. A whisper of strings*]

[*Screen legend: "The Crust of Humility"*]

Amanda [*Hopelessly fingering the huge pocketbook*]: So what are we going to do the rest of our lives? Stay home and watch the parades go by? Amuse ourselves with the glass menagerie, darling? Eternally play those worn-out phonograph records your father left as a painful reminder of him?

We won't have a business career—we've given that up because it gave us nervous indigestion! [*She laughs wearily*] What is there left but dependency all our lives? I know so well what becomes of unmarried women who aren't prepared to occupy a position. I've seen such pitiful cases in the South—barely tolerated spinsters living upon the grudging patronage of sister's husband or a brother's wife!—stuck away in some little mousetrap of a room—encouraged by one in-law to visit another—little birdlike women without any nest—eating the crust of humility all their life!

Is that the future that we've mapped out for ourselves?

I swear it's the only alternative I can think of!

It isn't a very pleasant alternative, is it?

Of course—some girls *do marry.*

[*Laura twists her hands nervously*]

Haven't you ever liked some boy?

Laura: Yes. I liked one once. [*Rises*] I came across his picture a while ago.

Amanda [*With some interest*]: He gave you his picture?

Laura: No, it's in the year-book.

Amanda [*disappointed*]: Oh—a high-school boy.

[*Screen image: Jim as the high school hero bearing a silver cup*]

Laura: Yes. His name was Jim. [*Laura lifts the heavy annual from the claw-foot table*] Here he is in *The Pirates of Penzance.*

Amanda [*Absently*]: The what?

Laura: The operetta the senior class put on. He had a wonderful voice and we sat across the aisle from each other Mondays, Wednesdays and Fridays in the Aud. Here he is with the silver cup for debating! See his grin?

Amanda [*Absently*]: He must have had a jolly disposition.

Laura: He used to call me—Blue Roses.

[*Screen image: Blue roses*]

Amanda: Why did he call you such a name as that?

Laura: When I had that attack of pleurosis—he asked me what was the matter when I came back. I said pleurosis—he thought that I said Blue Roses! So that's what he always called me after that. Whenever he saw me, he'd holler, "Hello, Blue Roses!" I didn't care for the girl that he went out with. Emily Meisenbach. Emily was the best-dressed girl at Soldan. She never struck me, though, as being sincere...It says in the Personal Section—they're engaged. That's six years ago! They must be married by now.

Amanda: Girls that aren't cut out for business careers usually wind up married to some nice man. [*Gets up with a spark of revival*] Sister, that's what you'll do!

[*Laura utters a startled, doubtful laugh. She reaches quickly for a piece of glass*]

Laura: But, Mother—

Amanda: Yes? [*Crossing to photograph*]

Laura [*In a tone of frightened apology*]: I'm—crippled!

Amanda: Nonsense! Laura, I've told you never, never to use that word. Why, you're not crippled, you just have a little defect—hardly noticeable, even! When people have some slight disadvantage like that, they cultivate other things to make up for it—develop charm—and vivacity—and—*charm!* That's all you have to do! [*She turns again to the photograph*] One thing your father had *plenty of*—was *charm!*

[*The scene fades out with music*]

Appendix **B**

AN ACTION CHECKLIST

Here is a checklist that summarizes the material on action we covered in Part Two. These are the questions you should ask yourself in the earliest phases of your rehearsal process.

I. **The Givens: What, Who, Where, When:**

    A. *What* happens in this scene?

        1. What is the *main event* of the scene? How does it move the plot of the play forward? How does it contribute to the play's meaning?

        2. What *changes* in the world of the play as a result of this scene?

    B. *Who* is in this scene?

        1. What is the *general* relationship?
        2. What is the *specific* relationship?
        3. Does your relationship *change* in this scene?
        4. What is discovered about your character in this scene?

    C. *Where* is this scene?

        1. How does the *physical* environment influence what happens?
        2. How does the *social* environment influence what happens?

    D. *When* is this scene?

        1. How does the *historical* time influence the scene?
        2. How does the *season of the year* influence the scene?
        3. How does the *time of day* influence the scene?

II. Scene Structure

A. What is the *main conflict* of this scene? How does it relate to the overall conflict of the play?

B. What is the *breakdown* of the scene, beat by beat? Be specific about each beat change.

C. What is the *crisis,* the moment after which the conflict must be resolved?

D. How does this scene grow out of preceding scenes? How does this scene lead into following scenes?

III. Objectives

A. What is your *superobjective*?

B. What is your *scene* objective? How does it relate to your superobjective?

C. Break down your *beat objectives* in sequence. Do you begin to feel the logic of their sequence or *through-line*?

D. Examine the sequence of your *immediate* objectives through the scene. Express each in a transitive verb as "SIP" (singular, immediate, and personally important); try to think of each as a desired change in the other character.

BIBLIOGRAPHY

Aristotle. *The Poetics,* trans. Kenneth A. Telford. Chicago: Gateway, 1961.

Artaud, Antonin. *The Theatre and Its Double.* New York: Grove Press, 1958.

Bach, George. *Aggression Lab.* Dubuque, Iowa: Kendall/Hunt, 1971.

Bacon, Wallace A., and Robert S. Breen. *Literature as Experience.* New York: McGraw-Hill, 1959.

Ball, David. *Backwards and Forwards: A Technical Manual for Reading Plays.* Carbondale: Southern Illinois University Press, 1983.

Barton, John. *Playing Shakespeare.* London and New York: Metheun, 1984.

Bates, Brian. *The Way of the Actor.* Boston: Shambhala, 1987.

Beck, Julian. *The Life of the Theatre.* San Francisco: City Lights Books, 1972.

Beckerman, Bernard. *Dynamics of Drama.* New York: Drama Book Publishers, 1979.

Benedetti, Robert. *Seeming, Being, and Becoming.* New York: Drama Book Specialists, 1975.

———— *The Director at Work.* Englewood Cliffs, NJ: Prentice-Hall, 1984.

———— "Zen in the Art of Actor Training," in *Master Teachers of Theatre,* ed. Burnet Hobgood. Carbondale: Southern Illinois University Press, 1988.

Berne, Eric. *Games People Play.* New York: Grove Press, 1964.

Birdwhistle, Raymond. *Introduction to Kinesics.* Louisville: University of Louisville Pamphlet, 1957.

Boleslavsky, Richard. *Acting: The First Six Lessons.* New York: Theatre Arts Books, 1933.

Branden, Nathaniel. *The Disowned Self.* New York: Bantam, 1973.

———— *The Psychology of Self-Esteem.* New York: Bantam, 1971.

Braun, Edward. trans. and ed. *Meyerhold on Theatre.* New York: Hill & Wang, 1969.

Brockett, Oscar G. *The Theatre: An Introduction,* 4th ed. New York: Holt, Rinehart & Winston, 1979.

Brook, Peter. *The Empty Space.* New York: Atheneum, 1968.

Bullough, Edward. *Aesthetics.* Stanford, CA: Stanford University Press, 1957.

Campbell, Joseph. *The Masks of God.* New York: Viking, 1959.

Cassirer, Ernst. *The Philosophy of Symbolic Forms,* trans. Ralph Manheim. New Haven: Yale University Press, 1953.

Chaikin, Joseph. *The Presence of the Actor.* New York: Atheneum, 1972.

Chekhov, Michael. *To the Actor.* New York: Harper & Row, 1953.

Cohen, Robert. *Acting Power.* Palo Alto, CA: Mayfield, 1978.

Cole, Toby, ed. *Acting: A Handbook of the Stanislavski Method.* New York: Crown, 1971.

Cole, Toby, and Helen Chinoy, eds. *Actors on Acting.* New York: Crown, 1970.

Crawford, Jerry. *Acting in Person and in Style,* 3rd ed. Dubuque, IA: Wm. C. Brown, 1983.

Dewey, John. *Experience and Nature.* La Salle, Il.: Open Court, 1925.

Ernst, Earle. *The Kabuki Theatre.* New York: Grove Press, 1956.

Esslin, Martin. *Brecht: The Man and His Work.* New York: Doubleday, 1960.

────── *The Theatre of the Absurd.* New York: Doubleday, 1961.

Feldenkrais, Moshe. *Awareness through Movement.* New York: Harper & Row, 1972.

Gielgud, John. *An Actor and His Time.* New York: Penguin, 1981.

Goffman, Erving. *The Presentation of Self in Everyday Life.* New York: Doubleday, 1959.

Gorchakov, Nikolai. *Stanislavski Directs.* New York: Funk & Wagnalls, 1954.

Green, Michael. *Downwind of Upstage.* New York: Hawthorn, 1964.

Grotowski, Jerzy. *Towards a Poor Theatre.* New York: Simon & Schuster, 1968.

Guthrie, Tyrone. *Tyrone Guthrie on Acting.* New York: Viking, 1971.

Hagen, Uta. *Respect for Acting.* New York: Macmillan, 1973.

Hall, Edward. *The Silent Language.* New York: Doubleday, 1959.

Halprin, Lawrence. *The RSVP Cycles.* New York: George Braziller, 1969.

Harrop, John, and Sabin Epstein. *Acting with Style.* Englewood Cliffs, NJ: Prentice-Hall, 1982.

Herrigel, Eugen. *Zen in the Art of Archery.* New York: Vintage, 1971.

Jacobson, Edmund. *Progressive Relaxation.* Chicago: University of Chicago Press, 1938.

Johnstone, Keith. *Impro: Improvisation and the Theatre.* New York: Theatre Arts Books, 1983.

Jones, Frank Pierce. *Body Awareness in Action.* New York: Schocken Books, 1976.

Joseph, Bertram. *Acting Shakespeare.* New York: Theatre Arts Books, 1960.

Kalter, Joanmarie. *Actors on Acting.* New York: Sterling, 1978.

Kirby, E. T., ed. *Total Theatre.* New York: Dutton, 1969.

Kuritz, Paul. *Playing.* Englewood Cliffs, NJ: Prentice Hall, 1982.

Lang, R. D. *The Politics of Experience.* New York: Ballantine, 1967.

Lao Tsu. *Tao Te Ching.* trans Gia Fu Feng and Jane English. New York: Vintage, 1972.

Lessac, Arthur. *Body Wisdom: The Use and Training of the Human Body.* New York: Drama Book Specialists, 1978.

Lewis, Robert. *Advice to Players.* New York: Harper & Row, 1980.

────── *Method or Madness?* London: Heinemann, 1960.

Linklater, Kristin. *Freeing the Natural Voice.* New York: Drama Book Specialists, 1976.

Lowen, Alexander. *The Language of the Body.* New York: Collier, 1971.

Maslov, Abraham. *Motivation and Personality.* New York: Harper & Row, 1954.

May, Rollo. *The Courage to Create.* New York: Norton, 1975.

O'Connor, Gary. *Ralph Richardson: An Actor's Life.* New York: Atheneum, 1982.

Olivier, Laurence. *Confessions of an Actor.* New York: Simon & Schuster, 1982.

Otto, Walter. *Dionysus.* Bloomington: Indiana University Press, 1965.

Perls, Frederick S., Ralph F. Hefferline, and Paul Goodman. *Gestalt Therapy.* New York: Julian Press, 1951.

Ram, Dass. *Be Here Now.* New Mexico: Lama Foundation, 1971.

—— *The Only Dance There Is.* New York: Doubleday/Anchor, 1974.

Redgrave, Michael. *In My Mind's I.* New York: Viking, 1983.

Richards, Mary Caroline. *Centering.* Wesleyan: Wesleyan University Press, 1964.

Sainer, Arthur. *The Radical Theatre Notebook.* New York: Discus/Avon, 1975.

St. Denis, Michel. *Theatre: The Rediscovery of Style.* New York: Theatre Arts Books, 1960.

Sapir, Edward. *Language.* New York: Harcourt, Brace & World, 1949.

Schechner, Richard. *Environmental Theatre.* New York: Hawthorn, 1973.

Schlauch, Margaret. *The Gift of Language.* New York: Dover, 1955.

Shurtleff, Michael. *Audition.* New York: Walker & Co., 1978.

Spolin, Viola. *Improvisation for the Theatre.* Evanston, IL.: Northwestern University Press, 1963.

Stanislavski, Constantin. *An Actor Prepares,* trans. Elizabeth Reynolds Hapgood. New York: Theatre Arts Books, 1936.

—— *Building a Character,* trans. Elizabeth Reynolds Hapgood. New York: Theatre Arts Books, 1949.

—— *Creating A Role.* trans. Elizabeth Reynolds Hapgood. New York: Theatre Arts Books, 1949.

—— *My Life in Art,* trans. J. J. Robbins. New York: Theatre Arts Books, 1952.

Suzuki, D. T. *Zen Buddhism.* New York: Doubleday/Anchor, 1956.

Suzuki, Shunrya. *Zen Mind, Beginner's Mind.* New York: Weatherhill, 1970.

Trungpa, Chogyam. *Cutting through Spiritual Materialism.* Berkeley: Shambhala, 1973.

Watts, Alan. *The Book: On the Taboo against Knowing Who You Are.* New York: Random House, 1972.

Wellek, Rene and Austin Warren. *Theory of Literature.* New York: Harvest/Harcourt, Brace & Co., 1942.

Willet, John, ed. *Brecht on Theatre.* New York: Hill & Wang, 1964.

NOTES

LESSON ONE

1. Erving Goffman, *The Presentation of Self in Everyday Life.* (New York: Doubleday, 1959), pp. 71–74. Copyright © by Erving Goffman. Reprinted with the Permission of Doubleday & Company, Inc.
2. Brian Bates, *The Way of the Actor.* (Boston: Shambhala, 1987), p. 7.
3. Bates, p. 9.
4. Bates, p. 16.
5. From an unpublished letter.
6. Constantin Stanislavski, *My Life in Art,* trans. J. J. Robbins (New York: Theatre Arts Books, 1952). Copyright © 1924 by Little, Brown & Co., and 1952 by Elizabeth Reynolds Hapgood. Used with the permission of the publishers, Theatre Arts Books, 153 Waverly Place, New York, NY 10014, and Geoffrey Bless Ltd., London.
7. From David Mamet, *Writing in Restaurants.* (New York: Viking Penguin, 1986), p. 116. Copyright © 1986 by David Mamet. All rights reserved. Reprinted with the permission of Viking Penguin Inc.

LESSON TWO

1. Frederick Perls, Ralph Hefferline, and Paul Goodman, *Gestalt Therapy* (New York: Julian Press, 1951), p. 134. (Dell Paperback, 1964.)
2. Perls, Hefferline, and Goodman, p. 33.

LESSON THREE

1. Mary Caroline Richards, *Centering* (Wesleyan: Wesleyan University Press, 1964), p. 38–39. Copyright © by Mary Caroline Richards. Used with the permission of Wesleyan University Press.

LESSON FOUR

1. Raymond Birdwhistle, *Introduction to Kinesics* (Louisville: University of Louisville Pamphlet, 1957), pp. 29–30.
2. Edward T. Hall, *The Silent Language* (New York: Doubleday, 1959), p. 43. Copyright © 1959 by Edward T. Hall. Reprinted by permission of Doubleday & Company, Inc.
3. Hall, p. 42.
4. Bates, p. 114.
5. Wallace A. Bacon and Robert S. Breen, *Literature as Experience,* (New York: McGraw-Hill, 1959), p. 32.

LESSON FIVE

1. Margaret Schlauch, *The Gift of Language* (New York: Dover, 1955), p. 3. Reprinted with the permission of the publisher.
2. Edward Sapir, *Language* (New York: Harcourt, Brace & World, 1949), pp. 8–9.
3. Sapir, p. 5.
4. Bacon and Breen, *Literature as Experience,* p. 286.
5. Ernst Cassirer, *The Philosophy of Symbolic Forms,* trans. Ralph Manheim (New Haven: Yale University Press, 1953), p. 148.

LESSON SIX

1. Alan Watts, *The Book: On the Taboo Against Knowing Who You Are* (New York: Random House, 1972), p. 6.

LESSON SEVEN

1. August Strindberg, "Notes to the Members of the Intimate Theatre," trans. Everett Sprinchorn, *The Tulane Drama Review,* 6, no. 2 (November 1961), p. 157. This material is also copyrighted by The Drama Review, 1967.
2. Richards, p. 25.
3. Mamet, p. 20–21.

LESSON EIGHT

1. Constantin Stanislavski, *An Actor's Handbook,* trans. and ed. Elizabeth Reynolds Hapgood (New York: Theatre Arts Books, 1936), p. 8. Copyright © 1936, 1961, 1963 by Elizabeth Reynolds Hapgood. Used with the permission of the publisher, Theatre Arts Books, 153 Waverly Place, New York, NY 10014.
2. Constantin Stanislavski, *Building a Character,* trans. Elizabeth Reynolds Hapgood (New York: Theatre Arts Books, 1949), pp. 218–36. Used with the permission of the publisher, Theatre Arts Books, 153 Waverly Place, New York, NY 10014.
3. Constantin Stanislavski, *Creating a Role* (New York: Theatre Arts Books, 1961), p. 62. Used with the permission of the publisher, Theatre Arts Books, 153 Waverly Place, New York, NY 10014.
4. Stanislavski, *Actor's Handbook,* p. 9.

LESSON NINE

1. Stanislavski, *Actor's Handbook,* p. 9.
2. Mamet, *Writing in Restaurants,* pp. 26–27.

LESSON TEN

1. Stanislavski, *Actor's Handbook,* p. 138.

LESSON FOURTEEN

1. Stanislavski, *Actor's Handbook,* pp. 137–38.

LESSON FIFTEEN

1. Oscar G. Brockett, *The Theatre, An Introduction,* 3rd ed. (New York: Holt, Rinehart & Winston, 1974), pp. 39–40. Reprinted with the permission of Holt, Rinehart & Winston, Inc.
2. Brockett, pp. 39–40.

LESSON SIXTEEN

1. Mamet, p. 76.
2. Jan Kott, "King Lear or Endgame," *The Evergreen Review* (August–September 1964), p. 55.
3. Moshe Feldenkrais, *Awareness through Movement* (New York: Harper & Row, 1972), pp. 45–46.

LESSON SEVENTEEN

1. Stanislavski, *Building a Character,* pp. 218–36.
2. Stanislavski, *Building a Character,* pp. 218–36.
3. Stanislavski, *Building a Character,* pp. 218–36.
4. Stanislavski, *Building a Character,* pp. 218–36.
5. Stanislavski, *Building a Character,* pp. 218–36.

LESSON EIGHTEEN

1. Alexander Lowen, *The Language of the Body,* (New York: Collier, 1971), p. 32.

2. This list is adapted from Nathaniel Branden, *The Disowned Self* (New York: Bantam, 1973), pp. 111–14.

LESSON NINETEEN

1. David D. Burns, *Feeling Good* (New York: Signet, 1980), pp. 11–12.
2. Stanislavski, *Actor's Handbook*, p. 56.
3. Mamet, p. 127.
4. Stanislavski, *Building a Character*, p. 70.
5. Stanislavski, *Building a Character*, p. 70.

LESSON TWENTY-ONE

1. Stanislavski, *Creating a Role*, p. 62. Used with the permission of the publisher, Theatre Arts Books, 153 Waverly Place, New York, NY 10014.
2. Nikolai Gorchakov, *Stanislavski Directs* (New York: Funk & Wagnalls, 1954), p. 77.

LESSON TWENTY-THREE

1. Strindberg, "Notes to the Members of the Intimate Theater," p. 157.
2. Quoted in an interview.
3. From an unpublished letter.
4. Mamet, pp. 20–21.
5. Mamet, p. 19.
6. Mamet, p. 21.
7. Stanislavski, *My Life in Art*, pp. 217–218.

AFTERWORD

1. Gorchakov, pp. 40–41.

APPENDIX

INDEX

Note: This index does not duplicate items listed in the Contents.